Advance Praise for

F YOU VERY MUCH

"A meaty cry for human decency, wrapped in a deliciously hilarious hot dog bun. I plan to read it again and then force-feed it to my neighbor, my mother, and my college roommate. If you care about people and enjoy a good laugh, I politely encourage you to read this book. Immediately."
> —Adam Grant, bestselling author of *Originals*

"A brilliant book."
> —Jon Ronson, bestselling author of *The Psychopath Test*

"A very funny and wise book about the blatant rudeness that surrounds us. Danny Wallace in top form."
> —Matt Haig, bestselling author of *Reasons to Stay Alive*

"Hilarious."
> —GQ

F YOU VERY MUCH

UNDERSTANDING
THE CULTURE OF RUDENESS—
AND WHAT WE CAN DO ABOUT IT

DANNY WALLACE

A TarcherPerigee Book

tarcher*perigee*

An imprint of Penguin Random House LLC
375 Hudson Street
New York, New York 10014

First published in Great Britain in different form as *I Can't Believe You Just Said That* by
Ebury Press, an imprint of Penguin Random House UK 2017

This edition published 2018

Most TarcherPerigee books are available at special quantity discounts for
bulk purchase for sales promotions, premiums, fund-raising, and educational needs.
Special books or book excerpts also can be created to fit specific needs.
For details, write: SpecialMarkets@penguinrandomhouse.com.

ISBN 9780143132196

Printed in the United States of America
1   3   5   7   9   10   8   6   4   2

Book design by Elke Sigal

For Mum and Dad

(The only two people I can honestly say
I've never seen be rude to <u>anyone</u>.)

Contents

Introduction   *ix*

Prologue—The Hotdog Incident   *1*

CHAPTER 1   The Rudeness Effect   *11*

CHAPTER 2   Going Viral   *18*

CHAPTER 3   Bad Manors   *30*

CHAPTER 4   Lip Service   *51*

CHAPTER 5   Rudeness and Power   *63*

CHAPTER 6   Rudeness and the Sexes   *81*

CHAPTER 7   Rudeness and Outrage   *95*

CHAPTER 8   Rude Health   *103*

CHAPTER 9   Rudeness and Revenge   *117*

CHAPTER 10   The Troll   *140*

CHAPTER 11   Rude Rage   *156*

CHAPTER 12 Lost in Translation 176

CHAPTER 13 Juvenile Behaviors 198

CHAPTER 14 Policing Rudeness 212

CHAPTER 15 Rude by Nature 229

CHAPTER 16 Sense and Incivility 240

CHAPTER 17 The Honesty Clause 254

CHAPTER 18 Rude to the End 271

Acknowledgments 287

The Wallace Report 289

Notes 295

About the Author 303

Introduction

In 2015, after 27-year-old Omar Hussain left his job at a Morrisons supermarket in Buckinghamshire and fled the United Kingdom to join the radical terrorist jihadist group ISIS, he was extraordinarily disappointed to find out how rude they all were.

We all get annoyed at our colleagues from time to time, but for Omar Hussain the everyday rudeness displayed by those simultaneously plotting to bring down the very tenets of Western civilization was a step too far.

In a blog he wrote in his first few months in the desert, he complained in no uncertain terms about the "bad manners" of his fellow radicalized death-cult militants.

Under a series of numbered headings on Tumblr, the bearded and bespectacled Hussain launched a blistering attack on Arab administrative skills.

"There is no queue in any of their offices," wrote the furious Briton. "You could be waiting in line for half an hour and then another Arab would come and push in the queue and go straight in."

When serving his peers dinner after a long day of terrorist training in the desert, Omar was shocked to be "pounced upon by everyone in the room. I therefore refused to give *anyone* food until every single one of them was sitting down in their seats. Unfortunately, I had to treat them like primary school students."

Poor Omar just hadn't known what he was letting himself in for. In subsequent blogs and tweets, you can tell he was becoming withdrawn. He talks of loneliness; he has trouble peeling potatoes; he spends his free time trying to find chocolates or feeding a local cat called Lucy.

What Omar perceived as the rudeness of others really affected him: this kind of behavior was not what he signed up to ISIS for, and it was wearing him down.

It only got worse.

"In the West, it is common knowledge to walk out of a room wearing the same pair of shoes that you wore while entering the room. Nay, it is common sense!" he wrote at one point, and you *know* someone's annoyed when they use words like nay. "However, here in Sham, our Syrian brothers [. . .] believe that everyone can wear each other's footwear. Sometimes you would enter a building and when leaving, you would see the person with your shoes walking 100 yards ahead of you and it can be quite irritating."

Of course, these things happen in war. But Omar suddenly found himself in a world in which men would simply stand three feet away and stare at him while saying nothing, and even where terrorists would "casually take your phone off charge to charge their own phone."

Omar expected better of ISIS. He didn't like how they would be so "childish in their dealings and mannerisms," nor how they would rifle through other people's property without asking first. They were always invading his space, and they talked far too loudly when he was trying to sleep.

As far as he could tell, they didn't find their own behavior rude at all.

We all have our own standards when it comes to rudeness.

· · ·

Politeness is extremely important to me, though sometimes I wonder if I set the bar too high.

I feel rude if I sneeze on a plane. I have lost count of the number of times I have apologized to garbage cans or lampposts if I've walked into them. If a *dog* looks my way as I walk through a park, I feel ashamed if I don't smile or nod a hello. I don't think I'd last five minutes with ISIS before I'd be straight to Human Resources!

But never was I more aware of my own standards of rudeness than on the day—and immediate aftermath—of what we'll call "the Hotdog Incident."

All I wanted was a sausage. What I got instead was an afternoon of incredible stress and the desire to do something about it. The desire, as it would turn out, to write this book. Initially I tried to exorcise my demons by composing a scathing 200-word review. But 200 words did nothing. There was too much I still wanted to say—and know. Something that began as a little silly took on a serious edge. What started as a few print-outs left by my bed in London soon became documents in ring-binders arranged in my office.

And all of this purely to try and understand exactly what happened between me and a complete stranger over an emulsified sausage.

In the following months, as my interest in the question of why people are rude became an obsession—and winning an argument became writing a book—I would start to realize that we are on the edge of something truly dangerous. I found myself calling upon the expertise of behavioral psychologists, psychiatrists, psychotherapists, bellboys, cab drivers, moving men, sociologists, journalists, ethicists, political strategists, neurologists, lawyers, baristas, waiters, politicians, NASA scientists, a limo driver called José, and at least one expert in cooked meat production.

Simultaneously, as I read more studies and familiarized myself with a whole new world of research and investigation, I began to discover I was part of a hidden community of "rudeness nerds," working diligently in the shadows to figure out why we are the way we are—and what it means.

And it's not pretty.

I'll be honest with you: I thought I had a pretty good handle on rudeness. What I wasn't expecting to find was what a threat it poses to our happiness—and maybe even to our continued existence on this planet. Its effects are potent, damaging, and, scariest of all, contagious. In the coming pages, I'll show you how rudeness affects the way our brains work, how it clouds our judgment and how it worsens our choices. We'll see how experiencing it can make us less effective at our jobs, and make us worse fathers and mothers, sons, daughters, and friends. We'll meet people who'll show us how rudeness can stop us trusting, and make us barbed, suspicious, and vicious. How those in power use it to keep us down.

If any of the things I've just told you happened because of something scientifically traceable—a mosquito bite, say, or a worm scratch—I am certain the world's governments would leap into immediate action. There would be constant panic and 24-hour rolling news coverage and someone would have quarantined Simon Cowell.

But as it is, for now it's just you, me, and this book.

Think about that for a second.

. . .

One thing before we get started. This is not a book about etiquette. I couldn't care less about etiquette. You can burn every etiquette book in the world as far as I'm concerned, so long as it's done safely and not downwind of anybody trying to enjoy their garden. I don't think we need to pull out chairs for people. If there's a puddle, I'm not going to take off my brand-new cape and lay it down for you to step on, though if I were wearing a cape in the first place you'd have every right to be rude to me.

However, I do think if someone's walking through a door behind us we could hold it open for them. I do think if we're in line in a Syrian post office, we should absolutely wait our turn, and if a radical extremist tries to elbow his way to the front, we have every right to sigh and tut.

That's the difference between etiquette and politeness. Etiquette is outdated; politeness is all we need, and this book is both a warning and a rallying cry for civility. We need politeness because it is right, it lifts our spirits, it makes things better, it lubricates the day and helps everything run smoother.

And we need it now more than ever, because things are getting worse.

·   ·   ·

Don't tell me you haven't felt it too. This "New Rudeness" is global. It's in the air, it pours out of our phones, tumbles from our TVs, dominates the cultural conversation, and I firmly believe it threatens to overwhelm us.

Passive aggression. Road rage. Over-the-line commenters. Spitters. Line-jumpers. People who are #justsaying or *Only Being Honest* or *Not Being Funny But*.

We seem more stressed, more time-pressed, tired, fed up, angry, and put upon. We seem more resentful, envious, self-obsessed, racist, and, yes, sad. We think less, react more, and run and jump to conclusions just so we have one, where once we might have ambled to see what happened along the way. We are self-entitled, knee-jerking, know-it-all thunderdicks.

We are ruder than we've ever been, and it's becoming a runaway train.

> **We are ruder than we've ever been,**
> **and it's becoming a runaway train.**

You get one nasty TV judge, and suddenly they can't commission a single show without one. You give one awful person a newspaper column, wait until he or she writes something that in civilized countries would be rightly deemed sociopathic, and we don't fire them; we give them a talk show on a minority satellite channel. We find ourselves at a point in time where suddenly we admire politicians who come up with put-downs instead of policies. Why? Because we find them "refreshing." We mistake their rudeness for "honesty," because we confuse "honesty" with "opinion," in much the same way as bores at dinner parties confuse cynicism with wit.

Of course, it's tempting to think only "other people" are rude. But the truth is, we're all at it.*

Some go out of their way to be rude, like the coal-hearted newspaper columnist desperately scrabbling around on deadline for thuggish ways to insult whoever's looking weak, just so one day she can line her

---

* And I should be clear: I am not above behaving rudely myself. When this book comes out, there will be a slew of eager-eyed people lining up to say, "Ah! But once I said hello to you in a pub and you flipped me the bird," or something. Well, first off, I don't believe you, but somewhere there does doubtless exist a tape recording of me absolutely losing my shit with a customer service rep from BT Broadband, which I imagine is played back in conference rooms for training purposes, nationally, almost every single day.

own coffin with slightly more expensive felt. Like the millionaires on Saturday-night TV making more money and generating more fame by humiliating those with mental health problems who just want a tiny slice of the hopeless dream they're being sold by the very people who'll never give it to them.

I'll touch on those people—because of their influence and because I can't stand them and because it'll be fun—but thanks to the meat-based Incident that could just as easily have happened to you, or your mother, or your neighbor's ex-wife, I want to focus on the *everydayness* of rudeness too. The tedious, beige mundanity of a rudeness that is now everywhere.

The wearing, draining, energy-sapping *pointlessness* of it all.

The New Rudeness is like a suffocating blanket, and this book an attempt to pull back the covers. I think we are at a point in time where we reward the wrong things. We celebrate incivility, we admire it, we joyfully kick our legs and laugh as we actively sink ourselves deeper into the quicksand of society's lowest cultural ebb.

Let's have fun finding out why!

Human beings are fundamentally good. We're a terrific bunch. But we slip up all the time. And I know what you're thinking. Something pretty terrible must have happened to me to make me go this far, so far that I had to write a whole book on the subject.

And you'd be right.

That something terrible was the Hotdog Incident.

Prologue

The Hotdog Incident

Allow me, please, to paint you a picture of beauty and serenity.

A small middle-class town—one I won't name—on a typical British summer bank-holiday weekend. By which I mean in the past 24 hours there had been a genuine risk of death by hailstone.

Lunchtime. Crisp air had worn holes in our stomachs, and in among the cobbles and chip shops and delis and abandoned, turned-up Fairtrade organic ice-cream cones, I led my small family toward something I'd spotted through the thin drizzle.

A tiny diner.

A freshly painted beacon of hope in muted, middle-class tones.

"Let's get a hotdog!" said my five-year-old son, which is not unusual for him.

"Yeah! Let's get a hotdog!" I replied, which is not unusual for me.

So I made an important decision. This would be where the family had lunch. This would be where we'd buy hotdogs.

This would be a mistake.

. . .

"You have to pay up front," said the woman behind the counter, hands on hips, barely looking at me, already somehow aggrieved.

She was in the midst of middle age and wearing her hair in a bun, over heavy eyeshadow and two carefully painted pursed red lips.

I looked at the price of our hotdogs. They were expensive. But we were hungry and already here and I did as I was told and paid up front, even though you don't pay for food up front.

There were no seats, and no ideas were offered, so we took a table outside and waited in the wind.

"This weather is wonderfully bracing!" said my son, though he phrased it "I'm cold."

I reassured him we'd have our hotdogs soon. I'd had hotdogs before. Hotdogs take no time.

Through the window, bored, listless families stared past each other. A kid toyed with his phone. His mum made him put it away but, when he did, she didn't speak to him.

I noticed none of them had any food.

"None of those people have any food," I mumbled, as gray clouds seemed to gather above me.

The woman in the eyeshadow at the counter had disappeared.

Twenty-five minutes passed.

. . .

"Just wondering about my son's hotdog!" I said, walking cheerfully inside when I spotted the woman was back.

She scowled.

Then she put both hands on the counter and leaned closer, and it got worse.

"There are TWO OTHER TABLES AHEAD OF YOU," she barked, eyes cold. "And we COOK TO ORDER."

This was not the response I was expecting.

"Cool!" I said, surprised at the volume of her response and the approach, and I rushed back outside to my wife.

"So there are two other tables ahead of us," I told her, as she rearranged our baby to prevent frostbite. "And the thing is, they cook to order."

"What does that mean?" she said. "Maybe it means we should go somewhere else."

She was right.

But *wait*.

"I had to pay up front!" I remembered. "It was like taking out a second mortgage."

Why had this woman made us pay for our food before we had our food? She had trapped us!

"Maybe *I'll* go in and ask," said my wife.

"No!" I said, because I'm the dad, and I'd already started this.

The woman bristled as she sensed my tiptoeing. She did not look up, preferring instead to try and burn a hole in her order book through wilful staring alone.

"Hi, uh, it's just that if we could get a *rough* estimate on time," I tried, trying not to wake the beast, "it would really help us."

"TEN MINUTES!" she yelled, throwing her book down. "You'll have EVERYTHING in TEN MINUTES!"

It was like instead of my polite and staggered sentences she thought I'd kicked the door in, taken my trousers down, and yelled, "Hey dickhead! Cook me a sausage!"

Behind her, a silent woman joylessly shunted meat around a grill. She looked like one big sigh.

"So should I wait . . ."

"*YES,*" she said, indicating the door.

.   .   .

Back outside, I clapped my hands together and pretended everything was absolutely fantastic.

"Perfect!" I said. "Everything in ten minutes!"

My son looked at me like I'd just said I enjoy stamping on badgers. Ten minutes is six weeks in kid years.

I scrabbled about in my pocket for something for him to play with. I gave him an old train ticket. He looked at it and handed it back.

.   .   .

Twenty minutes later and still nothing had happened.

Nothing.

Well, a seagull briefly landed on a garbage can, but that's not the same as getting a hotdog.

"We'll soon be approaching an hour!" I said in disbelief, but trying to remain positive, because I *really* didn't want to go back in again.

And then—a miracle!

A teenage waitress silently walked out with a plate.

"Hi," I tried, but word had obviously spread. The girl did not even look me in the eye. I was obviously a *troublemaker.*

She dropped the plate to the table and on it sat a tiny, overcooked, junior hotdog.

It looked embarrassed to be there.

Next to it were two wet leaves and a single cherry tomato.

"*Oh God,*" I thought, heart sinking. "*I'm going to have to complain.*"

Inside, diners looked at us sadly.

I glanced down and saw my son had eaten half his hotdog already. Maybe this would all be over soon.

"So where's *our* food?" asked my wife.

"*Oh God*," I thought again.

.   .   .

I reasoned that I needed a human shield so took my son with me for protection. But the very second I opened the door and activated its tinkle—a tinkle that had long since lost all sense of joy—the woman began physically to seethe.

In a cartoon, she'd have had steam coming out of her ears.

Somehow, by asking where a hotdog *I'd already bought* was, I had become the country's most difficult customer. I would not have been surprised to have turned on my television that night to see this woman being interviewed about me.

"You don't understand how it works," she barked as I got nearer, voice rising, already incandescent at my cheek. "We COOK everything TO ORDER."

My son took a step back.

It was time for me to take a step forward.

"Look, we've been outside for an hour," I said, trying to sound firm. "I'm just asking for updates."

"You've been outside TWENTY MINUTES," she said. "I know because I *checked*."

She made a "Ha!" face.

The whole place fell silent.

I've seen the films; this was becoming a standoff.

"It's been a *lot longer than twenty minutes*," I said, gaining confidence. Part of me could feel the room on my side. Enough for me to try raising *my* voice. "It's been an HOUR!"

She closed her eyes, revealing acres more eyeshadow.

"It has not been an HOUR," she said, opening them again, knuckles whitening against the counter's edge, "and YOU DON'T KNOW HOW IT WORKS!"

"I DO know how it works!"

"WE COOK EVERYTHING TO ORDER!"

"Why do you keep SAYING THAT?" I yelled, throwing my hands up in the air. "Well done on cooking to order! JUST LIKE EVERY OTHER RESTAURANT IN THE WORLD!"

My son was staring up at me now; not her.

"Do you think I've never ordered something and then they COOKED IT? I've done that almost everywhere. It's NOT AS IMPRESSIVE AS YOU THINK!"

"You've been here *twenty minutes*," she hissed again, ignoring my exceptional point, but everyone there knew this was a lie. The brilliance of it, though, was that it was impossible to *prove* I'd been there an hour.

But wait!

"My *receipt*!" I said, and I pulled it from my pocket and held it aloft, like Sherlock Holmes producing the crucial evidence at the last possible second. She made me pay up front! Hoisted by her own petard!

"According to this I've been here *one hour and one minute*!"

I'm a *genius*!

"And one hour and one minute," I added confidently, "is *too long to wait for a hotdog*!"*

The woman let out a bitter laugh. She was beaten, she knew it, but there was time for one parting shot, as she scowled and pointed at my wife and baby shivering outside and said, "You're probably the sort of people who queue up for *40 minutes* for FISH AND CHIPS."

---

* At this stage no national surveys had been done to confirm this.

Now, to this day I have absolutely no idea what that meant, but let me tell you, it sounded *very* insulting.

"Right!" I said, deciding to regain control, my mind now sharpened and the way forward clear in my head. "*Cancel* it! I want to cancel my order!"

Ha!

"You can't!" she spat.

"I can!" I said. Consumer rights! "I want a refund!"

"You can't have one," she smirked. "Because your *cheeseburger* is ready."

I DIDN'T ORDER A CHEESEBURGER!

Oh, hang on, my wife did.

The woman prodded a cheeseburger toward me with one long nail. It was in a little plastic basket. But the woman's face said it all: she thought she had *won*. Around us, people stared, watching the spectacle, enjoying the power struggle, but none yet willing to lend a hand.

"Well, I'll pay for the cheeseburger and my son's hotdog, then," I countered. "But I want a *refund* on my hotdog."

And then something happened.

It was like something exploded behind her eyes.

Her shoulders quivered, and she shook her head, and she did the *unbelievable*.

She looked at me and said, "Actually, do you know what? You *can't have it*."

She dragged the cheeseburger back toward her.

She was keeping the cheeseburger!

"I WANT YOU OUT!" she yelled.

"You want me *out?*"

"I'm not doing this," she said, hands on hips, head shaking. "You can't have your hotdog!"

"But I've *paid* for that hotdog!"

"No. I'm not having this. OUT."

What the . . . ? I—a man who tries to be polite, a bewildered man, a man who just wondered where his hotdog was—was being *thrown out of a diner*!

With no hotdog!

In front of my *son*!

I watched in disbelief as she furiously tossed coins onto the counter instead of hotdogs. And as I scrabbled to pick up the price of a re-funded, reconstituted sausage and turned and began to walk, I caught sight of her "TIPS" jar and almost laughed. My head was confused and spinning from the injustice, from the unwarranted aggression, from the unexpectedness of it all. Why was she being so RUDE?

I noticed my hand begin to tremble. This woman had broken the rules. This woman had *broken the rules*.

"You think you know how it works," she muttered again. "But you *don't*!"

"You think you can cook a hotdog, but you *can't*!"

"WE COOK TO ORDER!"

"You DON'T COOK AT ALL!"

"Go eat some FISH AND CHIPS!" she yelled, and at last I reached the door.

"Maybe if you didn't spend so long getting ready every morning," I spat back, pointing at her hair, her eyeshadow, her pursed red lips, "you could put the hotdogs on!"

My cheeks were burning, my head was throbbing, one hand was shaking, and as I found myself outside in cold and spitting rain I had a moment of complete and absolute clarity . . .

What was I doing?

What the hell was I doing?

All I'd wanted was a hotdog. And now here I was trembling in the rain. I had no idea what my next move was supposed to be. Nothing made sense. How had it come to this, and so quickly? Was there *any-thing* that woman or I could have done to avoid this situation?

Well, obviously there was.

She could have cooked a damn hotdog.

But what on Earth was I teaching my son?

"They're very rude," said my little boy to a stranger outside, as we gathered our things, watched by all inside, and as I struggled, confused, to focus on whatever I was supposed to do next. "I didn't even *like* my hotdog."

SUGGESTED ACTIVITY

With your friend, why not undertake the following role play?

One of you should pretend to be a person who wishes to buy a hotdog.

The other should pretend to be a person whose job it is to sell hotdogs.

See if you can work together to find a solution that solves both problems while avoiding conflict.

You have 3 attempts and 90 minutes.

CHAPTER 1

The Rudeness Effect

What I did next

Not long ago, I read a book called *Dying to Wake Up: A Doctor's Voyage into the Afterlife and the Wisdom He Brought Back.*

In it, the former cardiac anesthesiologist Dr. Rajiv Parti recalls the incredibly unusual events of December 23, 2010.

Rushed to UCLA Hospital suffering from a severe infection, Parti found himself in dire need of emergency surgery and was immediately put under.

Not long after, Dr. Rajiv Parti died.

The surgeons acted swiftly. They did what surgeons do. They brought him back.

But just before they did, he says, some very strange things happened to him.

First, his world was plunged into complete darkness, and moments after that he found himself traveling to another realm entirely.

When he looked up, Dr. Parti says he was shocked to see a big black cloud, flashing in the distance from lightning. There followed loud and terrifying rolls of thunder.

And then came the screams.

Loud, piercing screams of anguish and torture. Dr. Parti realized he was surrounded by burning, tormented souls that began to writhe around him, engulfed in a fierce and unstoppable fire that now raged all around.

Then someone made him lie on a bed of nails, he says, which really hurt.

He was confused; disoriented; poked with needles. And then he was made to walk toward a fiery canyon, he says, thick smoke coating his nostrils and scratching at his lungs.

From there, high up on the edge of some kind of precipice, in a world that smelled of burning meat, he was made to survey all the many horrors that lay beneath.

Dr. Rajiv Parti was amazed to find himself, in his own words, at *the lip of hell.*

In subsequent press interviews about his day in hell, there's even been talk of strange horned demons with crooked teeth scurrying around, seemingly threatening him with an eternity of pain, though oddly these didn't make the book.

However, here's the point.

Despite all that—despite the horned demons and the terrifying screams of anguish and the beds of nails—do you know what was the first thing that occurred to Dr. Rajiv Parti?

The *very first thought* he had, as he surveyed vast, endless burning fields of agonized bodies and human suffering and soul-scarring screams?

He says he thought about how rude he'd been to a woman who'd come to see him about her arthritis recently.

That's what he thought about. He thought about how rude he'd been.

He'd been really dismissive, and he shouldn't have been. He hadn't paid attention to her *at all* as she talked. He just wanted to get on with his day. He'd really been ever so brusque.

And as he stood at the very lip of hell, and as Satan himself must have been warming up his sulphuric fork and wonky-teethed demons began circling around him, Dr. Rajiv Parti stared into the raging heart of hellfire and thought about all the *other* times he'd been a bit rude to people.

· · ·

Answer this: when was someone last rude to you?

I bet you remember very well, and I bet you told other people about it. No one wants to hear about a great holiday you had, where your flights were upgraded and the hotel gave you a suite and the weather was beautiful and the drinks were free and you got to know your favorite rock band who were staying at the same place and they invited you to New York to sing on their next album.

But if some guy on a train spilled your coffee and just went back to reading his newspaper without apologizing—*that's* a story.

"What did you do?" your friends will ask, wide-eyed. "Did you say something?"

Each of us can recall with startling accuracy minor rudenesses thrust our way by strangers in the past. Perhaps we cringe when we think of times we know for sure we were needlessly rude to someone else. But a story about rudeness has the power to muscle its way to the front of any conversation. Imagine a scientist arriving at a TV studio in order to announce a cure for all known diseases. I am absolutely certain that as they got their notes together and prepared for the most important speech of their life, they'd still take a moment to tell the bloke who took their jacket what an absolute tit their taxi driver was.

Sharing stories is a fundamental part of the human experience, and no day-to-day stories are more powerful or relatable than stories of injustice and rudeness, because when a stranger is suddenly and inexplicably rude, they break the rules and burn a bad memory onto your hard drive.

We are fascinated by rude behavior. We listen to our friends re-count their tales of bad service or angry commuters with glee. We clap our hands on the table and shout "GOOD!" when we hear they stood up for themselves. We clap our hands on the table and shout "NO!" when we find out they did nothing.

When the Hotdog Incident occurred, I found myself talking about it a lot. I needed to offload. It was an experience that didn't just stay with me; it pretty much moved in.

And can I tell you something? Within 24 hours, I had done some-thing absolutely insane.

As I drove past the diner again—and even though it was now empty and dark and closed—*I gave it the finger.*

I flipped off *a building.*

Instinctively.

A 38-year-old man.

This was not normal.

And what must the building have thought? "For 60 years I have stood proud on this corner, serving the community, never saying a word, never once a complaint—and then I get flipped off by an early middle-aged man in a Volvo."

It doesn't stop there.

Even as we headed back to London, I felt affected. I kept saying things to my wife about that woman. I kept using the word "unbe-lievable" in various ways. "Unbelievably rude!"; "*U*nbelievable be-havior!"; "Unbel*ievable!*"

I kept protesting my innocence, often completely out of the blue. "I did nothing wrong!" I'd suddenly shout, as a new thought struck me or the injustice hit me again.

The long highway drive did nothing to rid me of my frustration. In fact, now I decided that on some level other drivers were going *out* of their way to get *in* my way. We hit traffic jams that compounded my mood. I sneered at other cars. I seethed. And when I got home, and span the cap off a bottle of wine so quickly I'm surprised it didn't set something on fire, I did something worse than flipping off a building.

I went online.

I looked at TripAdvisor for pretty much the first time in my life.

I signed up.

And I wrote a *withering* review.

Another way of putting this is: I was obsessing.

Rudeness *had* me.

But at least know this: the night I got home and wrote that review and drank wine and pressed "Publish" and clicked "Refresh" and "Refresh" and "Refresh" a few hundred times, willing my harsh words to appear, I also took a good hard look at myself.

I am not, by nature, an angry man. But now I had found an anger. A snarling rage, a sense of injustice and impotence and a hunger for revenge.

I can't blame the Hotdog Incident on its own. Looking back, perhaps it was the straw that broke the camel's back. It was just one heightened rudeness too far in a city and world and civilization I felt had become less . . . civil. The more I rolled the events around in my head, the more other examples started crashing in on me. Examples I'd written off as being part of a bad day or tried to ignore.

Rude people in restaurants. On the bus. That executive at that dinner in Edinburgh that time. That six-year-old in the park who swore at my son. Bitchy emails. Unnecessary insults.

All of it came tumbling down—a brief personal history of rudeness—and as my wife went to bed and I sat up late, I realized it was making me unhappy. I didn't want to be unhappy.

Something had been smoldering. But now the idea caught fire.

Maybe I could do something about all this. Maybe I could use this anger. Maybe I could try and understand why these things happen to us all. Maybe I could start with the Hotdog Incident. I could unpack it, unpick it, look at it from every angle. And maybe by doing so I could somehow put it right. For hotdog lovers everywhere.

So yes, I took a good hard look at myself that night.

And then I decided to take a good hard look at you, too.

. . .

As the first few days passed, and I began, I had another realization. How could I judge where we should be if I didn't know where we already were?

So I did something that at the time felt entirely natural.

I picked up the phone and approached a leading national polling company.

In return for several thousand pounds, they told me they could conduct a countrywide survey of 2,000 people aged 18 and over on "Rudeness and Its Effects in Everyday Life."

Immediately and excitedly I began writing the questions for what would soon become known in my household as "The Wallace Report." This would be my own state-of-the-nation survey. Because if, as I suspected, rudeness is getting worse, then how bad is it already?

I had so much I wanted to know because I suspect in some ways I wanted to know if I was still normal.

Is it *normal* to want revenge? Is it *normal* to be so affected by something as trivial as an argument over a hotdog?

Within a week, the results were back (see page 289 for the full Wallace Report). I threw myself into them. Immediately I discovered some worrying things.

> **Is it *normal* to be so affected by something as trivial as an argument over a hotdog?**

Try this one for size.

Thirty-eight percent of people surveyed said that they themselves had been rude to someone in the last seven days.

That is simply not good enough. Those people are letting the rest of us down.

Worse, a little over one in five (21 percent) actually consider themselves to be a rude person. That's how they think of themselves. "Rude." As a *defining characteristic*. Like a badge of honor. Fine, but I wouldn't open your match.com profile with it.

True, that still leaves nearly 80 percent who, like you and me, say they're just trying to get on, stay true to our unwritten social contracts, and are therefore surprised and bewildered when rudeness is foisted upon them. But *still*.

I pored and pored over The Wallace Report and found it fascinating, because it focuses not just on those big moments but on smaller, more specific ones too. Rather than overwhelm you, I'm going to pepper the answers of the public throughout this book to give some sense of our present-day attitudes to the New Rudeness that sweeps across our world the way a drunk clown sweeps across the first row of a circus audience, throwing not delightful buckets of glitter our way, but spraying us instead with a hosepipe full of his own filth.

I'm sorry if you found that rude.

But how does rudeness sweep across the world?

Does rudeness spread?

Incidentally, I emailed Dr. Rajiv Parti on a number of occasions to ask him if he'd be willing to talk with me about that evening spent at the lip of hell when he realized he would have to mend his ways, but so far he has rudely ignored me.

You have to wonder what it's going to take with that guy.

CHAPTER 2

Going Viral

Was there just something in the air that day?

On August 9, 2010, JetBlue Airways flight 1052 from Pittsburgh touched down in New York City, and flight attendant Steven Slater picked up the public address system to make an announcement.

The announcement was quite unusual.

He'd had enough, he said. He'd had enough of one rude passenger on the flight in particular, and he'd had enough of rude passengers in general.

He'd been in this business nearly 20 years, he said, though he used more swear words—and he could take no more.

"I'm done!" he yelled.

And then he grabbed two beers from the drinks cart, pulled open the door, activated the emergency slide, and jumped out of the plane.

Stunned passengers watched him bounce down the chute, then stand up and stroll away, across the tarmac, beers in hand.

And an American folk hero was born.

Steven Slater had done what everyone in the service industry fantasizes about doing when faced with a rude public—he had resigned in the most spectacular way possible. He would make news across the world. His story would be mentioned on every late-night talk show to huge cheers from the crowd. He started a national conversation about rudeness in the workplace. People would make T-shirts with his face on them. He would be branded a champion of the working man. He would also be suspended and receive a $10,000 charge for repacking the slide.

His colleagues said later that Steven Slater had been having "a really bad day." Admittedly, it got worse when a reported 50 police officers turned up at his house to arrest him.

Yet it all added to the sense of a bona fide people's champion: here was a normal guy pushed to the limits through no fault of his own.

Considering my embarrassing/justified outbursts when arguing about hotdogs, I considered whether I might be like Steven Slater. Maybe I, too, was just a man who'd been pushed too far, like in a middle-class, meat-based *Falling Down*.

What's interesting is that maybe—just maybe—that small incident in that little diner that day could have *global ramifications*.

.   .   .

In Roger Hargreaves's classic text on civility, *Mr. Rude*, a very rude man named Mr. Rude stops being so rude when a lovely man named Mr. Happy just keeps smiling at him.

Sorry for the spoiler, but it's a wonderful lesson, though not one likely to catch on any time soon on planet Earth.

The truth about rudeness turns out to be a little more complex. And as I soon discovered, there are others as interested in this as I am. Scientists, psychologists, and academics who see rudeness not just as an amusing character trait in a sitcom hotelier, but as something to be taken seriously and rigorously investigated.

Some days it just feels like rudeness is in the air. And that's closer to the truth than you might think.

One recent study, in fact, led by Trevor Foulk at the University of Florida, suggests that rudeness is contagious. Literally. It spreads just the same way the common cold spreads.

So that's what's dangerous about the backhanded compliment in the office, the sarcastic sneer, the unnecessary outburst to an innocent but on-the-edge flight attendant: they're catching. They're catching faster than you'd catch something off Mr. Sneeze.

If you've been rude to someone recently, don't beat yourself up. You probably caught it. And becoming a carrier is worryingly simple: you just need to have *seen* some rudeness.

You start to understand how serious this might be when you consider that the more people who see that same moment of rudeness, the more carriers there suddenly are.

From now on, let's call the woman who was rude to me "Madam Hotdog." Partly because that describes her in a very easy and shorthand way, and partly because she'd hate it. Now let's say ten people in that diner saw Madam Hotdog being rude to me.

Those ten witnesses are now—according to the latest behavioral science—*much more likely to be rude to someone else.*

And if they are, and if each of those ten subsequent moments of rudeness is witnessed by a fresh ten people, you start to see how the butterfly effect might just take place, and how my hotdog moment might still prove to be the turning point that eventually brings down the very foundations of Western society.

That day, Madam Hotdog and I actively made the innocent bystanders in that diner ruder by unwittingly releasing a fresh puff of rudeness, there to be observed and "caught" and spread by others. How?

"When people come into contact with rudeness," says Trevor Foulk, when I put this to him, because I'd suddenly realized I had the power to put things to people, "the part of the brain that processes rudeness 'wakes up' a little bit . . ."

Foulk says it's this nonconscious stirring of your rudeness antennae that means if someone's rude to you, it's now more likely that the next time you find yourself talking with somebody, you'll be primed for both giving and sensing rudeness yourself.[1]

I agree with you: it sounds crazy. It sounds unlikely we're that simple; that you will literally be rude to the next person you talk to because your Snidey Sense has tingled. What if it's a clergyman or a weeping orphan? But just as the Hotdog Incident proved to me as I became angrier and grouchier and quicker to judge, the rudeness is now within you, nearer the surface than it was, and it takes far less for it to bubble up and spill over into the next conversation, encounter, or standoff.

What's scary is that no matter who you think you are, your own rudeness is right there, waiting for someone to needle you, and even if you know this, controlling it is more or less beyond you. Whatever thin layer of civility we have is easily scraped and grazed. Gaps start to appear. You begin to perceive the world in a different way: you begin to see rudeness where none was intended, and then you act rudely yourself. You don't even have to witness rudeness repeatedly: one moment of exposure is enough. It's like someone sneezing directly in your face.

Rudeness is airborne; a hidden yawn, passed from person to person until it stretches around the world.

And it happens all the time. The Wallace Report tells us that British people feel someone's been unnecessarily rude to them an average of twice a week. That's 104 times a year. And each time it happens, know this: it makes *you* a little bit ruder too.

· · ·

Foulk and his colleagues had their report published in the *Journal of Applied Psychology*, and in it they explained a number of experiments they'd undertaken.

In one of them, a group of volunteers was happily working away in an office when an actor walked in to join them, as if he was a late participant. He was subjected to a moderate, scripted diatribe by the person in charge.

"What is it with you?" the acting man acted, aggressively. "You arrive late, you're irresponsible. Look at you; how do you expect to hold down a job in the real world? I need you to leave."

Cue awkward looks and quiet shuffles.

But it was then that the study really began, and here is what it showed.

The people who witnessed the outburst became not only less effective at the work, but also more sensitive to rudeness in general. Which means that even if someone else's subsequent behavior was pretty neutral, it was more likely to have been found "rude" by that group of people. A moment like that deeply affects us. It makes us more cynical of other people, warier of their motivations. Once someone has been affected or infected by rudeness, that little smiley face, or that kiss at the end of the email, is far more likely to be seen as sarcastic or aggressive.

Yes. An aggressive kiss.

The idea that we can "catch" behaviors has been around a while, and it's not just to do with rudeness. Here's a happy example for your next dinner party: if a friend of yours has recently divorced their partner, you are now 75 percent more likely to get divorced yourself.[2] You're welcome.

As people, we learn from each other and bolster each other's behavior either consciously or subconsciously. Like a computer virus, rudeness buries itself deep in our minds and skulks around in the shadows.

To demonstrate this, at one point Foulk and his team showed a video to a group of study participants. The video showed someone in an office being unnecessarily rude to a colleague. Another group of students was shown a perfectly polite video of perfectly normal office people being perfectly ordinary with one another. Both groups were then asked to reply to an email, which was written in neutral tones. The group that had witnessed the rudeness was far more likely to reply to this very everyday email with genuine hostility.

This happens to us all. I once received a perfectly neutral email asking me when I planned to deliver some work that ended "Many thanks" with a full stop on the end.

This is what it said:

If you could get me that document today that would be great. Many thanks.

It nearly drove me to despair.

"How *dare* they write 'Many thanks' with a full stop?!" I remember thinking. "It's so passive aggressive! Dismissive! Presumptuous! Oh, don't *ask* for the document, oh no. Just *assume* I'll send it. Oh, 'you'll do exactly what I say, *Many thanks*, full stop.' *Screw* this guy!"

In reality, it is theoretically possible he was simply ending an efficient email using a globally recognized term and correct punctuation. Nevertheless, I found it rude. And think about that phrase: I *found* it rude.

Maybe I found it because I was looking for it.

. . .

Foulk and friends suggest the toxic effect of rudeness—some actually call it a neurotoxin—lasts an entire week. It can spread like wildfire around a contained office, leading to general hostility, lower morale, poorer performance, and worse coffee.

I'm serious about that. The people who witnessed that latecomer getting told off made more mistakes in simple tasks afterward.

In fact, it's been shown that even when the rude behavior is mild at best, it impairs a person's basic ability to think.

This is why often our first reaction to rudeness is to be flustered.

The day of the Hotdog Incident? I couldn't think at first. The rules had been changed. I was going in for one thing, then dealing with another. I had to take a moment to change gear.

Generally, when surprised by rudeness, we need that moment to process; we need to delve deep into the files at the back of our minds and pull out a barely used instruction manual.

But Foulk would argue that the rudeness I experienced that day might not have been randomly aggressive at all. It could simply have been a natural response, triggered by some other event that could easily have happened five minutes, or five days, before.

Maybe the woman just couldn't help it. She was infected.

*   *   *

In a parallel study, doctors Amir Erez and Christine Porath tested three different "rudeness" scenarios involving 275 students.[3] The students had to brainstorm creative uses for a brick.

There were other things they had to do, like anagrams, but creative uses for a brick was my favorite.

Again, the idea of a latecomer was used because we've all been late for something and it's easy to relate both to being late and to being annoyed at someone's lateness.

This guy showed up six minutes later than he was supposed to, made his excuses, and was immediately dismissed and sent away. That's all the control group saw.

But another group saw the latecomer dismissed, followed by the experimenter going crazy, rudely complaining about how all the students at the University of Southern California were completely un-professional compared to those at other universities.

A further bunch of students arrived to be greeted by a passive-aggressive person at a desk saying *"Can't you read? There is a SIGN on the door that tells you the experiment will be elsewhere. But you didn't even bother to look at the door, did you? Instead, you preferred to disturb me and you can clearly see that I am busy. I am not a secretary here; I am a BUSY PROFESSOR!"*

I think describing yourself as a busy professor is not something a busy professor would do. Imagine a policeman walking around saying, "I am a busy policeman!" Are you, mate? Because you definitely sound like you've just found a uniform somewhere.

Then there was a final group who was asked just to *imagine* these scenarios.

Compared to the control groups who, remember, were unaware of any of this rude behavior, the groups who witnessed rudeness did far worse on their tasks.

Somehow, that rudeness created a roadblock in their minds.

Those who witnessed the latecomer being talked about rudely solved 33 percent fewer anagrams and came up with nearly 40 percent fewer ideas for creative uses for a brick.

Those who met our "busy professor"—who still sounds like he was wearing a trench coat and a fake mustache—were 61 percent worse at anagrams and produced 58 percent fewer ideas for unusual brick use than those who had not been treated rudely at all.

Frighteningly, even those who just *imagined* incivility suffered.

Just imagining rudeness makes you *worse at thinking up uses for a brick.*

This could decimate our building trade. Which is why it's so lucky builders have such a reputation for polite chitchat and manners.

Now you can see why businesses are so keen to train their managers not to offend anyone when giving out even the mildest criticism: it's not to protect their feelings but to protect the bottom line. They can't afford the roadblocks in people's minds.

If rudeness spreads, then keeping us all in cubicles and windowless strip-lit offices and encouraging us to eat at our desks and communicate by faceless email is like saying, "From now on, we're all going to work in a disease factory." One report I read was virtually pleading with businesses to consider whether they really needed internal emails, so often so easy to misinterpret.

No matter how polite we'd like to be, no matter how nice we like to think we are, receiving or witnessing rudeness makes us more cynical, less trusting, and even less empathetic.

> **Witnessing rudeness makes us more cynical, less trusting and even less empathetic.**

Because in that same study involving creative uses for bricks, like scientific Columbos, Amir Erez and Christine Porath had time for just one more thing.

They purposefully had someone "accidentally" drop something.

Nearly three-quarters of people who had witnessed no rudeness immediately tried to lend a hand. Of course they did; they're not animals. But of the people who had been treated rudely by the busy professor? Only 24 percent felt inclined to help.

Part of this is learned behavior. Office managers who receive what they feel is unfair treatment from their own manager tend to replicate it, handing the very same treatment down to their employees in turn.[4]

And slowly, a culture of rudeness starts to drown an office, a workplace, or a corporation.

· · ·

But that at least should be the end of it: someone says something thoughtless or rude, and you have a bad day at work.

You go home. Watch TV. Eat a samosa. You forget about it.

But you don't.

You've done this, I've done this, everybody's done this, but now it's science: infected people take the rudeness virus home with them.

Those who do feel drained; more emotional; they may snap at their partners.

Their partners, now infected, take that contagious rudeness back to their own office, free to infect others. As a team from Baylor University in Texas puts it, we are "sending ripples of rudeness" far beyond our own circles.[5]

Okay. And *then* it's over.

Except now comes the rudeness hangover.

That's not a technical term, by the way, but it's the best one I can think of to describe what happens next.

That night, when you get home, you cannot recover in the way you need to. You might not realize it's happening and, even if you do, you may not be able to put your finger on why, but your emotional state will more than likely have been altered.

I'm telling you all this because that's exactly what happened to me after the Hotdog Incident. I was snappier. I did feel drained. That wine couldn't have been opened any quicker. And there was that anger.

To get over a day at work you need a certain amount of psychological detachment; to do other things and think other thoughts. But when even vague memories of rudeness are burrowing about in your head, kicking at your synapses, bruising your brain, your recovery time is diminished. You can't switch off. Things play on your mind. Your sleep might be affected because you haven't wound down in the same way. You wake up grouchier.

A study of 171 people in the legal profession[6] showed that after-work recovery was lower on days in which people experienced rudeness at work, and that this continued to the next morning.

I told you: it's a hangover.

It can lead to disaster. It can even, if unchecked, lead to depression.

Even just on a basic scale, concentration plummets, taking productivity with it. It's even been shown that people learning new skills—the ukulele, say, or Esperanto—couldn't focus on these tasks as well as they could on "normal" days.

Rudeness is directly contributing to the *death of the ukulele*.

It is draining. It wears us down. It leaves us tired, stressed, upsetting our partners, and unable to do our best work.

Rudeness, I mean—not the ukulele.

And remember: most of the time it doesn't even need to have happened to us for it to affect us; we can have just been aware of it.

The simple fact that you are reading this book—you nerd—means that the part of your brain that is sensitive to rudeness may receive a boost in activation. Not only will you be more aware of rudeness—so I better apologize for calling you a nerd—but quite without realizing, your brain is dredging up memories of rudeness or moments you associate with it.

Reading this book, it's probable you now perceive the world as slightly worse than the person closest to you who is not reading it.

Put simply, just by reading about rudeness, this book is actively making your life worse.

If we are rude to other people, we are literally making the whole world ruder. It is a sickness. A zombie rudepocalypse.

> ## It is a sickness. A zombie rudepocalypse.

And this is how the world will end.

In all seriousness, rudeness can lead to devastating events, which can ruin careers and lives.

It certainly ruined flight attendant Steven Slater's career. But not for the reasons you'd imagine.

After all the press hubbub and the talk-show gags and the rumors of a TV reality show, Slater's story began to fall apart.

No one could find the woman who'd supposedly been rude to him. Nor could anyone find a passenger or fellow crew member to corroborate any of it. It turned out he may have been drinking and had mental health issues, as well as ongoing family problems. His former employers rounded on him, saying he'd put people's lives in danger. Emergency chutes open at an incredible rate; he could have killed someone on the ground. The plane had to be taken out of service, who knows how many innocent people's days he'd ruined with his own rudeness ripple effect.

But that side of the story is not the one that everyone has heard.

A man finally having enough; finally standing up against rudeness—that's something we all *want* to have happened because rude things have happened to all of us, and we've all wanted to do something crazy in response.

In fact, standing up to rudeness can be a beautiful thing—as we shall look at next, when we consider the story of one man and his very powerful bottom.

CHAPTER 3

Bad Manors

Was I not expecting rudeness out of the city?

In 1993, students at the Colombian National University in Bogotá, dissatisfied with the way the university was run, turned up to confront the rector, then 42-year-old Antanas Mockus.

The students were hostile, they jeered, they rudely booed, they numbered in their thousands, and they wouldn't let him speak.

Frustrated, Mockus did something he'd never done before.

He strode up to the edge of the stage, unbuckled his belt, turned around, dropped his trousers, and mooned them.

It was a powerful gesture of defiance. It was also a really weird thing for a rector to do.

The students were shocked. Were they being rude or was he? Was he just showing them how rude *they* were? *Why had the rector shown them his arse?*

It became a national scandal. Shocked citizens shook their heads and shrugged sadly at TV reporters. Hundreds of thousands of words were written about Mockus's bottom. He was forced to resign. He left the university in disgrace. He'd been caught with his trousers down.

But Antanas Mockus's bottom would go on to save thousands of lives and change people's behavior in a way that no one saw coming.

Eighteen months later, he would be mayor of Bogotá, and he would have at his disposal a powerful weapon.

An army of mimes.

                              *   *   *

I bet you read that last sentence a couple of times just to make sure it wasn't a mistake.

Let me explain.

In 1994, Bogotá, Colombia, was in danger of descending into chaos. It was widely known as "the worst city in the world"; a violent place of corruption and filth.

Antanas Mockus's bottom had led to him being seen as a maverick. A man who lived with his mother and enjoyed a chinstrap beard, but who would stand up and act honestly and tell people his feelings. He ran as an independent, and when he became mayor owed nobody money or favors. He set up his own staff, made up of the country's brightest minds, and told them to think differently.

The 6.5 million citizens of Bogotá had no pride in their city any more. They were acting violently because no one was condemning their violence. They were littering the streets because no one showed them why they shouldn't. They were selfish, unthinking, and helpless.

But Mockus had faith in them.

And to show this, one of the first things he did was dress up in a superhero costume and take to the streets as "Supercitizen," scrubbing away rude graffiti and picking up other people's rubbish. He was literally cleaning up the streets.

Granted, from the footage I found, he looks like a man having some kind of breakdown. But here was a man showing the world how to take personal responsibility.[1]

The people were inspired. They saw in him what they'd lacked before: a moral leader. Someone putting down rules that would make life better for everybody.

There was method to his madness. Mockus wanted to create a kind of dialogue about the way we treat each other. He wanted people to participate in society—the way we all participate when we respect one another and put rudeness to one side.

"Knowledge empowers people," he said. "If people know the rules, and are sensitized by art, humor, and creativity, they are much more likely to accept change."

One early scheme empowered citizens to comment on whether someone else was behaving in the way they would like to be treated.

Mockus printed 350,000 cards—on one side a red thumbs-down, on the other a green thumbs-up—and distributed them widely.

If you saw someone helping someone else with their shopping, or holding a door open for someone, you would walk up and hold out your thumbs-up card.

But if you saw someone pushing into a line or yelling at a cashier, a bunch of you would get out your thumbs-down cards and hold them aloft—humiliating the rude person and forming your own sort of behavioral police squad.

Ordinary citizens had been given a voice. It was a radical idea because only radical ideas would work. And it did. People began to relearn the rules of polite social behavior. They learned what was rude again because, quite simply, they'd forgotten.

The roads were also a problem.

Bad drivers who would flout the speed limits and the law in general were killing thousands every year. Dangerous driving, pushy behavior and selfish maneuvering all contributed. So Mockus did what we'd all do.

He unleashed an army of mime artists onto the streets of Bogotá.

These mime artists—dressed in traditional black, their faces painted bright white—would highlight bad driving or rule-breaking, pointing their oversize white gloves at drivers and making horrified crying faces, or encouraging whole streets of people to boo them. They'd run behind people who were crossing a road illegally, mimicking their movements and ridiculing them.

The transit police were furious that rogue mimes were taking such liberties, just as you would be if your boss suddenly announced a series of mimes were taking over *your* job. But the transit police were known to have many members who were corrupt and bribable. So Mockus shut them down. Told them they were all losing their jobs. Now, this was obviously unfair on the law-abiding officers, so Mockus did the right thing and rehired 400 of them.

But *only* if they retrained as mimes.*

Elsewhere in Bogotá, other citizens had complained of rude, mean taxi drivers. Mockus told the people that if they found good, honest drivers, they should ring his office immediately and name them. He had hundreds of calls, and invited all the "good" taxi drivers to a meeting in which he named them all "Knights of the Zebra" and they discussed how to change the behavior of their rude colleagues.

Mockus fought against domestic violence. Championed community policing. Promoted civility. He dressed people up as monks and had them hang around near loud people to combat noise pollution. He noticed that the streets didn't feel as safe when there were fewer women on them. So he launched a Night Without Men, where women were encouraged to hit the bars and restaurants and the men were encouraged to stay at home with the kids. A female police commander secured the streets with an all-female police force. Around 700,000 women—free of the threat of uncivil behavior from men—went out

---

* I'd love to have heard their conversations with their partners that night.

that night. Huge groups marched down the streets of Bogotá. If they passed a house in which they could see a man making dinner for the kids or attending to his baby, they would stop and applaud.

Things just felt *better*.

And the impact of making people realize the effects of their actions in the city were huge.

Traffic fatalities fell by half.

Homicides were reduced by a third.

Sixty-three thousand people actually volunteered to pay 10 percent more in taxes, just because Mayor Mockus said it'd be nice if they would.

Inspired by his story, I decide to try and call Mockus one night from my house in London. I find a number, call it, ask if he's around. And over a crackly, echoey speakerphone in Bogotá that evening, he tells me that people did think he was "borderline crazy." He's a family man who's incredibly close to his mother, so I ask him what she made of it all.

"She was once asked what she thought of what I had done," he says with a smile in his voice. "She said, 'Antanas has done nothing.'"

"Nothing?" I say.

"She explained: 'Because if you think you have *done*, you will stop *to do*.'"

Mockus was inventive, creative, insane. He was moral. He was also right. His schemes were incredibly popular: 96 percent of people wanted his changes to continue. He had made people think about how to be better, how not to be *rude*.

History will show that Antanas Mockus had a world-changing arse.

. . .

Now, ordinarily, in a book like this, you'd have a whole chapter called something like "A Brief History of Rudeness" and it would delve into the changing world of villages to cities, from the African plains to

Victorian London, to the stifled 1950s to our parents' generation to prevailing attitudes of the present-day vis-à-vis social networking and blah blah blah.

But that sounds like a chapter both you and I already want to skip, and, really, I don't want to tell you about some guy who said something rude to some other guy in 1843 and the scandal that then swept through polite society, outraging men with mustaches and making all women faint.

I want to talk about you and me and today.

I think it's enough to suggest that in the old days—a technical term—when we were all living in very small communities, whether in the desert or a tiny French village, rudeness was risky. Reputations stuck. You couldn't annoy too many people. Before you knew it, no one was talking to you and they'd chase you out of the village, claiming your bad vibes were to blame for the annual wheat crop failing.

It's also not ridiculous to suggest that as we moved into larger areas, the ability to get away with rudeness has grown exponentially. Away from your regular "safe spaces"—your home, your workplace—all you encounter are strangers with nothing to lose by being rude to you.

The bus stop. The bus. The train.

The bus stop again.

"What do you care about those people?" you might think. "You'll never see them again!" But this has become an attitude taken on by a world in which suddenly we have far more opportunity to experience and undertake rudeness. We are the rude-rich.

You mustn't take my word for it.

Robin Ian MacDonald Dunbar, BA PhD DSc (Hons), has so many letters after his name that when you get an email from him, you worry he's had a stroke and collapsed on his keyboard.

He is head of the Social and Evolutionary Neuroscience Research

Group in the Department of Experimental Psychology at the University of Oxford, and his business card is therefore two feet long. He is a great communicator, and I met him once when we both received an unimpressive certificate for learning how to pour Guinness properly in a pub in Putney. I'll just leave that story there.

Dunbar is best known for formulating "Dunbar's number"—a measurement of the number of people with whom your brain can manage to maintain a stable relationship at any one time. It's a long and fascinating paper, but if you're pushed for time, it's 150.

I asked him whether, evolutionarily speaking, there is any benefit to us in having rudeness as a tool.

Here is everything in three paragraphs that it would normally take 3,000 words to explain.

Rudeness?! I would hazard the guess that this is simply part and parcel of the in-group/out-group effect. Because our natural community sizes are small AND your community is very important for your success and well-being, it is important to protect those relationships and that unavoidably forces you into an Us-vs-Them situation . . . because them-there-over-the-hill are weird, weird, weird, and you wouldn't want to get tangled up with them. Even for the price of a hotdog.

So perhaps being rude to strangers is a way of reinforcing your within-group bonds: you have limited time and energy and you want to confine as much of that as possible to the people that are really going to matter. And you are never going to see these idiots again, anyway. AND, what's more . . . them-over-there aren't to be trusted, so you're better safe than sorry.

Strangers are always a risk, even in these situations . . . because you just don't have any experience of their trustworthiness.

The exception that people always cite, says Robin when I press him further, is desert culture, "where unstinting hospitality is offered to strangers that haul up in your neck of the woods dying of thirst. And that's true, but people always forget that a) it's a reciprocal arrangement, so you help me now and I'll help you later; and b) there's a catch . . . once you've left camp, you're fair game."

He reminds me of the time in Scottish history when the MacDonalds of Glencoe offered shelter and food to the lost Campbell clan in 1692 . . . and were swiftly massacred. The Campbells may have gone on to make wonderful soups, but they were terrible houseguests.

So, once we were rightly naturally suspicious of outsiders. But these days, as we share bus seats and crisscross city paths a thousand times a day, we tend simply to ignore them because they just don't matter. We have honed our social groups. We are no longer in our delightful teens and early twenties when the very next person who walked into the room could be your new favorite person and BFF. We are older and wiser, we are set in our ways and tired, and in a time-poor world strangers become people of no consequence. They are nothing more than meaningless extras in the glorious movie of our lives, to be treated however we feel in the moment.

And that's just a shortcut to rudeness.

．　．　．

Every week, one million new people move to the cities of the world.

It's getting a bit crowded, though I prefer the word "cozy."

Safe at home, in charge of our own environment, rudeness is not generally an issue. Not unless you've got a roommate who's always nicking your Fanta or a neighbor who won't stop playing Bruno Mars.

But as we leave our private space for public, we understand we're expected to behave in a different way. We just do. We get it. And in those moments where someone bursts our bubble by acting in a way we don't expect them to, we respond by feeling stressed and branding them rude.

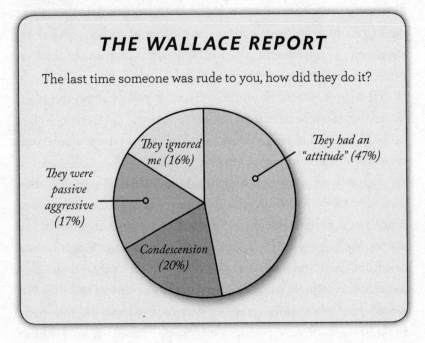

THE WALLACE REPORT

The last time someone was rude to you, how did they do it?

They ignored me (16%)

They had an "attitude" (47%)

They were passive aggressive (17%)

Condescension (20%)

Where the rudeness happens is important, too, and we'll get to that. But we are territorial. Even in what we know is a public space, we consider it somehow private. And yet other people will impact on us, either because they can't help it, they don't realize that they're doing it, or worse—because they don't care about you and your stupid life.

Strangers are everywhere, all the time, working to their own standards.

Darn strangers!

Like the stranger who brings a Big Mac meal onto the train so that everyone can watch and hear him eat it, pickles trickling from his mouth while the smell fills the carriage and our noses. The stranger in the coffee line who tries to nudge in front of you. The stranger who won't give you space at the cash machine. The stranger who reads your texts over your shoulder or who greedily snatches the newspaper you've barely put down.

There's the weirdo who thinks everyone on the bus wants to hear her crappy, tinny grime blaring out of a bright pink Samsung Galaxy; the waiter who makes a point of humiliating you by pretending not to understand why you ordered a "panini" and not a "panino"; the people who don't turn off the keystroke noises on their iPads and fill your world with tiny taps and bloody blips.

And the phones! My God, the phones. The people on their phones, loudly cackling at gossip or asking what they're having for tea tonight or showing off about how important or well-off they are, knowing that if this was a different time we would pretend they were witches just to watch them dunked in a lake.

Phones are particularly curious and are, I think, a wonderful micro example of how rudeness works in a city.

Once we understood the deal. It was simple. There was a phone at home, there was a phone at work. When it rang, it took priority. Someone was calling—*for a reason*. Now, all over the city, we're never off them, and while they connect us to the world at large, they disconnect us from the world around us.

The guy who just quickly steps out into the road at a pedestrian crossing while on his phone and won't even look your way to acknowledge you for not running him over in your car because he's on the phone to the friend he's 30 seconds away from meeting.

The woman in the line for coffee who won't answer the barista's simple and necessary questions about her order and will be furious when it arrives slightly wrong, and all because *can't you see I'm on the phone?*

These people get in our way, slow us down, and rudely slice off a piece of the world just for them. They are caught up in their own non-sense in a way that means they miss the communal things the rest of us are concentrating on, like the movement of a line, the flow of a pavement, or just not getting run over. One team of academics thought this "inattentional blindness" was so important and presumably frustrating that they dressed one of their team as a clown and popped him on a unicycle just to see whether a group of normal people on their mobile phones would notice a unicycling clown slowly circling around. Only 8 percent of people on their phones thought to mention it when asked if they'd just seen anything odd. Only 25 percent remembered it happening at all.

Again: this was a slowly circling *unicycling clown*.[2]

But here's what really irks us: the loud, private, public conversations we are forced to endure. Science has shown us why we find other people having a loud chat on their phone so frustrating and so rude: hearing half a conversation is proven more distracting than hearing a whole one.

It's why two people gossiping together loudly on a train might be annoying, but not necessarily rude. But one person loudly dominating the train car while speaking to an unseen party, never lowering their voice in consideration of others? That's rude.

In one experiment, a group of people were assigned a task and told to get on with it in total silence.

Then they were asked to complete a task while they also heard two other people having a loud conversation.

They managed the tasks equally well on both occasions.

But when they were played a tape of just half a conversation, their ability to perform the task diminished rapidly.

Lauren Emberson undertook the study while at Cornell University, and it came from a place of deep and earned annoyance.[3]

"When I was an undergraduate," she told me when I discovered this, "I rode the bus to campus for 30-plus minutes each way. When someone was talking on the phone around me, I found I could not tune out that conversation no matter what I did. I certainly didn't want to be listening to their often very boring conversations, but I couldn't seem to turn my attention away. I began to question why."

Well, it's this: imagine listening to an audiobook in which someone has edited out every other sentence. It would drive you insane. Our simple, monkey brains find it difficult to ignore only half a story. It doesn't make sense to us. Subconsciously, part of us tries to fill in the gaps, whether we want to or not. We think about the person invading our ears. We can't filter it out. Try reading this book while someone opposite is on their phone talking about whether Gary is ready to take on the role of Head of Acquisitions yet. You will literally read this sentence 60 times before you properly take it in.

Gary's not ready and, also, he's sleeping with Lorraine.

"Hearing half a conversation," says Emberson, "effectively forces a listener to pay attention to the conversation."

And that's precisely why we find it rude. This enforced witnessing, this *theft of control*, has a profound effect on our abilities to function up to our usual standards. It interrupts our thoughts and treads heavily on our lives. Some would say we should just ignore what Emberson calls "halfalogues," but the science just laughs and says: we literally cannot.

To prove it, researchers took 64 members of the public and exposed them to the very same staged conversation while traveling.

Now, half of these conversations were made by mobile phone, meaning that the travelers heard only half the conversation. The other half were performed by two people standing nearby, having the conversation in the "real world."

The results were clear: conversations on a mobile phone are much more noticeable—and therefore more infuriating—than genuine conversations.[4]

In the hum of the city, we are a mass, huddled together and doing our best to get where we need to be. We create situations that are the best possible for the most people possible: we sit in our seats, we share the armrest where appropriate, we keep our stuff in a neat little pile on the table in front of us, we make sure our bags aren't in anyone's way, we blush if we accidentally touch someone else's foot and disturb their peace.

When one of us whips out a Nokia and breaks out of the mass to begin a conversation unique to our own life, that is not on. Those around us see it as rude. You are no longer "one of us."

The problem is, cities flow—and "flow" is a word we'll hear again, when we take a trip to the Californian highways. But most of our use of the city is as wallpaper while getting from home to work, or work to home.

A million things happen that create the same distracting noise as the gossip on the phone.

People in cities are not worse than people anywhere else. But they are likely to be less similar because cities are by nature more diverse. We feel less responsible because there are more of us to share responsibility. And because there are more of us, we are each more anonymous. Three things that lead absolutely to a general sense of rudeness.

I once spent several months on a tiny island off the coast of New Zealand called Great Barrier. At the time, only 862 people lived there. You could easily go a day without seeing anyone, but when you did, God forbid you didn't say hello. When passing another car on thin gravel roads, a simple raise of the index finger said it all: *I acknowledge you, fellow traveler; I come in peace; may your journeys be fruitful; see you tomorrow.*

Only once did someone not return my heartfelt index-finger greeting. And look at the effect it had on me: here I am, ten years later, still banging on about it, to you, a complete stranger.

The thing that also really stuck with me after living on that island was just how much attention I paid to people when I saw them. I didn't just see them; I took them in.

When I returned to London—a city with a population 10,000 times that of Great Barrier—I mistakenly thought it would be a good idea to walk alone through Piccadilly Circus on my first day back. I found myself confused and shocked. I had to nip down a side street and have a pint on my own to recover. As thousands of people marched around me, I sensed my brain was trying to take them all in as individuals. But they weren't individuals anymore. They were just a mass. My brain had reset to a pre-city time in just a few months.

On Great Barrier, just as in any tiny community, acknowledging complete strangers is a social rule. But in London, or New York, or Berlin, or Tokyo, you'd be locked up if you tried it because human interaction in cities is as much based on ignoring one another as interaction on Great Barrier was based on acknowledging.

Just because society has evolved into cities doesn't mean our brains have had time to catch up. If we can't undertake simple tasks while hearing half a phone conversation, how can we deal with everything a Rome, Boston, or Taipei brings?

Just the noise itself is enough to change us as people. The sirens, the horns, the crazed cyclist kicking off a side mirror, the shouts of it all. When you bear in mind something called Urban Overload Hypothesis (coined by the brilliant American social psychologist Stanley Milgram), it's not too much of a stretch to think of the city as just one long mobile phone call we're constantly forced to overhear.

Imagine an old woman, standing at the top of some steps, her arm in a cast . . . she struggles with her shopping, and accidentally sends a bag of tin cans and apples cascading down the steps.

You want to help her, don't you?

You want to run to her right now!

Well, researchers tried a similar setup in the 1970s.

Eighty percent of people ran to help.

But that number fell to just 15 percent when, somewhere nearby, someone was using a lawnmower.[5]

Before, we saw how someone being rude directly to you can make you less helpful as a person.

But a *lawnmower*? The mere sound of a lawnmower can make us worse people? Old women could be flinging themselves off cliffs in the hope you'll notice, but if someone's edging their lawn, forget it.

In the insane noise and bustle of the city, we are, then, immediately less helpful to or mindful of others. Our cities seem less friendly, less personal, and—yes—ruder, precisely because that's what they are.

> **We cope with life by filtering things out.**
> **It's rudeness as survival.**

We cope with life by filtering things out. It's rudeness as survival. The way we ignore, pretend, act, or squeeze our eyes shut to fake sleep as a pregnant woman prays desperately for a seat on the bus. We are more likely to think someone else will help; we are less inclined to draw attention to ourselves; we are just trying to get away with it. We guard our precious bubble; we protect our anonymity.

．　．　．

In recent years in Japan, there has been a rise in the number of people wearing surgical masks as they travel to and from work.

It's slightly unnerving to walk through Yoyogi Park or over Shibuya Crossing and pass dozens of people hiding behind these small white masks. You find yourself holding your breath, just in case there's something catching. The most common accepted reason for people wearing them is that they're feeling a little under the weather and don't want to risk compromising other people. It is a selfless act, this extreme Japanese politeness toward strangers, and the very opposite of what we've come to expect in a city.

But more and more, different reasons for wearing them are coming to the fore. Maybe the real reasons. Some wear them for fashion, others to hide a pimple, but for many Japanese, wearing a surgical mask has become a way of coping with so many strangers, so many interactions, so many social expectations. A Japanese news agency study quotes one person as saying they just "don't like having to create facial expressions for people." Others wear masks and headphones together, so that no one can talk to them. Some just want to blend into the crowd of the city.

If they're used to most of their interactions being on email or apps or phones, suggests the Japanese writer Yuzo Kikumoto, they build themselves a thin cotton wall they can hide behind.[6]

Most people in Western cities don't wear masks—unless it's Gotham—but we do mask our civility. It is precisely—as Stanley Milgram puts it in his essay "The Experience of Living in Cities"—the way "the urbanite disregards the drunk sick on the sidewalk as he purposefully navigates through the crowd."[7]

As survival becomes more ingrained, growing cities develop a reputation for it.

"Tourists Find London Unfriendly"—Reuters

"New York Voted Most Rude and Arrogant City in U.S."—Daily Mail

"Moscow Voted the World's Most Unfriendly City"—Independent

"French Capital One of the Most Hostile Places for Foreign Visitors"—Scotsman

What Bogotá's crazy mayor understood was that we behave differently in a city if we no longer feel like the person who left the house that morning, but just part of a process. We don't feel that we have to stick to the rules if we don't feel there are any.

The Broken Windows theory popularized in the early 1980s by James Wilson and George Kelling—and which we'll get into the rights and wrongs of later on—says that if you leave one broken window unfixed on a street, more broken windows will soon follow.[8]

People will begin to assume that no one cares; that rules no longer apply here. Vandalism takes hold. Litter coats the streets. As recently as 2008, researchers at the University of Groningen in the Netherlands left money sticking out of a clean mailbox, and money sticking out of a graffitied one. Their results showed that normal, everyday people were twice as likely to steal someone else's money if it was from a graffitied mailbox.[9] One disorder leads to the next. It escalates. The world becomes microscopically harder, meaner, grubbier.

Let a broken window stay broken and, soon, everyone's dumping old mattresses there and a cat's on fire. Fix it, like Mockus, and maybe you'll have a city that can take pride in itself again.

Once more, we see that rude behavior begets more of the same and worse. It spreads, filling out the lines of our subway maps, trailing a line like a bus route across the city.

Only two things have been systematically proven to change this, and it is on these two things I am forced to suggest that, as we move forward, we must now rely.

Ourselves.

And mime.

CASE STUDY:
TRAIN OF THOUGHT

I'm on a packed train when the woman sitting next to me starts rustling about in her bag.

Her phone's going off.

A few people offer her comforting smiles as she panics, trying to find it.

"Hello, Jan speaking," she says, flustered, pressing the phone to one ear and the palm of her hand to the other. "Dave? Did it come through?"

She pauses, dramatically.

Actually, it's not a pause, is it, she's just listening to Dave.

"It *didn't* come through?"

Bloody hell. Whatever was supposed to come through didn't come through.

"Are you sure? Have you checked?"

I'm sure Dave has checked. It would be a weird thing to just guess at: "Oh, hi Jan, I'm just ringing because I decided to guess that the important document didn't come through. Have I checked? No, but as I say, I had a guess."

"Oh, lordy," says Jan, tutting. "Well, isn't that just the way?"

She gets out a lip balm and starts balming her lip. I try and go back to reading my book, but I can't. I'm now as involved in this loud conversation as Jan is.

"Tell you what, Dave, can you be a star and log in for me?"

It takes so little to be a star these days. One day Simon Cowell will start a show where people have to just log in for each other from increasingly impressive distances.

"Yeah, it should be right there on my desktop."

The lip balm goes back in the bag, and everyone waits for Dave to get to Jan's computer.

"How's Stacey getting on?" asks Jan, but because we can't hear Dave, I guess we'll never know. I hope she's not dead.

"Are you at my computer?" she says, jangling a bangle, like she's warming up for this. "All right, I'll give you my password."

She's going to give Dave her password. Here. On a train. In front of everybody else. This demonstrates extreme confidence. Jan's got some bold moves. That's obviously why she's in charge of Dave.

"Ready?"

I immediately feel uncomfortable. So does everyone else. A man leans into his book. A woman pretends to study the clouds. We don't want to hear your password, Jan! It's your password!

Why are some people so open on trains? Do they forget everyone else is there? Do we not matter? Even if you know we are all of us about to *know your password*?

I mean, honestly speaking, this password is of very little value to the other people on this train. I think I speak for everyone who has found themselves in Jan's close orbit this morning that it is unlikely any of us will ever break into her office, find her computer, and log in on her behalf. Even in a misguided shot at stardom. But the point is, we *could* do that now, if we wanted, couldn't we?

"It's nutnutnut100."

It's WHAT?

"Nut . . . nut . . . nut . . . 100."

It's NUTNUTNUT100?

The man leaning into his book brings it closer to his face.

That woman is trying really hard to stare at clouds.

I can't help but frown.

Jan casts me a sideways glance, and I pretend I'm frowning at some fluff that isn't on my jeans. I flick it away.

"Yep," says Jan, "is it there?"

All I can think about is nutnutnut100.

How did that become Jan's password? Is "nut" the only word she can remember? Is she just really into nuts? Is she a nut nut? But that still leaves one "nut" spare. Maybe she's someone who's just really into *nut* nuts. She's a nut nut nut. She's nuts about them.

I can't stop saying nuts.

"All right, then, Dave," she says, and now I think about poor, sweet Dave. He's got to walk around the office all day knowing that Jan's password is nutnutnut100. How's he going to stop himself from telling literally all his colleagues? What about Stacey? If she's at death's door this'll finish her off.

"Okay, bye then, Dave," says Jan. "You're a star, thanks."

She hangs up, and then everything is quiet.

I accidentally make eye contact with the cloud lady and she stifles a smile. The book man doesn't seem to have turned a page in ages but just sits there, his eyes staring madly.

I know what we're all thinking. We're all thinking nutnutnut100.

The cloud lady is about to laugh. This is a disaster. There's nothing wrong with telling everyone your password is nutnutnut100. The cloud lady is going red. I can't be here when she starts laughing.

And then the whoosh of the automatic doors and the familiar glassy jangle of the snack cart.

I know what's about to happen. At some point we're going to be offered nuts.

I grab my coat and quickly move seats.

Some things are best kept to yourself, Jan.

CHAPTER 4

Lip Service

How could bad service make me flip off a building?

Speaking as a man who's flipped off a diner, I have become very interested in the psychological effects of rudeness and why it turned me crazy.

Flipping off a building is never something to which I aspired as a child, and certainly not something I thought I'd be doing in my late thirties.

The fact that I felt so strongly about the Hotdog Incident—and considered an inanimate object somehow an enemy—stems once more from surprise.

Think about the terminology we use to describe rude events: "I was the *victim* of rudeness," for example; "It happened *to* me." There is a certain helplessness there, and finding out more about how rudeness works in the bustle of a city—where we're all a little more helpless than normal—reminded me of a place I knew 20 years ago.

When I first moved to London, a particular restaurant in Chinatown called Wong Kei was nursing a national reputation for incredible rudeness. I read a review of it in the *Evening Standard* on the train home from work one night.

"It sounds brilliant," I remember thinking. "They treat you so badly!"

Surly waiters would shunt you around, barely looking at you, impatiently demanding your order, castigating your choices, banging plates of food down in front of you, giving you your bill before you'd asked for it, literally chasing you down the street if you didn't leave a big enough tip.

Wong Kei seemed to go against everything the service industry so pompously declared it stood for. It was a novelty. It seemed refreshing. I decided to take a friend and go, because rudeness is fun, and even the name seemed playful, like it was putting on an act, like it was an entertainment somehow.

I lasted approximately eight minutes.

A tiny, furious Chinese woman pushed me up some stairs to a vast room, which was empty apart from a table of maybe eight people who sat in near silence.

"You sit here," she said, pushing me toward them, and when I asked if we could possibly sit at a different table, as we weren't with these guys and didn't want to gatecrash, she yelled, "NO!"

It soon became clear that the eight other people weren't together either. They were just four separate couples who'd all been made to sit together so at the end of the night the woman wouldn't have to clean as many tablecloths.

All four couples were now just sitting, awkwardly silent, praying their food would come and this would all be over soon.

I think a bad sign for a restaurant is if you have eight customers sitting in awkward silence praying it will all be over soon.

As it turns out, rudeness wasn't fun. It was just rude.

Wong Kei closed shortly afterward. It reopened only when they'd managed to find some friendlier waiters. I found that people stopped talking about it. It had lost what made it unique, its word-of-mouthness gone, just another Chinese restaurant in an area made up entirely of Chinese restaurants. Even today, the new manager wonders whether not being awful to people was the right move. "Maybe there was an issue with rude staff twenty years ago," he told a newspaper. "But I don't think so anymore. I don't know whether that's a good thing or not."[1]

You can imagine him shaking his head sadly as he said that, and then walking off into a more modern, customer-centric Chinatown, staring at the ground.

Some of the restaurant's reputation must obviously be down to cultural differences. There are obviously differences in global attitudes to rudeness, and we'll come to them, but maybe it's why when foreigners think of Britain, it's not long before they think of a nation of butlers. Quiet, attentive, polite. A friend of mine has been a waiter for many years, and he is good. He takes it very seriously. He says that a good waiter remains unseen, unnoticed, there before you realize you need him, and gone when he's done what he needs to do. Your glass remains invisibly topped up, and the conversation with your friends flows just as freely, because everything a host normally does is taken care of.

The United States is a country famed for its service industry, but what to an American diner is the height of politeness can, to a British person, seem overbearing and, yes, even a little rude.

They are not being polite to you—they are being polite *at* you.

They dominate, they perform, they interrupt, and though they are only interrupting to check you are having a nice time or ask where you're from, they are still interrupting. They lean over you to ask if you need things to make a point of you knowing they are actively getting you what you need. You get the feeling that if you had a little piece of broccoli stuck to your mouth, they might simply lick their fingers and thumb it off. Their attention can be tiring and physically and mentally intrusive, and I honestly think this kind of politeness is rude. It is performance politeness. It's "Look how polite I am!" versus being polite, and it comes at a cost. About 20 percent of your bill.

But in North America, when someone is genuinely impolite, you really notice it.

Ask Darren Dahl, Professor of Marketing and Behavioral Science at the Sauder School of Business in Vancouver.

"Now the problem with a hotdog," he tells me, wisely, "is that it's not aspirational."

I find this very rude but decide to keep talking to him. Particularly because a few years ago, in downtown Vancouver, he met his own Madam Hotdog: a woman who worked in the luxury Hermès store and who in the blink of an eye and the shake of a head would become the catalyst for his own subsequent research.

Darren walked into the shop simply to buy some grapefruit after-shave. He didn't tell me why he wanted grapefruit aftershave, though I guess it's more aspirational than a hotdog. Behind the counter sat a cold-looking woman in designer clothes, who took one look at Darren, "in a ratty T-shirt and ripped jeans," cast him a withering glance, shook her head, and looked away.

In that moment, Darren Dahl felt tiny. Unimportant. Unworthy. Unwelcome.

"The scowl said, 'You can't afford to be here. This is not for you,'" says Darren. "I wanted to show her that wasn't the case."

Darren ended up buying twice as much grapefruit aftershave as he went in for. Darren Dahl left that shop owning more grapefruit after-shave than literally anyone else on Earth. Darren Dahl must have smelled of nothing but grapefruit for years.

But later that day, as he sadly surveyed his hundreds of dollars' worth of bottles of designer grapefruit aftershave, Darren wondered why on Earth he'd done that.

"It's not like when I was in that diner I ended up buying twice as many hotdogs as I wanted," I tell him, and he reminds me again of that word: aspiration.

Darren aspired to be someone who wore grapefruit aftershave. And when someone told him he wasn't, he opened his wallet to win.

But why hadn't he just left? Gone somewhere else? Or not bought any grapefruit aftershave whatsoever?

He decided to study his own behavior, and what he found is depressing. We are far more likely to want to buy and use products from the very people who treat us with disrespect just for wanting to buy and use products from them.[2]

Dahl has called this rejection-into-profit the "Pretty Woman" effect, for obvious reasons. However, this effect won't work if you're buying knock-off Armani aftershave from your corner shop. Who cares what that guy thinks?

For rudeness to drive us to spend, we first of all have to aspire to be part of that gang. We have to be impressed by Givenchy or in awe of Armani.

"The research shows that if it's something you really want and you don't have it, you will put up with rudeness. If they're saying, 'You're not good enough for this,' you'll say, 'Yes I am—watch'—and BAM!"

And that "BAM!" is the sound of you ending up with North America's largest individual supply of citric aftershave.

The mere look of the salesperson plays its part, says Darren. The way they're dressed. Their makeup. Their hair. For us to spend, they must represent the brand we so desperately want to be accepted into.

But it all sounds so . . . childish. I put it to Darren that this must go all the way back to the "in" crowd at school. That this is an insecurity; that he was trying to *buy* her respect that day.

"Yes," he admits. "That is part of it."

Brands are powerful signifiers for our personalities.

* * *

As we grow up, we start to truly believe that certain brands represent certain qualities.

A Mercedes, for example, jet black and shiny, might in childhood have spelled out the idea of success to us. Owning a business, being a success, making money. If we're cut off on the highway by someone in a blacked-out, blinged-up Mercedes Benz, we're more likely to think this is a rude gesture by someone who doesn't care about us. It's emotive. They achieved what we couldn't. We're nothing to them because they're successful. They cut us off because on some level we're a failure.

An American academic named Jack Katz covered exactly this in a celebrated piece called "Pissed Off in L.A."[3] It touched a nerve with American drivers, and after reading it I thought about it constantly as I drove around the streets of London. Why were people in LA, or London, or Lichtenstein, so nice on their driveways—yet such beasts in their cars? Many people began to realize they had a very different idea of themselves from the reality they showed to strangers. If you asked anyone how long they'd wait before they beeped at a car that hadn't moved off at a green light, they'd probably say "five or six seconds." I tried it the day I read Katz's piece. The light turned green and I didn't move. I was beeped at in less than two seconds.

I immediately email Katz and politely demand a chat. He says if I'm ever driving around Los Angeles I should look him up.

But back to Darren and his surfeit of cologne.

Luxury brands rely on creating a social distance. They sell a lifestyle they need us to want. And now we know that Darren's research shows that if you walk into a shop and your insecurity about whether you should even be in there or not is confirmed, you are far more likely to spend.

You are not, however, likely to go back.

Seventy percent of us, according to the Wallace Report, think that if someone in a brand-name shop is rude to us, it absolutely affects our opinions of the brand as a whole. Nearly a fifth of people said that the last time someone was rude to them, it was while shopping.

A moment of rudeness can damage a brand. People think negatively about Luxury Inc. as a business if they were once treated rudely by someone wearing Luxury Inc. in a Luxury Inc. store.

And bad customer service is estimated to cost the U.S. alone around $41 billion a year.[4] How?

- Nearly 60 percent of the "ideal" consumers who experience bad or rude service—people aged 25–35—then share that experience online.
- 89 percent stop giving those businesses money altogether.
- And just as a cherry on top, 95 percent of them then tell their friends.[5]

These are our greatest weapons in the fight against rude customer service.

Psychologically, it cuts deep. Even just witnessing store staff being rude to someone else entirely is often enough for us not only to have a lower opinion of that brand and never revisit the shop, but also to start generalizing about what the other individual members of staff are probably like as well.[6]

Just like I did during the Incident, when I made my assumptions about the sad-faced woman shunting meat about in the background. I guessed she was probably rude because her brand ambassador was rude. That sad-faced woman might have been an absolute angel.

But Darren also thinks it's why an increasing percentage of luxury goods are bought online. Rudeness keeps us at home. It stops us feeling special.

From the everyday experiences we've had since school—in-groups, the need for acceptance—through to the respect we demand as adults, we no longer want to have to deal with the rejection of the devil wearing Prada. Or, in Darren's case, Hermès.

As we'll discover in a few moments, we are constantly engaged in power struggles both minor and major.

And that way rudeness lies.

CASE STUDY: BOTTOMS UP

My wife and I have arranged a babysitter and are at a restaurant, which so far is quite quiet.

"This is nice," she says. "We should do this more often."

"Definitely," I agree, knowing that with two kids there is a just above zero chance we will do this more often.

I move my coat as a man and his family arrive and sit down at the table next to ours. They could have picked anywhere. They chose right next to us. That's fine. That's a normal thing to do.

"The babysitter was okay, wasn't she?" I say, a little quieter now that we have company. "I had to talk to her about her exams while you were getting ready. I always end up talking about their exams. And then I have to say things like, 'Oh, that sounds like a good choice' when they tell me where they're going to university. For all I know I am doling out terrible advice. Perhaps I am *ruining* young lives."

"Good," says my wife.

Then: "MICHAEL!!!!" bellows a man, from across the room, and he stomps toward our table.

I give my wife a look.

"HOW *ARE* YOU?" says the man, shaking hands with the man at the table next to ours. "DO YOU HAVE EVERYTHING YOU NEED?"

I dunno why he's still shouting. He's inches away from the other guy. And they're literally holding hands.

"Yes, absolutely," says Michael. "Great place, by the way."

"Thank you," says the man, and he puts his other hand over his heart, because that's the only way to show thanks are sincere.

My wife raises her eyebrows. Guy must be the manager.

"You remember Kate?" says Michael, pointing at his wife, and while all this is loudly happening, my wife and I sit silently and chew on our bread, because we don't want to interrupt this great meeting, and anyway it'll be over soon.

"Yeah, been here about six months," says the manager, trying to sound bored but knowing it's impressive, and then he reels off a list of other fancy restaurants he was at beforehand, and then he *leans down onto their table and extends his bottom backward.*

This man's bottom is now just inches from my wife's face.

All I can see is my wife's face and this man's bottom.

"So," says my wife, "you know what you're going to order?"

No! I don't know what I'm going to order! And doesn't she realize? Can't she tell she's just inches from a strange bottom?

The manager continues to blather on about places he used to work for so long I feel like standing up and shouting, "Yeah? Well I used to work at *Argos* in the nineties!," and then Michael's wife starts showing off her knowledge and saying things like, "Oh, you must know Tom, then?" and then they both start passive-aggressively competing about who's known Tom the longest or worked with him the closest.

I widen my eyes and nod subtly to my wife's left. She looks. She sees the bottom. She turns back, horrified.

"It's a bottom!" I mouth.

I should say something. After all, we're paying customers. It's obvious how loud all this showing off must be for us because there's hardly anyone else here.

But it's the manager's bottom. And if I say anything, not only will I be insulting the manager, but I'll be ruining this wonderful reunion between Michael, Kate, and the owner of the bottom.

"Well enjoy—I'll see you after," says the manager, finally, and I am so relieved because that means I don't have to cause a fuss. Surely now, as he leaves, he'll turn and glance at us and give us an apologetic look—one that says, I'm so sorry for being loud and invading your wife's personal space with my bottom. And then we'll become friends and he'll invite me to become a shareholder.

But no. He turns, barely registers us, and skips off.

"He didn't even say sorry," I seethe, as Michael and Kate try and make their kids impressed by having met a loud man.

I spot the manager over my wife's shoulder. He's talking to a waiter and pointing in our direction. Moments later, the waiter heads toward us. He's carrying a bottle of wine!

"Oh!" I say, delighted.

"What?" says my wife.

The waiter walks straight past us and delivers the free wine to the table next to ours.

"From Mr. Smith," he says, and Michael and Kate coo over it.

I start to realize why I'm annoyed. It's not because of the loudness and it's not because of the bottom. It's because every time the manager makes these people feel special, he makes us feel unspecial. Like they are the aristocracy, enjoying *all* the power, and we are the norms. I have *no* power. I feel like singing that song from *Les Mis*. We're special too! WE'RE SPECIAL TOO!

I reach for more bread, but we've run out.

"Let them eat cake!" the manager would probably say.

The waiter tries to uncork the bottle, but it's a struggle. He places it between his knees and bends to pull.

His bottom is now right next to my wife's face.

There is zero chance we are doing this more often.

CHAPTER 5

Rudeness and Power

Who's more rude—the powerful or the powerless?

When I was at school, we had to do a Model United Nations.

I guess a lot of schools do it. You get a country—Namibia, say—and you research it. You find out what's important to it, how it makes its money. You stand up for its interests and debate with people representing other countries, and in front of everybody you're forced to hammer out shared interests and to try and avoid conflict.

That's not what happened at my school.

I can't remember how we all ended up with the roles we had to play, but let's say it was by lots. Someone got Belgium. Someone got Russia. And then we ran out of tables, so I was made a security guard.

The role of the security guard in a Model United Nations is not one you hear much about, which is very surprising, so let me tell you my main role. I had to help keep order while ensuring the safe passage of messages between different countries.

This was a system open to abuse.

After a while, it was clear that some of the security guards like myself were fed up of being gruffly beckoned over with a click of the fingers so that we could pass pointless notes between countries. There was nothing about trade deals or lifting of sanctions in them. It was just France telling Italy to bug off. The U.S. declaring war on Spain. China reminding Iraq he still owed him 50¢ for that Mars Bar.

It's probably just like it really is, but look—we were security guards, not page boys.

Well, we put our foot down. We had to take this seriously. We started vetting confidential notes, or refusing to take them. I remember Belarus telling me I was a tit straight after.

This lack of respect for a recognized authority figure like me doing such an important job irked the whole of the Ralph Allen School Model United Nations security team. Our authority was being consistently challenged by some jumped-up pencil pushers, bean counters, and bureaucrats who weren't on the front line like we were and had probably never even seen real action like this before. We weren't having it. We puffed out our chests, shushed them, or reported them to our higher-ups, like Mr. Simmons the geography teacher; a nice man but not one really experienced in high-level international negotiations.

Very quickly, two factions formed. It was them and us. It was like the Stanford Prison Experiment, except in a school gym with children who were just pleased to be out of math.[1] It became very unpleasant very quickly.

Now I see why: we had turned into little tyrants.

Even my own friends turned on me. To this day I can't look at William Sansom without thinking he should really have respected my authority more that day. You were a total dope that afternoon, William.

· · ·

There is a darker side to this.

According to academics like Nathanael Fast, power without status can lead not only to rudeness, but to abuse and even violence.

The relationship between the status of a job and the power it holds is fascinating. It can be the key to why the woman in the bank is so rude to you, or why your torturer turns the screw just a little bit tighter.

The more I looked at what happens between a customer and a server, say—which, after all, is how my interest in this world began— the more I wondered how our behaviors change as our power increases.

> **A small amount of power and very little status can have devastating effects.**

A study called "The Destructive Nature of Power without Status"[2] has shown that if it goes unchecked, a combination of a small amount of power and very little status can have devastating effects.

Those with high power and high status tend to be fine, says Fast. CEOs. Presidents. Police chiefs. "But it was people who had power and lacked status who used their power to require other persons to engage in demeaning behavior."

On ground level, we see this all the time.

The airport security person barking at you to take your belt off when you're still miles away from the metal detector. The fire safety officer who yells, "YOU NEED TO MOVE OUT OF THE WAY!" (I don't *need* to do anything, mate; you'd *like* me to.) People in hats who are sticklers for the rules. Essentially, low-level authoritarians with just enough power to tell us we have to do something, but not quite enough power to make us.

The problem, the academics explain, is that feeling low status in itself leads to "threatening and aversive" behavior. But add to that a little bit of power, and you'll find it "frees people to act on their internal states and feelings."

If those internal states and feelings are already strong enough, bad things happen.

Things far worse than not getting your 50¢ back for that Mars Bar.

. . .

We look to other people for a clue as to how we are perceived, just as Darren Dahl did the day he ended up with more grapefruit cologne than anyone else in the world.

In 1902, Charles Horton Cooley came up with "The Looking Glass Self," the notion that we use other people's expressions, behaviors, and reactions to define ourselves.

We all do it automatically to see how we're doing in life, like a sort of never-ending performance review. Any little interaction can bring with it a myriad of emotions—Pleasure! Guilt! Embarrassment!—and it's through this kaleidoscope that we ultimately develop our sense of self.

If that's true, imagine if we're already paranoid that people don't respect us. When they then go on to act in a way that seems to prove it, it's a tinderbox; a shortcut to rudeness of our own.

A deputy manager might just be more naturally inclined toward rudeness than a manager. An HR person . . . well, we know all about those. A detective is far less likely to be on the receiving end of rude behavior than a beat cop. But a beat cop will still get more respect than, say, a traffic agent, or the guy who sits in the booth at the parking garage, or the woman who won't cook you a bloody hotdog.

But that's when the civilian and the Little Tyrant are on more or less the same level.

When the person of little status has real power over you, it can lead to some very dark places and go far beyond rudeness.

* * *

I speak about this with Nathanael Fast. He works at the University of Southern California, is one of America's "Top 40 Professors Under 40," and an expert in power, status, and consequences.

He's also about to run out the door of his home in San Pedro to coach his son's all-star baseball team.

"What you say about the hotdog lady," he says, excited, "I think everyone has experiences like that. Like umpires . . . I think of umpires and it's exactly the same thing. You just go out to ask them a question or clarify a rule—that's all!—and what you get is just the same. Sometimes it's all you can do not to get thrown out of a Little League game."

"It's strange, isn't it?" I say. "All you're trying to do is ask a question. But it's immediately taken as a slight. 'Don't question my authority!'"

"Those people can't hear anything but disrespect. And it was experiences like that that led me and colleagues to take a look at it."

What Fast and friends found was that for years we have been saying that power corrupts. In fact, he says, "Power liberates."

Power allows people to act in whatever way they choose. It's when status gets involved that this goes wrong. For a long time, we saw the two as interchangeable.

They are quite different.

Power is having control. But status is the admiration associated with having that control. When you lack status, you tend already to feel disrespected.

So those who lack status but wield power—"whether the hotdog lady, or the umpire at the game, or the guy at the Department of Motor Vehicles . . . that is a bad combination."

It's bad because people who feel they have no status often assume you feel the same way about them.

"The problem is they experience that pretty much every day. So when you come along with your question, you're just *one more person just like all the others*, so any question you ask can easily be perceived as rude or disrespectful."

The rude person behind the counter thinks *you're* the rude one, based on a lifetime of experience. What they don't understand is that they are helping to create that rudeness from thin air.

"It becomes a vicious cycle of conflict. They have the tendency to treat other people in a demeaning way because of low status/high power. Then you become much more likely to treat them in the same way."

You see it all the time. The guy at passport control, already furious at you for not opening your passport correctly. The little moments in life where a weary stranger is desperate to make obvious some control over you. Jobsworths. Sticklers. Blotter jotters. But outside of those, it can create a toxic situation, which may stay with you for *years*.

"I remember in grad school, I was riding my bike," says Fast. "A police officer stopped me. He was *insanely* rude. That's a good example of having tons of power where the perception is, 'Most people are against me.' It's the epitome of power without status, and the violence that can sometimes emerge from that is frightening."

"So this woman in the diner might have been having a bad day," I suggest. "Maybe she'd already messed up an order or maybe it was all *just happening again*. Maybe she felt that although she had the power, I was disrespecting her authority just by approaching her and asking how long my hotdog would be. And maybe some of that comes down to a lack of confidence in her own abilities?"

"That's a very feasible explanation for sure," says Professor Fast.

Running a restaurant is an art. It can be overwhelming. Yet that day the conflict just felt inevitable. I have often asked myself whether there was anything I could have done to have made it more obvious I was not challenging Madam Hotdog's authority.

Fast tells me I could have complimented her.

I blink. It didn't really feel like the right time, I say. *You have kept me waiting in excess of an hour for a hotdog. That said, you have wonderful skin.* There's the possibility it might have felt jarring.

But "what we've tested is that an expression of gratitude toward an incompetent person really works. When an incompetent boss receives a message of gratitude from a subordinate—just a simple 'thanks for all you do'—we found that they are far less likely to give negative job evaluations. A very simple short form of gratitude [in these situations] makes a huge difference."

Sucking up to power works.

Sucking up to power works. And the best form of defense if you want to get on in society might just be to kill with kindness. We also need to be conscious that those without status know they're without status. The latest thinking says that bosses of people in low-status jobs should spare time to make their employees feel appreciated. And crucially, if you're a boss: let them know there is an actual career path that they are heading down. That this isn't it; they're not stuck.

• • •

Being appreciated does wonders, and changes the way we act. It gives us our own sense of power. Whether or not we feel valued and respected by our peers—or by the companies that employ us—informs our self-worth. It's outdated now, but once we enjoyed "kind business practice," where profit was the aim but by no means the only one.

In Victorian Britain, companies like Rowntree's and Cadbury paid comparatively well, offered security and sometimes even provided healthcare. In 1893, the Cadbury brothers even decided to buy a large plot of land, on which they'd soon create a village for their employees to live in.

Almost a century later we were in the 1980s. Everything was profits and shareholders. Workers were now just cogs in a machine, easily replaced when they became worn out. Ignoring legitimate concerns, browbeating employees—this was corporate rudeness, and it spread like a rash. For many it would become intolerable, this feeling of powerlessness, constantly under stress, like the system is bullying them, living with a constant and very real threat of being fired at any time.

In the wrong state of mind, and at boiling point in a high-pressure environment, a sense of rude treatment, of insecurity, of being under the thumb, can make a person do things the rest of us can't understand.

It was Patrick Sherrill, a 44-year-old postal worker from Edmond, Oklahoma, who reportedly found himself in just this type of situation in 1986. It was Patrick Sherrill who arrived at work one day with a bag full of weapons, and went on to give the world the phrase "going postal."

Just being slighted or wronged can have devastating effects.

Every year in the U.S., hundreds of people are killed in cases of workplace violence. In 2014—the latest statistics available at the time of writing—307 people were killed in a category known as "shooting by other person—intentional."[3] It happens pretty much everywhere. Curtain and linen mills. Pottery manufacturing. Car dealerships. Insurance agencies. Child day care. Nail salons.

In the shadow of another shooting, this one at an engine plant in Seymour, Indiana, in 2016, the head of the National Institute for the Prevention of Workplace Violence attempted to explain what happens in cases like these, and what he blames it on is alarmingly mundane.

The majority of these homicides occur when workers feel "slighted or wronged."[4]

Such weak words.

Slighted. Wronged.

But worryingly often, our sense of self relies on the most mundane of moments.

. . .

As we finish up, Nate Fast tells me about a friend of his who would often have to deal with a notoriously rude man. The rude man was in charge of paying back staff's business expenses. You wanted to be on the right side of this man. But remember: he was notoriously rude.

So Nate's friend made an effort. Whenever he had to go and see this rude man, he would bring him a snow globe from wherever he'd just been in the world.

The rude guy loved it. He became less rude. And all his friend's expenses were repaid in full, on time, and never queried.

"So I should have given Madam Hotdog a snow globe?" I ask.

"Well, we haven't tested the snow globe theory *specifically*," he says, and then Nate Fast is off, to annoy another umpire.

. . .

We fuel our engines on respect. And we don't have to look too far back to see how status, respect, and rudeness can impact the world in dramatic ways no one could ever have seen coming.

Donald Trump's campaign for the White House saw something extraordinary and unique in U.S. politics.

In the same way that a barrage of rude judges suddenly refreshed the stale variety-show format, a rude politician thundered onto the scene and treated the whole thing the same way. Voters went for it. It felt refreshing to them. Dumb to everyone else.

In recent years, a river of hatred toward "political correctness" has turned into a flood. "Why can't we say anything at all to whomever we choose about whatever we like?" scream the red-faced, sign-wielding, New Rudeness mobs, furious that someone else's feelings might be worth the same as their own.

Now, I'll avoid talking about political correctness too much—just as I am going to do my best to avoid the national tragedy that is the acceptance of "banter" as a form of witless and rude communication—but perhaps we can just agree on its fundamental principle. (Can I still say "fundamental"?)

Political correctness has really only ever been a system developed to protect those in a vulnerable position by discouraging those in the majority from needlessly, rudely offending them. Disabled people. Black people. Muslim people. Political correctness in its simplest form just means choosing your words more carefully, but so frothy-mouthed is the horde they can't see the logic for the bile. "These bloody do-gooders!" they spit. You'll notice that political correctness is a phrase that often goes hand-in-hand with "do-gooders." People hate do-gooders. These bloody do-gooders, doing good. Well, what's your chosen alternative, mate? Do-badders? Do-nothings?

So here was Trump—a powerful, rude man—just saying whatever he felt like during his presidential campaign. Railing against political correctness. Sneering at the do-gooders. Whether he believed what he said or not didn't seem to matter. He just stood there. Shouting rude things. On television. Seemingly making it up, like a mad, drunk old uncle ranting on Facebook. Hopping from one half-thought-out insult to another.

He insulted Mexicans by implying many of them were rapists.

He did a "funny" Indian accent.

He insulted women by calling some of them ugly, or implying that if they asked him a tough question they were probably menstruating.

He did an impression of a disabled journalist with a withered hand. While in the same room as him.

He was unpleasant, boorish, thuggish, and rude. Anyone who wasn't him was a loser, a clown, a failure, sad!

It's just banter, mate! Get a sense of humor!

But look how far he got: president of the United States. People were willing to believe that a man who didn't seem to know what his next word was going to be was a man also capable of bringing peace to the Middle East, negotiating trade deals with Russia, and paving all our streets with gold, when all the facts said we should be impressed he could tie his own shoelaces. Which to this day I don't think anyone's really checked.

Why? How?

We'll talk more about Donald J. Trump later—because how could we not?—but the reason for so much of his success is simple.

Rude people get ahead.

Sad! Dickheads.

Rude people do not find themselves constrained by all the normal rules that you and I tend to feel obliged to abide by. They don't have to say please or thank you because, really, what's in it for them?

But the side effect is that the rest of us aren't appalled; we're impressed. On some level, we *invite* them to trample all over us.

In one simple experiment at the University of Amsterdam, a strange man strode into an office that wasn't his and poured himself a cup of "employee only" coffee. At no point did anyone think to stop him. No one questioned him. It was merely assumed that this complete stranger with a pompous face was powerful enough to feel fine doing it.[5]

Just projecting authority—and rude people do, whether they have it or not—will get you ahead.

Our unwritten rules of social behavior work against us precisely because they are unwritten. Disrespecting them—whether it's interrupting, speaking louder than everybody else, ignoring input, not reacting to jokes, calling people clowns—instills in other people the mere idea that you can *afford* to.

Rudeness is one of the purest forms of power play; an effective way of controlling a situation, asserting your own superiority, and showing other people how very special you are.

> **Rudeness is one of the purest forms of power play.**

Remember the kid at school who was rude to the teacher? You'd never do that, would you? But remember how weirdly impressed you were? Trump's schoolyard bravado was played out in an international playground, and every time he did it, he bought himself more fuel to keep going.

It didn't impede him. It promoted him. It promoted him to the highest office in the world.

We're impressed by rude people. We put them on a pedestal, and they let us.

But, in general, we don't actually *like* them.

We don't like them because, particularly at work, they make our lives worse.

Ninety-eight percent of Americans say that they have experienced rudeness in the workplace. That's nearly everyone. That's people working on Wall Street as well as in Buddhist retreats. Though I suppose if you're going to be given the silent treatment anywhere, it'd be there. More than a quarter of people asked by the Wallace Report said that the last time someone was rude to them it was in the workplace. Nowhere in our lives is power more at play than at work.

The problem is compounded by ego. Ours, and that of the rude person.

Powerful people see themselves as "other" from the group. They're an individual. Us, though? We're just a group.

This has been shown to be a particular problem when it comes to the upper classes.

You know who I'm talking about.

In London, they hang out in Kensington and wear red trousers. Only the upper classes wear red trousers. That's not a scientific fact, by the way, but it might as well be.

Psychologists at the University of California, Berkeley, studied our red-trousered friends and found what we had always merely assumed: that wealthier people *do* tend to be more selfish in their behaviors and consequently . . . rude.

Much of this important scientific work—like all the best scientific work—involved hiding in bushes.

Paul Piff—who despite his name is not a magician, but an assistant professor of psychology and social behavior—led the study.

In the first one, the psychologists concealed themselves near a crossroads in San Francisco and spied on drivers who were supposed to stop at the stop sign and wait their turn before moving off. They judged people by the model, age, and appearance of the car. Immediately, they found that those in less classy, or "normal", cars broke the rules less than 10 percent of the time. More than 30 percent of the time, those in the most prestigious decided they didn't have to wait their turn.[6]

Then there were the pedestrian crossings. We all know the rules. You see someone waiting to cross, you politely bring your car to a halt and let them. In the United States, you get a ticket if you don't. Piff and pals found that people in the cheapest or oldest cars were most likely to obey the law and polite rules of society and stop. But people in the posh cars drove on, ignoring the waiting pedestrian, around 45 percent of the time.

In their heads, *they* are important. *They're* on their way somewhere. *You* can wait.

Spurred on by these results, subsequent studies found out that the higher a person's sense of "class" and power, the more likely they were to lie, to cheat, and even to steal sweets that had been left out for children in a neighboring laboratory.

Can I just say that again? The better off you feel, *the more likely you are to steal from children.*

When I speak with Piff, I am immediately struck by how passionately fascinated he is by rudeness, and how the way we feel about ourselves determines the liberties we take with others. How we behave in the wild. He's done "40 or 50" different studies on how power changes us, and what causes people to be nice to each other, versus mean or rude. He's found that "the more money people have, the less likely they are to share it. That poor people tend to be more generous. The wealthier you are, the more narcissistic you are. The more likely you are to think the world would be a much better place if you could just rule it."

He's found that the richer you are, the more likely you are to cheat at silly little games to win silly little prizes you really don't need. To those people, "getting ahead of others is more moral than breaking the rules is immoral."

.   .   .

This immediately reminds me of something.

Let me take you back to the evening of a friend's fortieth birthday party. He is a broadcaster and had invited all sorts of people. The great and the good. One such person was a well-known and glamorous woman you can often find in the newspapers. I will keep her anonymous, but let's just say she is a very well-connected heiress and socialite.

My friend Marc was also there, who is neither well-connected nor an heiress, and probably thinks socialite is some kind of precious metal.

Marc was trying to take his place at the table for dinner, but the heiress was blocking his path. She was leaning back and sitting on the dinner table, talking to a couple of well-to-do men. The problem was, she was sitting with her arse on Marc's plate.

The plate that Marc would soon be eating from.

Marc, a *very* polite man, tried quietly to draw her attention to this, mainly by apologizing for bringing it up.

The heiress looked at him, looked at where she was sitting, and weighed things up.

Was the fact that this man—whom she didn't recognize so couldn't possibly *be* anyone—was complaining about her sitting on his plate worth stopping her conversation for?

Or even moving?

She looked back at Marc, said, "I won't be long," then just went back to talking to her friends.

Marc had to stand there and wait until she'd stopped sitting on his plate.

(Months later, that anonymous woman's brother ran for political office. Neither myself nor Marc voted for him, and it was in large part because of his sister's arse. Rudeness can therefore now also be said to damage the democratic process itself.)

The problem is that at no point did that anonymous heiress—let's call her Ladybottom Tabletops—seem to consider her actions rude.

A Dutchman called Gerben van Kleef found that powerful people see themselves in a very different way. He found that when asked where they get their inspiration or what inspires them, powerful people tended not to write about others, but to write more about themselves. They would just write about how brilliant they are and how they inspired themselves with their own inspiring actions.

Then, in face-to-face conversations, they were made to hear other, less powerful people's tales of inspiration: tales of recovery, or achievement, or redemption, or heroism.

The powerful people listened quite patiently, but then afterward said that, actually, they found their own stories more inspiring.[7]

Paul Piff found almost comical levels of self-entitlement. "We'd ask people how much they'd agree with the following statement: '*If I was on the* Titanic, *I would deserve to be on the first lifeboat.*' And the wealthier and more powerful you are in society, the more likely you are to agree with over-the-top statements like that."

When U.S. television network MSNBC asked Donald Trump whom he'd be talking to about foreign policy—which globally renowned intellects and high-powered brains would he be taking advice and counsel from should he make it to the White House?—Trump replied: "I'm speaking with myself, number one, because I have a very good brain."

He then added: "And I've said a lot of things."

We've all said a lot of things, mate.

So there's the ego of the powerful. There's also that of the "victim."

By ego, I don't mean arrogance; I just mean the sense of self-worth that is challenged when someone treats us badly. It's easy to feel powerless in the face of apparent contempt from a superior. Even that word—*superior*—irks us on some level. Being disrespected implies we are powerless, and in a work situation it's a brave person who retaliates. You can't remonstrate with your boss the way you can with someone pretending to sell you a hotdog.

And yet you and I both know that employees feel better about themselves when they don't just take it.

The trick is passive aggression—the low-level, pleasing, everyday rudeness that we suspect infuriates the most. It's a clever rudeness; indirect, beneath the surface, and hard to prove. Maybe it's not performing a task as well as everyone knows you can. Being obstructive or sulking. Blaming, self-pitying, ignoring. It is satisfying for one party, infuriating for the other.[8]

But more than that, someone who strides into their boss's office and sternly demands a raise is likely to be paid more than someone who just takes what they're given. That's what scholars from Ohio State University found—and do you know what? The same study showed "rude" people are also likely to have a better credit score than polite people, because polite people tend to be the ones applying for store credit cards just to make a salesperson happy, or who trustingly lend money to friends and family members less responsible than themselves and then end up suffering as a result. It seems agreeable people are (weirdly) therefore less likely to pay their bills on time, while rude people just look out for number one.

Perhaps Madam Hotdog saw in me a financially unattractive agreeableness that day. Perhaps that's why she asked me to pay up front—to prove I could afford her meats.

But even ignoring all that, the one thing with which we can't argue is that people feel better about themselves if they stand up to rudeness and demand respect back.

Soon, we'll see how far people will go, and some of it gets strangely dark, strangely quickly. But all this jibes with what I did that day in that diner.

Here was someone in a position of power: the guardian of the hotdogs.

It was her place, her rules.

"The woman with the hotdog," says Piff, "she's in a position of power and status vis-à-vis you. Who knows what she's like in other contexts? But here she has got an ability to express control. She's not dependent on her relationship with you. But you are totally dependent on her to help you get food. And it's in this type of situation where you can get some of the most interesting and pernicious effects."

Power seems to corrupt or liberate, I decide, depending on which side of the counter you're standing.

Madam Hotdog had it, with or without status, yet I had nothing but a vague fumbling motto like "The customer is always right," which is not even something I believe. But I'd already paid; I was an impotent, perceived troublemaker in a position of weakness.

What I did in response to her rudeness was try and scrabble about to regain some control. Stand up for myself. Get her to respect me. *Rebalance the power.*

But the cycle had begun. The rudeness was in the air, and neither of us could back down or disarm each other with a compliment or a smile because of our egos.

There are constant power struggles happening in our everyday interactions. When they pass without incident, we all understand the unspoken rules of society and just try and get on. When they end up in rudeness, it's because one or other of us overplays our own importance whether through a lack of self-confidence or thoroughbred arrogance.

Either we allow those people to remain numb to the needs of others, or we challenge them.

Because, as far as humans are concerned, power is everything, hierarchies are everywhere, respect is all, but snow globes work wonders.

CHAPTER 6

Rudeness and the Sexes

*Would I have been less surprised if
Madam Hotdog had been a man?*

Remember Omar Hussain, the terrorist who was furious that other terrorists would use his phone charger without asking?

More recently, and on the other side of the playing field, a woman called Carolyn Stewart was coming to the end of a five-year stint analyzing ISIS targets for the United States Central Command.

Stewart harbored a hunch that some of her reports were not being taken as seriously as they should have been, and that the rising jihadist threat was greater than was being made public. The army veteran spoke up.

Soon, related or not, though some say it most definitely is, this analyst in an extremely important job at a crucial time found herself in court.

The reason she was there—along with a two-star general, a military judge, and the third-highest ranking person at the Defense Intelligence Agency (DIA)—was to find out whether she had sworn while at work.

This was an outrageous accusation because no one in the military had ever sworn before.

Yet according to reports from the courtroom, at a time of great international conflict and when ISIS were taking over the town of Palmyra, Stewart was accused of taking issue with a colleague who refused to adjust a target order, and then swearing at them.

A government lawyer was there to go over it all with a fine-tooth comb. The lawyer wanted to know precisely what Stewart had done with the papers she had been holding in her hands at the time, for example: "Did she toss the papers down or place them down?"

She was also accused of using a swear word on another occasion, and just one short year after that, she allegedly swore at a subordinate when it turned out they hadn't filled out an overtime report correctly.

Stewart herself admitted she "may" have used naughty words at times at work. It's easy to see how she may have felt stressed, what with ever such a lot to think about, but this, the government argued, had led to a toxic work environment.

The DIA chief of staff concluded that while Stewart's behavior did not, in fact, qualify as creating a hostile work environment, it was still rude and "unbecoming." Stewart was reassigned to a job in cyber security.

Unbecoming.

It's difficult for an outsider to see how that word might be used to describe a man charged with the same responsibilities.

Whether or not it had anything to do with Stewart's reports, the fact that she was being singled out for swearing at work in this way is worth considering.

. . .

The writer and public relations coordinator Alayna Frankenberry recently made a rallying call for women at work everywhere.

"We're expected to water down our statements when we mean to assert ourselves," she wrote. "To do everything we can to avoid being called a bitch. And how have we been rewarded for playing nice? Of the Fortune 500 companies, women run 4 percent. Of the Fortune 1000, 4.1 percent. In short, it's not working out."[1]

Be a bitch! she is saying.

Be forthright! Assertive! Aggressive! Because it pays to be rude!

And we know it does. Remember, rude people do tend to earn more because they dare to ask for it. Buoyed by confidence and not bothered if they offend, they generally make bigger, bolder, *ballsier* demands during salary negotiations.

If you are a rude woman, however, and you're sitting there all proud of yourself, arrogantly flipping the bird at everybody as they walk past, know this: it doesn't pay as well as it should.

Rude men? They're having a grand old time.

A trio of American universities looked at the earnings of 10,000 workers over a period of 20 years. They found that rude women earn 5 percent more than nice women.

Well done, rude women.

> **A rude man will earn 18 percent more than a nice woman.**

But a rude man will earn 18 percent more than a nice woman.

Well done, rude man!

Hang on, though—because that still means that even if you are a rude woman, and you love being a rude woman, and you are the best rude woman at being a rude woman that any rude woman has ever been, being a rude woman will *still* earn you 13 percent less than being a rude man.[2]

Rudeness works far better for bastards than bitches, but none of this means that men are actually deep down ruder than women. What it means is that women don't act as rudely. Why?

Because the rest of us find them "unbecoming" when they do.

.   .   .

Kieran Snyder—who is a woman even though she's named Kieran—is a tech entrepreneur and Seattle business owner who had a hunch about all this.

She's brilliant because, instead of just having that hunch and getting on with her day, she did something about it. She started gathering information. It's something she's done before. Once, she overheard a conversation at work in which one woman complained to another woman about a colleague's habit of interrupting everyone in meetings. It was deeply annoying, very frustrating, and, of course, rude. She said it was unfair, too: the women listen in meetings; the men interrupt. The idea fascinated her. And so she set to work. She defined an interruption as any "event where one person starts speaking before the other person has finished, whether or not the interrupter intended it." She attended every meeting she could, finding rooms as evenly split according to gender as she could. And then she sat back, listened, and kept track, over hours of conversation on the technology industry throughout a whole month.

What she found was that, generally, people interrupt a lot.

But men interrupt, cut off, and take over approximately twice as much as women.*

Not just that, but men are almost three times more likely to interrupt a *woman* as they are a *man*.

---

* During the first presidential debate between Donald J. Trump and Hillary Clinton in September 2016, Trump interrupted Clinton 25 times in the first 26 minutes alone. He went on to clock up 51 interruptions in 90 minutes. Clinton interrupted Trump just 17 times.

Of the 102 interruptions from *women* that Snyder logged, an incredible 89 of them were women interrupting women. That's 87 percent of the time.

However, when the woman is the most senior person in the room, she will interrupt everyone, all the time.

"And I fit that classification," Snyder tells me when we speak. "Lifelong interrupter. And I thought that was interesting: the women who manage to succeed in this male-dominated industry, all of them have fairly assertive styles of communication. And I wondered if there was a connection."

Her results seem to suggest there is. But remember her use of the word "assertive" there. We'll get back to that.

What Snyder's interruption study seems to show is that "women don't advance in their careers beyond a certain point without *learning* to interrupt."

And yet our attitude toward women who do is different from our attitude toward men who do.

You'll hear it a million times about women who rise to senior levels in business.

She's rude, she's bossy, she's ruthless, she's a bitch.

But men are generally *focused, determined, driven, aggressive.*

An aggressive male boss is accepted and even considered positive, while an aggressive female boss may be scary and make others uncomfortable.

In the 1970s, the linguist Robin Lakoff argued that all this starts in childhood. If a little girl starts talking like a little boy, swearing or calling the dinner lady a poo-face, "she will normally be ostracized, scolded, made fun of."[3] But young women who learn to "talk like a lady" are celebrated. Talking like a lady means not interrupting; it means listening to what's being said, responding politely, not swearing or saying "poo-face" or using aggressive language; being deferential, using softening phrases like "Would you mind?" or "Would it be possible?" or "Please may I?" Women are allowed to complain, "but only a man may bellow in rage."

(In fact, a 2015 study showed that when men went off on someone, raising their voices and using strong language in a jury situation—a *jury situation!*—people were much more likely to be persuaded by their arguments. But if a woman did it, using the exact same opinions and language, people were far more likely to stick to their original verdict and brand the woman overly emotional and not to be trusted. It's why Reginald Rose wrote a play called *Twelve Angry Men* and not *Twelve Untrustworthy and Overemotional Women*.[4])

Women are screwed either way. Rude or polite. "If she refuses to talk like a lady, she is ridiculed and subjected to criticism as unfeminine," wrote Lakoff. "If she does learn, she is ridiculed as unable to think clearly, unable to take part in a serious discussion."

But here's what the very latest research shows.[5] Women *are* behaving more rudely. At least when it comes to language. They haven't just caught up with men; they're starting to outdo them.

Researchers took 376 people and asked them to record up to three hours of their normal, everyday conversations. Conversations about colleagues. Tax bills. Where to get lunch.

At the time of writing, only around half of the 10 million words that were submitted have been transcribed—and had they been mine they would almost all have been about where to get lunch—but what the results show so far is striking.

In the 1990s, data from studies on language showed that for every million words they spoke, men would use the F-word around 1,000 times. Women, so pure and sheltered, would use an F-word only 167 times.

The fresh data shows a dramatic shift.

A new generation of politer men now use "fuck" and its variants 540 times in every one million words.

Women? Five hundred and forty-f'ing-*six*.

·   ·   ·

So gender differences between what men and women can say without people fainting are starting to fall away. Look at how their behavior is judged, though, and the differences Lakoff was on about in the 1970s live on. It's great to say that women should find their inner bitch, but generally they've been raised not to *want* to be forthright, aggressive, rude. Those who have risen to the top have done so despite their upbringing, not because of it. Even among the top-tier businesswomen in the world, there is still the fear of being seen as rude instead of direct.

This fascinated Kieran Snyder.

She's been in the male-dominated technology industry since getting her PhD 15 years ago. "I was generally highly rewarded and quickly promoted. But my feedback in performance reviews generally always said, 'You're doing great work . . . but you're kind of a bitch.' I was encouraged to tone it down, make room for other people . . . and then I heard a friend of mine discuss two candidates he was bringing in for promotion."

One candidate was a man. Kieran's friend wasn't worried about the man. Everyone liked the man.

The woman, on the other hand, while a stronger candidate, was a huge concern.

"Her peers didn't like her."

The woman was seen as a little too forthright. A little too assertive.

"*Abrasive*."

Snyder had heard that word before. A thought struck her. She began to collect real data. She gathered 250 separate performance reviews in which people's performances at 30 different companies had been evaluated.

She found that while men were likely to be reviewed on their business results, women were more likely to be reviewed on their personality.

Almost 60 percent of men received feedback you could call critical. But for women it was 90 percent.

Men were given constructive suggestions, like "Take time to slow down and listen. You would achieve even more."

But women were given constructive suggestions and told to shut up. "You can come across as abrasive sometimes. I know you don't mean to, but you need to pay attention to your tone."

· · ·

Negative personality criticism showed up in 71 of the 94 reviews received by women, along with words like "bossy," "strident," "abrasive," "emotional," and "irrational." "Aggressive" was used for both men and women. For men, generally to say "be more aggressive." For women, "don't be so aggressive!"

And did you notice "abrasive" popping up again?

"'Abrasive' was interesting because it *only* turned up for women," says Snyder.

In fact, while not one man was apparently abrasive and were all as smooth and shiny as beautiful pebbles, the A-word showed up for women 17 times in 13 reviews alone.

For abrasive, by the way, read rude.

In fact, read pure rudeness. The word "rude" comes from the Latin *rudis*, literally meaning unwrought, or jagged, or unpolished, or—you know—abrasive.

"It's an association word . . . it means not playing along *nicely*," Kieran says. "It means opinionated. Aggressive."

"More likely to contradict the men in the room?" I ask.

"Yeah. It means giving opinions when it would be much easier for everyone else if you did not. Women sharing opinions is . . . unlikable. In an environment where women are so profoundly outnumbered, just speaking at all is read as abrasive."

So in business, a woman speaking her mind is rude. For a military officer, it's unbecoming. In a jury deliberation, it's untrustworthy. As a child, it's unladylike.

Let's not even start on video-game journalism.

No wonder women don't interrupt. They're far too rude already. The fact is: *we unfairly hold women to higher standards when it comes to rudeness.*

"I do think women in the workplace worry about negative characterization of their personality," says Kieran. "A man has to go really far down the 'bastard' path for there to be any repudiation. A woman only has to say she disagrees with you."

For a woman, merely speaking up or standing out is enough to make people nervous and incite character assassinations. When the Tory MP Anna Soubry made an emotional address at a Westminster rally, fighting back tears as she spoke to a huge crowd of young people, saying that Britain's decision to leave the European Union was a "terrible mistake" and urging the public to report hate crimes, which had seen a nationwide upswing since the decision, *The Times* columnist Tim Montgomerie immediately tweeted her to tell her to "stop moaning." Then fellow MP Nadine Dorries—also a woman—told her 30,000 followers that Soubry was drunk.

We patronize women for stating opinions, we tell them to stop moaning, and if they deign to persist, they're rude or drunk.

To quote Sheryl Sandberg, the CEO of Facebook and one of only 172 female billionaires in the world, "When a woman speaks in a professional setting, she walks a tightrope. Either she's barely heard or she's judged as too aggressive."[6]

I begin to wonder whether my judgment of Madam Hotdog that day—that she was so aggressive, so *abrasive*—could in some way have been informed by the fact that she was a woman. Would I have reacted differently if she'd been a man?

"I don't know," says Snyder. "I think it's possible. Without knowing the details of the hotdog vendor, another thing to ask yourself is would you have been more surprised if she was older or younger than she was, or a different race? We are generally more tolerant of assertiveness in younger women than older women. Not by much, but generally we are. We are generally more tolerant of assertiveness in white women than women of color. It's an interesting lens. If it had been a man, ask yourself: would you have written a whole book about it?"

I think about Kieran's question for a whole day.

And I conclude that yeah, I bloody would.

It was *deeply* unbecoming.

CASE STUDY: THE STORY TOPPER

I am at the party of a friend and it is important that I do well so that I reflect adequately on him. So I am telling a story to a man, and it is probably my Third-Best Story.

The man is watching me, delighted and enthralled, and I imagine how delighted and enthralled he will be when I move to the story's powerful conclusion, and all that that entails! How he will reel backward at the twist in the tale, appreciating it as at once a punchline and as an entrée for further discussion. I imagine the supplementary questions he will have, with which I will deal one at a time until all avenues of relevant conversation have been exhausted and the man is a twitching, juddering mess, his mind blown, his appetite sated.

It's a pretty good story.

And as I move into my final sentence, and I fix him straight in the eye, I go for the kill.

"And *that's* when he found out it was *someone else's*."

Boom! Thank you! You're welcome! Your round!

And the man looks at me, and for a second I think he is too shocked to realize what has just happened here, and then he nods almost imperceptibly, and he says, "Yeah, that's a bit like me, because . . ."

What? What does he mean, that's a bit like him? What's happening here? Why is he not a twitching, juddering mess? Why is his mind not blown? And then it hits me. The man is a *story topper*. He's trying to beat my story! He wasn't even

listening! All the while I was talking—with my neat little
turns of phrase and my tried-and-tested metaphors,
developed and honed until I was satisfied I had a new
Number 3 worth its place alongside the other children—he
wasn't even listening! He was just thinking about his own
story! Where are his manners? How rude can you get, to not
listen to another man's story? This is the height of societal
rudeness!

I watch his lips as he says whatever it is he is saying.
Surely sometime soon this "story" will be over. Then the art
will be taking my cue and segueing somehow into my
Second-Best Story. That'll teach him. It'll be a bold and
confident move, which will both scare and humble him. Why
top a story? Why not just let the story be? Now my Third-
Best Story is tainted. I hate story-tainting story toppers.

And then it looks like he's about to finish and I prepare to
top his story.

"So *that's* why we went by *coach!*" he says, and I nod ever
so slightly and say, "Yeah," and then say, "Talking of
travel . . ." and I'm in!

But what did I notice there? A flinch of pain behind the
eyes? A momentary narrowing? A shock of thought across
the brain as he realized the consequences of his actions?
Yes, sir. The topper can be topped. You thought you were a
topper. Well, here's your toppee license. For here is my
Second-Best Story, and oh, thou shalt feel thine humiliation,
sir. This story has been tested. *Road* tested. It's been told
across the globe, to prince and pauper alike. Just go with it.
Don't fight it. Head into the light . . .

"Which is why *that* was the last time my wife ever said boo to a goose!"

And we're done here. Nice one. Thank you. Mine's a pint.

And yet nothing. Not a smile. Not a twitch. Nothing. And ... my God ... here it comes. I can see it coming ...

"Yeah, that's a bit like *us*," he says, and I have never seen the like. He's off again. He's going to try and top the story with some old rubbish about him and his boring wife! He is incorrigible!

Well, he's asking for it now. He's asking for the big guns. He's asking me to wheel out Machine Number 1, Guinevere. She's not had an outing in quite some time. I've been resting that story. You have to do that with your number-one story. Your Best Story is for emergency use only. It needs to be untoppable and, once you start, unstoppable. You don't half-tell your best story. You don't start it unless you're committed and have absolute commitment from those around you. Your best story must be respected, listened to, appreciated. Otherwise the whole system is meaningless and arbitrary and not even a proper system, and you could never accuse it of that. Surely this man respects this? Surely he will listen?

I'm pretty sure he's nearly finished now. His arms have got involved. Hey, the people in my best story have arms. Maybe that's my in. And as he stops talking, I nod, and twitch a quarter-smile, and say, "Did I ever tell you about the time I ..."

And he stops me, there and then, and says, "Will you excuse me for just a minute?" and I say, "Of course!" and he backs away, through the party, and I have won, I have won, I have *won*!

Well done me. I topped his stories. I didn't even listen to his.

I pat myself on the back, because I *hate* people like that.

CHAPTER 7

Rudeness and Outrage

Or: it's not just me

One year, on my birthday, I heard mention of someone on the radio.

It was one of those "on this day" features, where they tell you about important things that happened on this very day in another year. Amazingly, there was no mention of my birth. But there was mention of a man named Gilbert Harding, who died on November 16, 1960.

He'd been a policeman. A schoolmaster. A *Times* correspondent based in Cyprus.

But in the 1950s—his heyday—he'd also been Britain's rudest man.

The TV show *What's My Line?* invited members of the public to turn up and perform a short mime that best demonstrated the job they did. After that, a panel of unusual personalities would politely ask yes or no questions to try and determine whether Mr. Simpkins was a postman or Mrs. Botherby was a potter. It was extremely gentle stuff for a Sunday evening. But viewers soon started to tune in not for the game, but for the gruff, irascible, unpredictable panelist Gilbert Harding.

He was not a man to suffer fools gladly. He was suspended from one TV show—which he was hosting—for angrily complaining about the lengthy introduction he himself had just given. He was once suspended for being drunk on live TV, which he said was true, claiming the weather had been bad lately and made his asthma worse, so he had obviously "overfortified" himself, as all asthma sufferers definitely do every time the weather turns.

Harding's forthrightness, impatience, and rudeness were a breath of fresh air in 1950s Britain. Being rude to someone else on television or radio was unthinkable, but here he was, not just thinking it but doing it, and becoming the UK's most famous man and first real media personality in the process. His appearances on TV won more viewers than the Queen.

But all this was at a time when people on TV had yet to separate their public self from their private self. Harding was rude when he felt like it. He wasn't when he didn't. Viewers soon began to want a guarantee that if they watched Harding on TV, they'd get the Harding they wanted: the rude one. Eventually, pressured, that was what he had to give the 12 million people who would tune in for him.

Harding began having to *manufacture* his rudeness. This is a vital moment in the history of television that leads us directly to where we are today.

Not that by our current standards it was even all that rude.

One of Harding's most shocking statements was when he told a contestant: "I am tired of looking at you."

There was uproar when that happened. Complaints. Newspaper outrage. How could he say something like that? Had he gone quite *mad*?

Once, he was about to interview the American actress Mae West, and was asked by her manager to try and sound a bit more "sexy" when interviewing her. He replied:

If, Sir, as you suggest, I possessed the power of conveying un-
limited sexual attraction through the potency of my voice, I
would not be reduced to accepting a miserable pittance from
the BBC for interviewing a faded female in a damp basement.

Now here's chef Gordon Ramsay replying to a guest in his TV
restaurant who's just asked for some extra pumpkin.

Right, I'll get you more pumpkin. I'll ram it right up your
fucking arse. Would you like it whole or diced?

Both are strangely elegant in their own way, though if you had to
guess which one came from the 1950s I think you'd manage.

The point is, just as people began to tune in to Gilbert Harding
for his rudeness, we tune in to Gordon Ramsay because we're waiting
for the bit where he swears or tells someone he's going to insert
pumpkins in their bottom.

Again, we have to think of the private self and the public self. Is it
real or for show? Is telling people he's going to insert pumpkins in their
bottoms how Gordon Ramsay built a multimillion-dollar restaurant
empire? Maybe. Though it's not *much* of a business plan.

But Gordon Ramsay telling people he is going to insert pumpkins
in their bottoms is *definitely* how he carved out a successful television
career.

We loved Nasty Nigel; Anne Robinson made millions when she
was offered a U.S. television deal based entirely on delivering ghost-
written sneers or calling people thick on *The Weakest Link*; we switch
on to see Simon Cowell berate hapless 65-year-old supermarket check-
out women who know they'll never be Lady Gaga but just want a nice
day out. We're amazed and impressed and *relieved* when any of them

actually says something nice to someone. People cry and there are standing ovations and the uplifting music swells and the guys from Coldplay can each buy a new wall lamp with the royalties.

Politeness is not the norm anymore; it's become the exception.

Gilbert Harding was loved and he was hated. Probably more loved. In one of his last interviews, reflecting on his life, he said his bad manners and rudeness were "indefensible." At his memorial, over 2,000 people showed up to Westminster Cathedral to pay tribute.

Will the same happen for Cowell? Ramsay? Robinson?

Rudeness, once incredible, is now pitifully disposable. Obvious. Factory-made and a predictable part of a glut of unimaginative television commissions. Right now, in some brightly lit break-out area of an office in Dalston, a team of people with no socks on sit brainstorming ideas for judges for a new celebrity sushi-rolling show, and one of them's about to say, "And of course, we'll need a *rude* one."

TV, radio, online—the content providers know we are drawn to the perversity and thrill of rudeness; we like people losing their cool; we are invigorated by someone else being the butt of a cruel jibe and the dark voyeurism of watching it happen unscathed.

It is poisonous. And it feeds people the lie that they don't have to try and be nice: not if they're *only being honest.*

.   .   .

Gilbert Harding was unexpectedly responsible for helping to set a new tone in broadcasting, and one I imagine he'd be horrified by.

But only a year or two after his death, up stepped a prescient woman determined to ward it off.

The media, she decided, was in a state of moral decline. If it kept going the way it was, then what might happen in the next 50 or 60 years? You'd end up with chefs threatening to insert winter vegetables into a paying customer's anus.

She was Mrs. Mary Whitehouse, a senior mistress at a school in Shropshire, and she was outraged, surprised, and disappointed.

But she was going to do something about it.

She was going to complain.

And when she made one of her very first complaints, *if only someone else had answered the phone.*

A duty officer at the BBC picked up, listened to her complaint, and then brusquely dismissed her concerns.

The officer didn't apologize. Didn't say they would log the call, or make sure a higher-up heard straight away.

They just said: "You could always switch off if you don't like it."

Somewhere inside Mrs. Whitehouse, a fire was lit. *You don't matter,* was the message she'd taken. *We don't care. You're just some woman. We're the BBC.*

Whitehouse, with her thick-rimmed glasses and cloud of gray hair, was enraged; insulted; belittled.

In that moment a campaign was born.[1]

She started phoning and writing to the BBC, arranging meetings with everyone from the director general's office to the head of the Independent Television Authority to the Minister of Health, Enoch Powell.

It turned out she had a problem with almost everything.

The children's television program *Pinky and Perky* featured two pig puppets who would sing songs in high-pitched voices and have adventures with friends like Bertie Bonkers.

Whitehouse didn't approve.

She saw an episode in which "Pinky and Perky were constantly unkind—to the point of callousness—to the grown-up in their program. This kind of thing could be the origin of the cruelty some find it hard to understand of juvenile delinquents toward the elderly and helpless."

It sounds like a comment you'd read under a story on a mad website. And all over middle England, alarm bells started ringing.

She created petitions, rang newspapers, organized town-hall meetings. Her campaign picked up pace.

Yet it didn't gain her the respect she was after. Still she was treated rudely by the media she complained about.

On May 6, 1964, after a large meeting in Birmingham Town Hall, *The Times* wrote, "perhaps never in the history of Birmingham Town Hall has such a successful meeting been sponsored by such a flimsy organisation."

Despite and because of reporting like this, Whitehouse became a national figure. She received over 18,000 letters over the next year from similarly concerned viewers. Within four years, 430,000 people had signed their names on her "Clean Up TV" manifesto.

And through it all, she focused almost entirely on the BBC.

Her reasons for not targeting the commercial rival, ITV, was that she had only ever "received nothing but courtesy from them and an objective reaction to the suggestions we have made. We ask no more."

But from the BBC?

"Our experience with the BBC has been quite the reverse."

Rudeness. Discourtesy. Disrespect.

The BBC had inadvertently set a tone to their dealings with Mary Whitehouse that they would come to regret.

And then they made it worse.

The BBC began being not just rude to her, but actively rude about her.

A serial program called *Sizzlewick* featured a character called Mrs. Smallgood—a very petty, repressed woman obviously based on Whitehouse. Another character was Ernest the postman. Whitehouse was married to an Ernest, and they lived in a house called Postman's Piece. In one episode, Ernest was unwell, suffering from overwhelming guilt after hitting a dog with a football. It was around the time the real Ernest was recovering from shock after hitting a young man with his car.

Whitehouse felt under attack. They'd made it personal. So she went on the offensive, fighting even harder, and the world felt her shadow grow. She rose in power and status, becoming a thorn in the side of the BBC. She was invited into the House of Commons; spoke up and down the country; was rung up by every paper whenever they sniffed controversy and needed a quote; her name cropped up in every review of the BBC's output; she and her organization were consulted ahead of parliamentary committees on broadcasting; she was backed by MPs, a whole roster of bishops, some chief constables, and the notoriously fun-loving Scottish Housewives Association.

In short, she became a massive pain in the arse.

Sir Hugh Greene, the director general of the BBC in the 1960s, thought she "would have been at home in Nazi Germany."[2]

Yet the BBC stood firm, kept poking fun, kept being rude about her.

At one point, commentator Ned Sherrin casually insinuated Mrs. Whitehouse could well be a lady of the night. She sued him for libel and accepted damages from Associated Newspapers, and it only fueled the fire. So did the obscene phone calls and the anonymous sweary letters she'd receive from members of the public.

To Whitehouse, Britain had become a place that was overwhelmingly rude in all sorts of ways. It was uncivil, insulting, base, too sexual, disrespectful, and dumbed down. She railed against the lyrics in Chuck Berry's "My Ding-a-Ling." Complained that *Doctor Who* set a terrible example to children thanks to "the brainwashed Daleks who chanted 'Kill, Kill, Kill.'" (They're not brainwashed, and I'm pretty sure it's "exterminate.") She saw hidden messages everywhere, asking whether, because the main character in a play about homosexual love committed suicide, this was "to move people to compassion so that they hastened to change the law and legalize sodomy?"

Doubt it.

Actually, I don't, but of course she saw that as a bad thing.

Ignoring the programs themselves, it was the rudeness White-house felt from the BBC in her first few dealings with them—and the rudeness she felt from them afterward—that directly led to her cre-ating this entire movement. She simply felt she wasn't getting enough respect; that her concerns were important; that she *must be heard*.

What you can never take away from Britain's protective great-aunt was her mission. Her fight. Her manners. Her commitment to the health of the nation.

As I investigated rudeness further, I began slowly to wonder—and with pride rather than horror—if one day I might be considered the Mary Whitehouse of hotdogs.

CHAPTER 8

Rude Health

Should I have just let it go?

H ere are six words you will soon read again.

ASTONISHING. AMAZING. TERRIFYING. DEVASTATING. HORRIFYING. SHOCKING.

And I stand by every one of them.

Rudeness wears its victim down. Psychologically, of course, but there's growing evidence that those subjected to the stress of incivility for too long or too often find their immune systems weakened. A weakened immune system can lead to a raft of major physical health problems like diabetes, cancer, and heart disease.

The *Journal of the American College of Cardiology* has shown that hostility has a direct link to heart problems[1] and rude, hostile words can even cause brain changes and long-term psychiatric risks for young adults.[2] According to the Wallace Report, well over half those asked—56 percent—feel that rudeness has indeed affected their mental well-being.

Even witnessing rudeness—or going over rude moments again and again in your head, just as I did in the days after my failed bid to buy a processed meat product cooked to order—elevates levels of hormones called glucocorticoids throughout the day. Too many can lead to a whole host of health issues, but one of the first effects is an increased appetite.

So now we can say that in addition to everything else, rudeness can make you fat.

But it can also affect your health in a much more frightening way.

. . .

Since not buying a hotdog, I have become a bit of a fan of an Israeli academic. I am also the only person ever to have typed that sentence.

Dr. Amir Erez is an expert in positivity and positive thinking. Or was, until he also became an expert in rudeness.

"This is kind of a strange story," he tells me when we speak. "Until seven or eight years ago I was not interested in rudeness at all. But I had to give a talk at the University of Southern California on the power of being positive. There I met another researcher, called Christine Porath."

I've also become a bit of a fan of hers. She's the woman who made people come up with new ideas for how to use a brick.

"We had lunch together," says Erez, "and she told me all about her research into rudeness and incivility, and I just told her that I didn't believe in any of this research."

"That was rude," I say.

"Yes! I said it in a very rude manner."

"So much for the power of being positive."

"I told her, why would it have any effect? These small insults? It's not violence, not aggression, just small incidents! And we're good at ignoring these minor things. Because otherwise we would walk around all depressed all the time. So I told her, no, I don't see much evidence for it."

"You mean scientific evidence?"

"It's all self-reported. People saying, 'Oh, this happened,' or 'That happened,' and they felt insulted and like it affected their performance and so on."

Erez said the only way he'd believe that rudeness had an impact was if Porath could actually induce rudeness and measure the effects it had. She struck back, saying fine, if you don't believe me, let's do it together. Each simply wanted to prove the other wrong.

"So this was essentially the academic version of a drunken bet?" I ask.

"It was. It was pretty much a bet. And she was right and I was wrong. Since then we've conducted many studies, and the effects are just absolutely amazing. Each and every time I conduct a study, I don't believe I will find much. But I always find something. And the effects of rudeness to me are astonishing."

It's astonishing, because what Erez found was that rudeness can kill.

"One of the reasons rudeness is so devastating is that it affects cognition. When people encounter rudeness they can't think in the same way. We know now that it affects working memory."

Working memory is important. It's used in reasoning, in decision making, and in determining our behavior.

"That's the part of the process where everything is happening. Planning, goal management, memory—pretty much everything is dependent on working memory."

In one of their studies, the team looked at attention. They found that when people experience rudeness, they miss obvious information.

"Even when it's in the center of their visual field. So I said to one of my friends, 'This is really scary. Can you imagine if this happened in surgery? Can you imagine if a surgeon was rude to an anesthesiologist, and the anesthesiologist now starts to miss information that's right in the center of their visual field, for like 30 seconds?'"

And as the words sank in, they decided they had to test it.

"And we found that it has devastating effects," he says, before pausing. "It is terrifying."

.   .   .

The study, "The Impact of Rudeness on Medical Team Performance," took place in Tel Aviv.

Erez and his colleagues gave 24 medical teams—each one comprised of one doctor and two nurses from neonatal intensive care units—one hour to diagnose and treat a sick baby.

It was all simulated, of course—and for the experiment they chose a case of something called necrotizing enterocolitis.

Put simply, that's a potentially fatal disease that moves rapidly around a premature infant's intestinal tissue. If it's not treated immediately, it begins to inflame the tissue, which starts to die. So does the baby.

Before any of the teams got to work, they were told that a leading expert from the United States would be observing them through a webcam. In front of the teams, a researcher then rang a fake phone number and played a message from that "expert."

Half the teams heard a perfectly normal message.

The other half heard this expert rudely inform them that he had observed other medical teams from their country and was "not impressed with the quality of medicine in Israel."

The simulation began. The teams got to work.

Ten minutes later, another message arrived.

Half the teams heard the expert say he hoped that the simulation would help them in their work.

The other half were told that based on their work so far, they "wouldn't last a week" in his department.

So what happened?

The teams that experienced no rudeness did just fine.

The teams that experienced rudeness fell to pieces.

They had trouble communicating, they couldn't work out how to cooperate, they forgot basic instructions, and they misdiagnosed the illness. The doctors asked for the wrong drugs. The nurses prepared the wrong things. They didn't ventilate the patient in the way they should have, nor did they resuscitate well.

Three outside judges appraised the results, without knowing what the experiment was all about. The difference in the quality of their work was incredible. What Erez discovered is that even one rude comment in a high-pressure environment decreased performance by doctors and nurses in a life-or-death situation by more than 50 percent.

The doctors who'd been treated rudely could well have killed their tiny patient as a result.

If you're a little brusque with the man in the hospital sandwich shop, he might hand you a cheese and pickle sandwich instead of cheese and ham.

Be rude to a doctor, and you might never eat again.

. . .

Now, rudeness in these high-pressure situations is one thing. As surprised as we might be by the results, they're understandable. But the banal drudgery of everyday rudeness does much the same thing, and once again the results can be just as scary. The reason we don't know about them is that, quite simply, no one's thought to trace them back to rudeness before.

We think people make mistakes when they're tired, when they're stressed, when they're going through a rough time at home. Rarely do we think they might be making mistakes because of an offhand comment or a cruel aside.

There was another simulation, more recently. This one lasted far longer than an hour, and took place over the course of a medical team's day.

They were made to encounter rudeness at the start of their day, this time not from a colleague, but from the presumably distressed mother of an infant. What Erez found was that the rudeness they experienced didn't just affect their ability to treat the woman or her child in the moment. Nor did it only affect the next person or problem they encountered.

"It affects them all day," says Erez. "They go through five patients afterward. And they just don't treat them appropriately. The entire day."

> **One moment of rudeness can affect *every single patient a doctor meets in their day.***

One moment of rudeness can affect *every single patient a doctor meets in their day.*

Medical errors are a major issue. In the United States, it's the third leading cause of death after cancer and heart disease: 400,000 people die every year because of them.[3] That's more than 1,000 people a day. Ten times that amount suffer from the serious complications that arise after medical mistakes: like the Minnesotan woman who underwent a bilateral mastectomy to treat a cancer she then found out she never had in the first place.

Then there's the financial cost—and the side effects. A report on the economics of health care quality and medical errors puts that cost at a genuinely unbelievable $1 trillion a year in the United States alone, with 10 million days of lost productivity thrown in for good measure.[4]

In Europe, the World Health Organization reports that medical errors consistently occur in 8 to 12 percent of all hospitalizations. You have a one in ten chance of it happening to you. One in 20 patients in Europe sit in the hospital with an infection they didn't arrive with and didn't really want. In Britain, these infections cost the country £1 billion a year.[5]

It suddenly feels like ambulances should be rushing people *out* of hospitals, not into them.

Yet most efforts to limit medical errors focus on improving the IT systems and "comprehensive systematic approaches to patient safety," which is another way of saying spreadsheets.

Erez thinks there's more we can do than agree to a software update on our Excel.

He suggests that the entire field of medicine is investigating the wrong things when it comes to limiting medical errors. It's social interaction, he believes, that needs the focus.

"It explains so much more of medical errors than anything else. In our last rudeness study, [rudeness] explained 40 percent of errors."

Rudeness clouds judgment. And a little-known side effect is that a doctor who experiences it will therefore find it much harder to adapt their thinking. Whatever the first diagnosis is, Erez says, that's what they'll be more likely to stick with, even when strong new information enters the frame. It's called a fixation error.

"If you give doctors an initial diagnosis—even if it's a diagnosis that comes from, say, the daughter of a patient, which is very unreliable—but then give them signs that actually point to a different problem, [you find that] people that experience rudeness don't move from their first, wrong diagnosis."

Put simply, rudeness fogs our brain and stops us processing new information properly.

Doctors know all about this. A survey of 4,530 doctors, nurses, and

> Rudeness fogs our brain and stops us processing
> new information properly.

hospital personnel showed that 71 percent of them believed that disruptive behavior—rudeness, abuse, condescension, or insulting personal conduct—led to real medical errors; 27 percent tied it to patient deaths.[6]

But rudeness isn't limited just to the medical profession, of course. Think of the number of times we put our lives in the hands of other people: the bus driver, the pilot, the guy who weighs us up before he straps us to the bungee cord and kicks us off a bridge. If any of them have experienced rudeness that day, their ability to do their job properly is compromised. It's a little like they've had a drink. With alcohol, though, there are clues: you smell the booze on the pilot's breath, you see the glassy eyes, you're aware of the sway, and maybe they're holding a kebab or talking to a mannequin. But even a sniffer dog can't seek out traces of rudeness.

Erez broadened his research to truck drivers and their daily interactions with their dispatchers. Those who experienced rudeness violated more safety laws. And we can't blame them for it. Their brain just wasn't able to cope with driving as well anymore.

Now, fair enough, if you're a young doctor, you're already underpaid, sleep deprived, unappreciated, overworked and stressed, and backed by a government that wants you to work harder for longer for less. Add to that some lunatic screaming obscenities in your face when you should have been on your break and, yes, your focus may waver. But the really scary thing about all this is the levels of rudeness involved.

It is incredibly mundane.

"It's amazing," says Erez. "We find effects even when you just prime it."

"When rudeness is just on people's minds?"

"So we'll give people sentences to reconstruct. And if those sentences have rude words in them, it influences people's working memory."

If even seeing a rude word slows you down, I ask him what constitutes a rude word. Are we talking about swear words? Or words that describe rude actions?

"Just words," he says, "like 'rude,' 'ignore,' 'bother.'"

I take a moment.

"As gentle as 'bother'?" I say.

There's a pause.

"Every time I get results, they are just totally shocking to me."

All of a sudden, rudeness seems a far more serious issue—this well of frustration and muddle-headedness that can arise from a mild insult, a banal word, someone not holding a door open for us or forgetting to say thank you. It eats us up, plays on our mind, clouds our judgment. So I tell Dr. Amir Erez about the Hotdog Incident, about how it stuck with me for days.

"What you describe with the hotdog is really interesting," he says, "because we all wonder—how should I have behaved in that moment? It's so surprising and shocking that someone could behave in that way. Often you don't react immediately precisely because it disrupts cognition."

Which is okay if you're a writer trying to buy a hotdog, but dangerous if you're a doctor, or a nurse, or a bomb disposal expert, truck driver, hostage negotiator, crane operator, parachute packer, fireman, juror, or a cleaner in a nuclear bunker dusting the big red buttons.

"We're trying to find some ways to control it," he says at one point. "To raise the threshold of people's sensitivity to hostility."

He throws this away, but it's fascinating. We can't do much about the rudeness that spreads like a cold. We'll never stop it, because it's already started, and it's out there—waves of it, infecting new people every day and being passed on all the time, as unstoppable as the tide. But maybe the trick is to protect against it.

Erez and his team tried a new idea. A simple 15-minute video game doctors could play at the very start of their day.

"It reduced the effect of rudeness on their performance."

I'll let that sink in.

Erez is developing a *rudeness vaccine.*

"It doesn't change the perception of rudeness. They still perceive the person who was rude as rude. But the rudeness did not affect them. [But for] other people not inoculated . . . it affected their performance tremendously."

The good doctor says the results of his experiments are the same in people all over the world. If nothing else, we can say rudeness unites us.

But if rudeness can lead to heart attacks, diseases, mistakes in the operating room, misdiagnosis, unnecessary deaths, cost hundreds of billions of dollars and pounds and euros and yen, and cause 40-ton trucks to miss stop signs, can we go on ignoring it?

If the world's getting ruder, it's getting more dangerous.

"Most people think it's not a big deal," says Erez. "Just like I thought."

But it's not overstating the case to call it a silent killer, I tell him. Yet people find rudeness amusing.

"They find it amusing," says Erez, "until they're on the operating table."

CASE STUDY:
SAY IT

I'm walking along a very long corridor in a very old building and there is a man walking very closely behind me.

We've been through one set of double doors already, and I have done the polite thing and given them an extra little push so that he can get through right behind me with the minimum of effort.

You must not call me a hero for this. Plenty of other people have done far greater things—saving lives, curing things, etc.—but you are right if you say that this is just a different *type* of heroism.

The only problem is, the man didn't say thank you.

Because that's what you do, isn't it? A stranger makes a small effort to make your life easier? You say thank you!

Not to worry, though, because we're about to hit a second set of double doors, and this will be his chance to redeem himself, and as we go through I give them that extra little push again but once more he says *absolutely nothing*.

Maybe I'm missing it. Maybe he's saying "cheers" or "thanks" or "ta" very quietly. How could you not say thank you? It's a reflex, isn't it? After all, I'm giving the doors an extra little push!

A third set of double doors is upon us. He must be going to the same place as I am. He must realize this too. Well, he has to say thank you now, doesn't he, because we may end up in the same room? He will know he didn't say thank you for my extra little pushes and he will be devastated.

And as we walk through them, I give them that extra little push, and I listen really closely, but the man does not say thank you!

Well, now I know exactly what I'm going to do.

When we get to the end of this corridor, I'm going to say, "Pfft, don't worry about it." But I'm going to say it in a really cutting way. It will be loaded with contempt, and dripping with sarcasm. "Don't worry about it" will become all he can think about, all day. He will lie in bed tonight staring at the ceiling thinking about "Don't worry about it." "Don't worry about it" will cause him radically to reassess his life. He will come to question his every decision he has ever made, and perhaps start to reflect on how he treats people. In time, he will realize he has been taking his wife for granted and neglecting his children. His work will begin to suffer. He will be overcome by an overwhelming sense of ennui. He will resign from his job, citing emotional distress, and spend his afternoons sitting at home in his pants wondering how he ever came to be this way. "Where is the bright-eyed young kid?" he will ask himself, wailing at his bathroom sink, staring into his own cold, empty eyes in the mirror, his mascara running down his face, even though he doesn't wear mascara; it just helps the image.

"Where is the young man setting out in the world, so full of hope and optimism?" he will scream as he bangs his fists against the mirror—shattering it, each shard now a grim taunt, each one reflecting the men he *could* have been.

Then his wife will leave him, taking the kids, because now she realizes that without his job, she never really liked who he'd become anyway. Theirs was a cold and lifeless marriage, fueled only by habit, she will tell him. When had they stopped talking to each other the way they used to? When had they stopped listening?

"WHYYYYY?" he will scream, as he drives his car aimlessly around in the dead of night—this "man," if you can call him that—searching for forgiveness the way he always used to search out the dollar, prepared to do anything to get ahead, no matter who he let down or what he sacrificed.

And he will know that all he had to do was say thank you to me as I pushed open some double doors for him that day and he could have continued living that lie.

"Don't worry about it" will be all he can hear, as he spirals down into the depths of his own self-loathing, a washed-up has-been living rough on a beach, forced to hang around hospital entrances so he might dash in and squirt some more alcohol gel onto his hands to lick off later, before the security guards, who would once have respected him, chase him away, the way they always do. *"Don't worry about iiiiit . . ."*

On reflection, maybe I shouldn't say it.

But I know I'm going to. He needs to realize. He can't go on this way.

And as we reach the final set of double doors, this is my moment. I am going to absolutely relish this.

I give the doors an extra little push, sending them swinging wildly open, and as I begin to peel off to the room I'm going to, I half-turn my head and sneer, "Pfft, don't worry about it . . ."

At exactly the same time as the man says, "Thanks, mate!"

I look like a terrible, sneering, sarcastic person asking far too much of my fellow man! What—did I expect him to say "thanks" each and every time?

Well—yes, of course I did.

"Don't worry about it!" I quickly say again, turning around and beaming, but this time in a panic and trying to erase all sense of sarcasm.

"Cheers," he says.

"Don't worry about it!" I say, giving him a big thumbs-up.

I feel such incredible warmth toward him for the simple fact that he wasn't horrible.

"Okay," he mumbles. "Bye."

I love that guy!

CHAPTER 9

Rudeness and Revenge

Or: why did I join TripAdvisor?

The BBC's children's television station CBBC—home of *Dennis the Menace*, *Danger Mouse*, and *The Dog Ate My Homework*—was very excited one day to send out a new press release.

It came from the channel head, Cheryl Taylor, and read as follows:

> Today we wave goodbye to our very hard worked green and black logo (it's been a sturdy companion for almost a decade) and say hello to a colorful and versatile identity that is box fresh and fit for purpose in a mercurial and constantly shifting media landscape.

You can just imagine how excited the children who read this quote in their Media *Guardian* or copies of *Broadcast* must have been. "She's right!" they'd have called across a crowded classroom at break. "A logo for a children's television network must be fit for purpose when you consider the mercurial and constantly shifting media landscape!"

The point is, the kids didn't care. Whatever. It was a new logo. A bit more colorful. A little more modern. So long as CBBC still had *4 O'Clock Club* on at four o'clock they couldn't care less.

But some people did care. Some people cared very much.

There was immediate, knee-jerk outrage. People HATED the logo. They hated it SO MUCH. They were personally offended by it. Why had the BBC done this to them in particular? Why would it DO that?!

Sure, they were largely in their twenties, with no children of their own, and holding down full-time jobs that might make watching *4 O'Clock Club* live just a little trickier without canceling meetings and so on. But you're missing the real issue: this was *their* Children's BBC. *Not the children's* Children's BBC!

I read the comments, tweets, and updates with fascination.

Still so upset by the fact they have changed the cbbc logo and jingle.

You are a 34-year-old butcher from Croydon.

The new cbbc logo makes me angry.

You'll live.

Who the hell changed the cbbc logo?

CBBC did.

First they change the cbbc logo and now it's off air at 9 p.m.

WHY ARE YOU WATCHING CBBC AT 9 P.M.?

It went on and on.

"Still can't get over cbbc getting a new logo what the heck is that about???" wrote one person, late at night, probably staring at the ceiling, still finding the idea of a new logo so absolutely mind-blowing that I pray they never see the moon, or someone tells them what electricity is. As they drifted into slumber, the impotent yells continued to echo around the chamber . . .

> The new CBBC logo is a DISGRACE!
> This has destroyed my childhood.
> My childhood is gone.
> Bye bye childhood.
> Childhood is literally over.

Me me me. My my my.
  I am important. My opinion matters. I will be heard.

·   ·   ·

There are a billion things written every day about the internet, outrage, and rudeness, so I just want to focus on a couple of things.

  The writer Paul Ford has spent years considering exactly what happens to us when we sit in front of a keyboard or reach for our phones in the face of any minor slight, whether it's to complain about customer service or to scream about a channel we stopped watching 15 years earlier changing its logo for a new generation who genuinely enjoy it.

"Why wasn't I consulted?"

He sums it up with the phrase "Why wasn't I consulted?" [1]
  It has, he says, become the fundamental question of the web.
  I think he's right. The internet is a beautiful thing—a never-ending

place of ideas—but it is also an IV drip that feeds us what we need: to be heard. To be heard on anything and everything. Whether we care about it or not.

When it was announced that 84-year-old billionaire Rupert Murdoch was to be married to 59-year-old former model Jerry Hall, the internet responded in the way you might expect. But whatever you think of either of these two people, you'd do well to convince me it was any of your business. Yet off we go, firing conjecture, snide remarks, knowing asides, sarcastic attacks. We assign motivations we can't justify to people we've never met. We include them in messages—a couple who'd just announced their engagement. We're rude to them and about them.

This isn't a defense of Rupert Murdoch and Jerry Hall, by the way. It's not about the "victims"; rather the perpetrators.

Because just as interesting are the people who think about this coupling, weigh it all up in their heads, and finally come to a conclusion like this poster's:

Fair enough. Good luck to them.

The fact this person thinks this opinion worth including in the cultural conversation speaks volumes about our inflated new sense of self-worth and our approach to the internet.

He is giving the couple his blessing.

Some guy. Sitting there. Sipping coffee at his keyboard. In Des Moines. He's saying they can get married. It's the decision we were all waiting for.

This sums up the "Why wasn't I consulted?" phenomenon.

It hit Paul Ford when he spent 18 months carefully curating a website for *Harper's Bazaar* and studied the immediate reactions it got from its brand-new users.

"Brace yourself for the initial angry wave of criticism," he wrote. "How dare you, I hate it, it's ugly, you're stupid. The internet runs on knee-jerk reactions. People will test your work against their pet theories: It is not free, and thus has no value; it lacks community features; I can't believe you don't use dotcaps, lampsheets, or pixel scrims; it is not written in Rusp or Erskell; my cat is displeased."

People were working from a standing start of rage. They did not see an individual trying his best. They were blinded; offended by his decisions; wounded by his fonts.

"The ultimate question lurks beneath these curses," he wrote. "*Why wasn't I consulted?*"

When I speak with him, Paul sounds wise but weary of the web.

"The person who sees the Google logo changing and becomes outraged . . . ," he starts, and I think he's about to start slating them, but instead he sounds like he understands them. "People are territorial animals, and I think this is very emotional. You have a huge global effort to brand things, whether it's a clothing brand or soft drinks. Billions of dollars are spent creating a relationship, and then they change the nature of the relationship. Humans, being territorial, felt they had some control or understanding and it's taken away. So it's like your girlfriend saying, 'I'm going to see someone else' or your mom saying, 'We changed your room.' It's a reminder that we're powerless when those things get changed. A lot of the relationships and control we think we have in the world are fake. By *pretending* you have a link with a soft drink company, we can have the relationship that we think we want."

When Google did in fact excitedly unveil a brand-new, yet very similar, logo one day, there was uproar. It was the subject of TV news items. Furious radio diatribes. A writer for the *New Yorker* magazine said that by unveiling a new corporate logo, Google "symbolically diluted our trust."

It is precisely that sense of powerlessness that drives us to demand we have our say.

. . .

This can go wrong in so many ways.

In 2016, when Delta Airlines cheerfully announced their brand new Delta Pulse scheme—where passengers could give real-time feedback during their flight to the airline staff responsible for their comfort and safety—everyone agreed it was a brilliant idea.

It would have been a brilliant idea, too, if it hadn't involved actual people.

The entire air-travel experience in general could have been designed as an experiment in cultivating rudeness. They try and make it better. New airports are more spacious, lighter. Some have free water dispensers so you can refill your bottles. There are children's areas, and "dignity" spaces for passengers to put their shoes back on without hopping around.

But still. The *rest* of it.

Let's make people line up for hours in confined spaces, make them take off their shoes, bark at them if they haven't put their laptop in a separate container or their makeup in a see-through bag we all know is too small. Let's get some underpaid, passive-aggressive staff to act like authority figures because they did a couple of training days in the conference room of a Hilton near a highway; let's make people take their belts off and then brush the genitals of randomly selected passengers; let's charge them $40 for a coffee and a disappointing croissant; let's crowd them all into a hot, confined space after taunting them by making them walk past Business Class; let's keep them waiting on tight seats which become tighter the second the guy in front hits "recline"; let's feed them weak, warm recycled air with all the power and strength of an old woman breathing on them from above while they work out whose thin metal armrest is whose; let's immediately run out of meal selections and offer them OF ALL THINGS Tofu Bolognese (American Airlines flight 119, June 18, 2016); let's be late; let's make them wait at little carousels for bags that won't then arrive. Then let's do passport control again!

For Delta Airlines and their Delta Pulse initiative, their mistake was not just in asking for "honest" immediate comments without understanding that, with the best will in the world, no one wants to fly anywhere—they just want to *get* there. A flight should never be memorable. If a flight is memorable, it's because something went wrong.

Delta's second, worse mistake was in accidentally allowing the feedback to be seen by staff unfiltered.

So employees were getting "honest" real-time feedback like:

- I hate this airline and your shitty flight attendants.
- The aisles are too narrow on your planes and my elbows kept getting bumped by the pudgy flight attendant who couldn't control the movement of her ass.
- The flight attendants on this flight were fabulous. What a nice change to have young, fresh, exciting crew on board instead of the old washed-up ladies who are bitter and there just to get their money before they retire.

I chose these three because they show three different types of rudeness. None is particularly constructive in its criticism. All are more about the person sending the feedback than the people it's about.

But this is another example of an outlet that should be a wonderful thing going wrong the second you add humans. Humans who overlook something.

As Paul says when we speak, though with no hint of sadness, "it is so easy for people to be their worst selves and forget the person on the other side is a human being."

                        .   .   .

Perhaps the rudest anyone has ever been to me on the internet happened on a beautifully sunny Friday afternoon one day several years ago. **I am about to tell you precisely the sentences that came my way and be warned: one of them contains an extremely rude word.**

I was sitting in our living room, the sun streaming through the trees outside the window, beside my then heavily pregnant wife. I remember thinking what a wonderful day it was. I felt lucky.

And then because there was nothing on TV, I idly checked Twitter and saw the following message.

YOU ARE THE WORST WRITER IN HISTORY AND IF I EVER MEET YOU I WILL PUNCH YOUR CUNT FACE.
#DannyWallacedeservesAIDS

Looking at it now, it doesn't seem quite as bad as it did then. It just seems a bit playground. But at that moment, this violent, ugly, all-caps threat from a complete stranger seemed far worse, far more shocking. Everything had been so lovely! And now a man seemed to hate me. Really hate me. Wanted to punch me. Said I deserved something no one on Earth actually deserves.

It played on my mind for days. What if I ran into him? What if he was the guy walking behind me at night? Or as I pushed my soon-to-be-born son around the park? I looked at the guy's profile. He had a website. I read his poetry. He didn't seem like he'd have a very strong punch. But the way things do, his face became familiar, burned into my mind.

The rage the internet stirs up and allows us to vent threatens to derail the thing that once made it beautiful. Newspapers, once so proud to welcome in the community and get a discussion going, are now wary of their own below-the-line commenters. Those who stick their necks out sigh as they press "Publish," knowing that whatever they say and no matter how clearly they say it they will be accused of racism, sexism, homophobia, stupidity, thoughtlessness.

And, as you already know, they have their favorite targets.

A study by the *Guardian* newspaper showed that although the vast majority of their comment articles were written by white men, the ones most likely to receive "abuse or dismissive trolling" were not. The ten attracting the most abuse were eight women and two men. Those two men—the only ones on the list—were both people of color.[2]

Paul Ford has watched this rise for 20 years, and enjoyed semi-regular death threats himself for the past 15.

And one day, he decided to provoke it. Stir the hornet's nest.

"Someone asked me to write a piece for *Elle* magazine," he says. "And I just decided to piss everyone off. I don't know what came over me. I wrote a piece I knew would enrage everyone."

Paul is the father of twins—a boy and a girl. In his article on the gender pay gap—the difference between men's income and women's income—he declared he had found a way forward. He intended to save money for his daughter. But not for his son. His son would be fine. It was his daughter he needed to give money to.

"This was custom-made for a shit show," he says. "I was invited on to national TV shows, but I took one look at the [initial] comments section, and it would say things like 'your wife is a whore who should die' and I decided not to go on TV. It pissed off the left *and* the right. On the left, because I was using my class to protect my children. On the right, I was favoring a daughter over a son."

This, for Paul, was a sort of internet swan song.

"It was me saying, 'I'm done with you.' It's easy to tweak the mob. They're right there waiting for it. They're hungry. They want to get angry."

And the mob can get angry about anything.

* * *

Not long ago, the *Oxford Mail* ran a perfectly ordinary story with the headline:

CHARITY SPRAYS NICETIES ON TOWPATH TO ENCOURAGE RIVERSIDE POLITENESS

Apparently, people weren't being as polite to each other as they could, and for some reason this was particularly prevalent near water.

The Canal & River Trust (CRT)—the charity that takes care of nearly 2,000 miles of waterways in England and Wales—initiated a new scheme designed to encourage civility.

They decided to try and encourage good behavior at a particular lock on the Oxford Canal by deeming it a "polite zone."

There are no real losers here. The reader thinks about their own behavior or the behavior of others, and the CRT—even if the scheme is completely ineffective—get a little exposure and perhaps some thanks for a pretty thankless task.

So polite, nonpermanent messages of encouragement were sprayed on the towpath saying things like "Smile and say hi as you go by!" and "This is a hat-tipping zone!"

They celebrated. They handed out free cups of tea to passersby. They even employed a "canal laureate" and asked him to write a poem about being nicer to each other, and he came up with positive and hopeful lines like:

Let others too enjoy its use—be like the duck, and not the goose!

It was all perfectly lovely. And a completely innocuous story. The whole scheme probably cost about 28 bucks. There was really very little to get angry about. Even if you're completely ambivalent about what happens near one lock in a regional canal you live nowhere near, you would still file this story in the "positive" box and think better of the Canal & River Trust. Some of you might even donate to a charity you'd never thought about before.

So I made a bet with myself about what I'd read in the comments that readers left underneath.

I really loved the first one.

Far better would be interlocking sheet steel piles and stabilized canal banks.

I love this because you just know it began with a sigh. I love it because of all the meaning that is loaded and hidden. You can hear the commenter rustling the paper and muttering it to himself as a weary aside, and then going to all the trouble of registering on the site, confirming his details, assigning a login, verifying his registration, going back to the news story, writing his comment as if it's a casual aside, then sitting back, safe in the knowledge that now everyone knows he knows something about canal banks. Now everyone knows he knows what interlocking sheet steel piles are. And if he doesn't explain what interlocking sheet steel piles are, that means he just assumes that everybody knows what interlocking sheet steel piles are, and they *don't*, so he is better.

But his comment continues.

This patronizing gesture may seem "nice," but it is largely unnecessary here as folk are already polite and considerate for the most part. But we are mostly not naive, nor hoodwinked by such insulting tokenism from the CRT.

What's interesting about this to me is the ability to claim you are nice, while purposefully not being particularly nice. And that it's possible to claim others are committing the crime of patronizing you, while at the same time patronizing them. It's taking the higher ground, it's saying, "I should be in charge," it's asking, "Why wasn't I consulted?"

The very next comment pays particular attention to the canal laureate himself, a well-meaning young man named Luke Kennard, recently named as one of the winners of the Poet Book Society's "Next Generation Poets" prize, and who I expect gave his time and work to the charity for free.

That "poem" is worse than a bad greeting card. I hope they don't pay much to the canal laureate.

Again, I don't think it's a full-time job, and it's not like you see many poets swanning around on the canals of Oxfordshire in a two-story yacht.

It goes on:

Rude people are not likely to heed this primary-school approach and may even become worse out of defiance.

I'll stop you there. At no time in history has being given a free cup of tea as you walk by a canal brought about a feeling of moral indignation and defiance in anyone. No one has ever been given a free cup of tea by someone and been so outraged by this primary-school approach that they have immediately decided to become actively ruder and push that person in the canal. All that happens is you think, "That was nice," and continue on your way.

They haven't finished.

Nice people don't need the advice, so this looks like a stunt to get free PR in the paper.

Well, of course it's a stunt to get in the paper. Canals just existing has never been enough to get into the paper on its own. But once again, it's fascinating to see someone behaving in a negative way while also taking great care to assert their own niceness.

The comments go on and on. There are jokes about how the Canal & River Trust may have communist sympathies. Someone attempts to hijack the conversation and steer it toward Oxford Council's "secret war against the people of the waterways." Someone calls the whole project "a reasonably harmless gesture" but still "beyond insensitive" for reasons I'm still trying to figure out.

And a final poster rails against the use of the slogan "Smile and say hi as you go by!" written on concrete in temporary spray.

This is basically appalling vandalism to the towpath; you'd hope the charity that has ended up responsible for the canals and their rich heritage would have a modicum of respect for them and not pull patronizing stunts like this, but no.

They finish with a flourish.

What a pointless and offensive project.

Pointless. Offensive. Appalling. Insulting. Patronizing. Unnecessary. Insensitive. Something that might actually make people worse than they already are.

I'm talking about the comments here, not the politeness campaign.

It's all so abrasive. Calling the CRT a charity that has "ended up" responsible for the canals rather than a charity that *took on* responsibility for the canals—as if there are just general groups of aimless charities sitting around under bridges waiting for someone to assign them a cause for which they "end up" responsible.

This is the kind of low-level, patronizing, passive-aggressive rudeness that clogs up our internet, fills our eyes, and drains our hearts.

Every word of it is designed not to berate others so much as to make the poster feel better about themselves.

Whole communities continue to evolve online whose sole purpose is to leave comments like this, and either agree wholeheartedly with one another (to feel better about themselves) or nitpick tiny holes in each other's arguments (to feel better about themselves).

What a truly pointless waste of time.

And it is everywhere. All the time. A constant barrage of rudeness. In the strangest, most innocent corners of the web.

Here are five completely innocuous stories taken from the *Mail Online*—one of the world's most popular websites and active online communities—below which I have included five real and completely typical comments in full.

The cutest brace face ever! Adorable golden retriever puppy who has to wear BRACES becomes instant online hit
Would have been better off putting it down.

Jolly hockey sticks! Countess of Wessex laughs at her best efforts as she joins the England team on the pitch

Sad shallow woman meaningless life

Suki Waterhouse opts for biker chic in shearling jacket and leather boots as she attends Coach's Paris Fashion Week party

she is an idiot

Comedian Jamie Kennedy reveals he has been dealing with secret heart problem for 35 years

Promoting something is he.

Wife confronts "cheating husband" after he tries to "hook up with her BEST FRIEND"

Typically manipulative women taking advantage of a man's friendly behavior.

Now granted, that last one was me.

And guess what—57 people liked it! And 108 didn't. I just wanted to see what it would feel like. I couldn't go so far as to actually insult anyone personally. I wanted to. I just couldn't. So I just insulted all women instead.

But here's the strange thing. As wrong as it was, and as playful as I was being, there was a certain sense of satisfaction I gleaned from those little green upticks, as well as those little red downticks, as I told myself it was an experiment.

I was joining the pack. I was taking my place in a community. No one said I had to get out; they saw that I was joining in and they let me. I was on their wavelength.

That is dangerous.

But even as I joined them, I couldn't help but wonder: who's doing it? Who, when writing "sad shallow woman meaningless life" on an internet message board under a story about the Countess of Wessex playing hockey, cannot see that perhaps they might in fact be writing about someone closer to home?

We have this idea that everyone's opinion is worth the same, and while that looks great on paper, it is not, of course, true.

Someone who asserts climate change is happening has the backing of 97 percent of the world's top climatologists. Someone who claims it is not has their mate Barry, who says it snowed when he was on holiday—so how can it be?

Some opinions are worth more than others. Opinions based on fact, or knowledge, or experience are worth infinitely more than opinions tossed out off-the-cuff online or after four pints of Stella.

But when it comes to how rudely that opinion is put forward, the person writing it is bulletproof: this is my opinion and that's the end of it. *Only Being Honest.*

And this is not just true of the amateur keyboard warriors who comment online. As long-established newspapers close and fold around us by the dozen, and the world stretches further online, journalists and professional commentaters have been forced to face an unpleasant truth: they're only worth the clicks they muster. Attract an audience, attract the advertisers, keep your job. Pieces saying how nice rainbows are or that the Education Secretary was wearing lovely shoes as she attended a meeting with local officials are nothing compared to clickbait screaming WHY RAINBOWS ARE A PIECE OF CRAP or full-scale shoe-based attacks on a woman with bigger things on her mind.

What's really sad is that we all know this, yet to cope we pretend it isn't true. That we *would* read an article about rainbows or nice shoes, when in reality nothing interests us less. And every now and again, to convince ourselves we are not part of this New Rudeness, we ask why.

When the rude writer Giles Coren was challenged on a piece he wrote labeling the outpouring of grief over David Bowie's death insane, some people felt moved to ask him why he felt the need to always be so condemnatory.

You could sense the sad shrug of his weakened shoulders as he replied, "Well, *you* don't have to write 1,200 words about something in the news every week. Not condemning things is a luxury I don't have."

Once opinion journalists sought to provoke thought; now they're forced to troll for reactions. And what provokes more knee-jerk, bankable reactions than rudeness?

· · ·

And through rudeness, I found myself joining them.

I surprised myself when I came home from the Hotdog Incident by joining TripAdvisor and writing my review.

I surprised myself mainly because of my motivations and how impure they were.

I was not writing this review to help other people. I wasn't trying to warn them off the diner or suggest places they might have a better time.

"No," says Paul Ford. "You wanted *revenge*."

I did. I wanted revenge.

And revenge is an interesting side effect of rudeness.

Ordinarily, what civilized human beings desire is justice. If someone kills our dog, we want justice. We don't want to kill that person's dog. If someone burgles our house, our first thought isn't to try and burgle them back.

But if someone is rude to us, it's not justice we immediately think of. We want to shove their rudeness straight back in their stupid rude face. We want to show strength. Fight. We want them to feel the way they made us feel.

"In that moment, with that hotdog," says Paul, "you needed to exercise and demonstrate your status. With your review, you were saying, 'I am a person who is worthy of respect, and whoever served me this hotdog didn't respect and understand that, and you need to be warned, dear reader, lest you walk into this trap in which your own status is not respected!'"

That is it. That is exactly what I was doing.

"Look, we can't help it," he says. "We're very status driven as human beings, and you felt that that was fragile at that moment, and that your position in life was meaningless."

I did! I *did* feel my position in life was meaningless!

"There are people who just get screamed at all day. A lot of them work in the service industry and their status is low. And they are reminded of it all the time. And they don't have the ability to say 'stop it.' But it's very tricky . . . see, you and I can go back to the zones where people respect us. That's the rest of your life. But that doesn't transfer to the restaurant, and it doesn't transfer to the guy on the street who yells at me as I go by on my bicycle. I feel like it should. 'I'm a big deal!' I wanna yell back. 'I have a good salary!'"

We have a need to be respected, and when we are treated rudely—especially by a stranger—we have a need to punish them. Ordinarily, this doesn't happen in the moment. We're confused or we can't think of the perfect comeback until we're halfway down the street.

According to the Wallace Report, this is how people reacted the last time someone was unexpectedly rude to them:

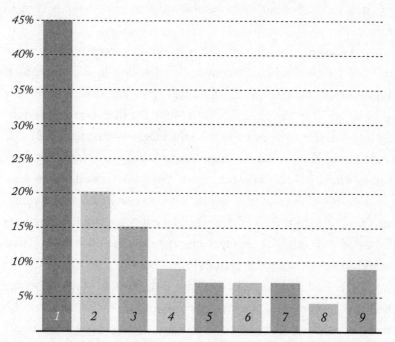

Respondents could give more than one answer.

1. *ignoring them (45%)*
2. *giving them a "look" (20%)*
3. *being rude back (15%)*
4. *being passive aggressive (9%)*
5. *shouting back at them (7%)*
6. *trying to respond with a "clever" comeback (7%)*
7. *trying to make them feel guilty (7%)*
8. *mumbling something under their breath (4%)*
9. *other (9%)*

Fourteen billion years since the Big Bang, and the best coping strategy we've come up with is pretending it didn't happen or giving a "look."

It is only after our looks have faded that our thoughts turn to revenge.

It doesn't matter what our status is. When a mere blogger wanted to Have His Say and loudly complained that he felt he'd been rudely kept waiting at a press launch for a new Tesla car, the unimaginably wealthy owner of the company, Elon Musk, felt that in itself was rude. So he personally intervened to have the blogger's order for an $80,000 Tesla Model X canceled. Revenge! And what's fascinating is, we don't think "what a jerk" or "how ridiculous." We think . . . well, fair enough.

Revenge is everywhere, rearing its head every day on every high street. A 2011 study showed that when an employee found a customer's behavior rude, they themselves began to engage in behavior that would *directly sabotage that person's experience.*[3]

It's the cashier who packs your eggs at the bottom of your shopping bag; the barman who doesn't quite fill your pint; the waitress who sprays your table while you're still sitting at it; the postman who weeks after you pissed him off still ignores the "Do Not Bend" on the envelope; the billionaire who cancels your car order.

Revenge is natural. To not want it is weird and it has ever been thus.

In fact, in 2014 archaeologists discovered what are believed to be the only two written examples of the ancient British Celtic language. They were pretty much just slagging someone off. They were discovered along with 128 other "Curse Stones" found at the Roman Baths in Bath, like the one that said:

Docimedis has lost two gloves and asks that the thief responsible should lose their minds and eyes.

. . . which I suppose is fair enough, if they were really nice gloves.

. . .

Revenge figures highly in the Wallace Report, precisely because it is such a fundamental human urge.

Of those polled, 47 percent of men and over 50 percent of women have wanted to take revenge on people who were rude to them.

If you're rude to two people, chances are one of them is now plotting to get you.

The scary thing is that we really do believe that revenge is a dish best served cold. We wait. We plan. We relish. And afterward, we are secretly proud. We also have the ultimate excuse: they were rude to me.

But here's the thing. If you walked into a pub and said, "You know that guy I plumb bathrooms with? I decided to eat his lunch, and then I hid all his equipment," people would think you had lost your mind. But that is a *real answer* in the Wallace Report.

In fact, try and imagine any one of these sentences without putting before it the phrase "Someone was rude to me so . . . ," and you'd think they were crazy.

I gave obscene gestures from my car.
I changed their Netflix password.
I turned all their possessions upside down.
I let a dog lick a sausage I was serving to them.
I rubbed my bag of fries all over their windshield.
I pointed out their flawed appearance in great detail.
I spat on their back.
Squealed on them.
Reported them for their untaxed and uninsured vehicle.
Sabotaged them.
I ignored them when they were looking for help.

I sent him some offensive letters.

I set them up to fail.

Humiliated them.

I smashed something they liked.

I destroyed their stuff.

I slashed their tires.

Keyed their car.

I smacked them in the mouth.

I punched them in the face.

That got dark pretty quickly.

Any one of these things is completely unacceptable in normal life. Some of them are criminal. In my survey of 2,000 people, 270 were only too pleased to tell me all about what they felt was an extremely justified response. From shouting at someone (8), to ignoring them (7), to getting someone sacked (2), to sleeping with someone's partner out of revenge for a perceived slight (1).

These are also things which, if done anonymously or even in plain view, can affect other people's lives very deeply. I mean, someone had to change their Netflix password back.

But this is a deep pot of unattractive emotion we're stirring. Most of these acts of rudeness-revenge are done from the shadows, the results of which aren't seen or witnessed, but just imagined and enjoyed. Within each of them is a deep, sad feeling of powerlessness.

I wrote my online revenge-review precisely because I felt powerless. I had no immediate way of getting my own back or turning to sabotage, and so I joined the sad ranks in the place the powerless go to find respect.

And I didn't care. As far as I knew, I would never darken her door again, or ever meet her again.

Talking of which . . . remember the guy who wrote me the terrible tweet? The one all in capitals?

Remember how I said I memorized his face?

Remember what he said he'd do to me . . . if ever he met me?

Well, guess what happened next.

CHAPTER 10

The Troll

The ugly consequence of rudeness

I n the hit 2006 film *Snakes on a Plane*, Samuel L. Jackson plays an FBI agent called Neville Flynn who, while on a routine flight from Hawaii, finds himself completely surrounded by snakes.

In one particularly emotionally charged scene, he is asked by other passengers to clear a whole cockpit of them.

This is when, completely fed up with these blooming snakes and probably thinking, "This is all I need!," Samuel L. Jackson utters the line:

Enough is enough! I have *had* it with these motherfucking snakes on this motherfucking plane!

It is an important turning point, and one which rings true if you're someone who can relate to clearing unexpectedly aggressive snakes out of airplane cockpits.

However, when the film came to be broadcast on television, worried censors thought the script was a little rude, and requested that line in particular be redubbed, which is how it came to pass that

Samuel L. Jackson, charged with the unenviable task of removing snakes from a plane, takes a breath and says:

Enough is enough! I have *had* it with these *monkey-fighting* snakes on this *Monday to Friday* plane!

Now, I think if you were on a plane full of snakes and a man suddenly lost his temper and started shouting that, you would assume the snakes must contain hallucinogenic venom and the man had been bitten on the bollocks.

Even if you didn't, you would still want to know how he'd jumped to the conclusion that these snakes had at any point been fighting monkeys, given that so far absolutely no one else had at any point mentioned monkeys also being on the plane. It's possible you might also have had some questions about why this particular flight only operates on weekdays.

I'm telling you this because there's some more bad language coming up, and for a moment I considered swapping the swear words for inoffensive replacements, because I know how delicate you are. But I think those words are important to the story.

By the way, not to spoil it, but Samuel L. Jackson gets rid of all the snakes and as a reward someone takes him to Bali and teaches him how to surf.

. . .

There is a theory often doled out about the internet.

"It's like the Wild West," they say. "It'll never change."

But just as every time I travel I question why it took a hundred years for someone to come up with the idea of putting wheels on suit-cases when we live in a world in which both things have long existed simultaneously, one day we will look back on these relatively early internet days and marvel at the apparent lawlessness. At how vicious we could be, how condescending, how rude, and at how the national and global tone changed with the rise of social media. We will find it unbelievable that someone like Caroline Criado-Perez—the woman who suggested to the Bank of England that they put Jane Austen on the new £10 note—could receive 50 abusive messages an hour for a day afterward. Or "24 hours of rape threats," as she put it.

On a typical day in the UK, five people are convicted for sending offensive messages on the internet. The average jail sentence is just over two months.

Most of those people clearly aren't well. And those who would pass psychological assessment would doubtless tell you it was out of character. They were drunk. They'd been dumped. They were angry. They wouldn't do it again. They're normally really nice, honest.

But we are now able to stretch into a stranger's life with just a few taps of a keyboard. It's a responsibility we haven't yet realized is a responsibility. How we do it and what we say rests with us, and we have to live by the words we use.

· · ·

Perhaps four months after I received my unusual tweet—**YOU ARE THE WORST WRITER IN HISTORY AND IF I EVER MEET YOU I WILL PUNCH YOUR CUNT FACE. #DannyWallacedeservesAIDS**—I was standing in a pub in the West End of London with two people I'd just worked with but didn't know that well.

I had good feelings about this pub. I'd gone there since before there even was a Twitter, or Facebook, or broadband. All dart boards and wooden floors and stained-glass windows featuring nineteenth-century boxers. There was a work crowd in. A famous actor stood on the street outside with his pint, smoking tatty hand-rolled cigarettes and laughing with fans.

I was just raising my glass to my lips when I turned around for some reason, and I spotted someone.

I spotted the guy who sent the tweet.

. . .

The day I'd received the tweet, my wife could see that something was off with me. I look at it now and it's meaningless. But on the day, when someone has taken the time to contact you in that way, it plays on your mind. It's like those first moments after unexpected rudeness, as Amir Erez told me, when your frontal lobes are off.

Twitter is the world's number-one trolling service. It has a problem, and it knows it. Their top lawyer, Vijaya Gadde, recently said they had been "inexcusably slow" in tackling abusive messages sent on their platform. That very day, a study of 134,000 rude or abusive social media messages sent to soccer players in just one season showed that nearly 90 percent of them happened on Twitter. Mario Balotelli alone received 8,000, more than half of which were racist.[1]

When I got mine, I replied to the guy, just saying, "Wow. You seem aggressive." And in part this was to give him an out. To let him turn it into a joke, or say, "Oops. Sorry." Or just somehow do something to take the sting out and make it better for us both.

But there was no reply. He just swaggered away, slapping himself on the back, smirking with his mates.

My wife asked to see the tweet, so I showed her.

Which is when she looked at the guy's profile and said something amazing.

"I *know* that name."

. . .

Seeing him here, live, in this pub, right now, the first thing that bristled through me was anger.

That guy. That absolute *monkey fighter.*

And then delight. Delight that he was here, but why?

I was delighted because I knew that I now had a range of options open to me.

I could ignore him, like a grown-up. Know that the best revenge is living well. I could just have fun with these two people and drink a pint and laugh, unaffected.

But the other side of my brain was saying . . . *do* something. Tell him. Let him justify his words. Let him see he can't always get away with it. Because I'd looked at his profile and it wasn't just me. He'd been nasty to lots of people.

I was also delighted because I knew that he knew who I was . . . while he had absolutely no idea that I knew who *he* was.

The power had shifted.

.   .   .

My wife is a former publicist.

When she saw this guy's name, she flipped open her laptop and found an old document.

It was a list of old publicity contacts.

She trailed one finger down the page until it stopped on one name in particular.

The guy was a writer too.

So now I knew. And suddenly I was in charge. I could make the decisions. I could let him go, or I could catch him out.

And then I looked at the people I was with. This was my first-ever pint with them. What would they think of me if I challenged the guy? They'd think I was brittle, delicate, that I take things too seriously, that I was somehow damaged.

But I wasn't. I was just a man who wanted revenge in the face of rudeness.

So I said, "Look, um, that guy in the corner with his mate . . ."

And I told them the story and that I might be about to do something.

And the glee in their eyes was exciting for a moment, but also told me maybe I was overstepping the mark.

So I resolved to do nothing. To be the bigger man. To let it go.

And then I turned around and he was standing right next to me at the bar.

. . .

Received wisdom tells us that the greatest ally of trolling on the internet is anonymity. The person whom you're saying is a travesty of a human being does not know who you are, and therein lies both your power and your clever escape. You can be in and out before they know it. Hit and run.

In fact, evidence is mounting that it is not anonymity that empowers trolls, but a lack of eye contact. Eye contact is vital to humans. It's the Looking Glass Self again, letting us know how we're being perceived by the other person, whether we've insulted them, hurt their feelings, crossed a line.

Researchers at Israel's University of Haifa asked 71 pairs of students who had never met before to debate a topic over Instant Messenger and come up with a solution. Some could see each other, others could not. Others still were asked to maintain constant and unwavering eye contact.

What they found was that people who could look into each other's eyes were only half as likely to say something hostile to the other person; those who were hidden from view were twice as likely to be hostile.[2]

Well, I was about to make *direct eye contact* with this man.

And I was about to become hostile.

. . .

We often write off the people who post abusive messages online. We imagine them as stinking reprobates, barking at their mums to bring them more bacon sandwiches as they sit scratching in their rancid back-bedroom hovels, firing off abuse at the woman on the sports channel for being a woman on the sports channel, and also being a woman so far out of their league it's a different sport. They were bullied at school, they've never had a girlfriend, they hate women and the middle classes, they don't wash their hair and think deodorant is a madcap, left-wing affectation.

But this guy, standing next to me at the bar, this guy we'll call Steve . . . he looked normal.

Glasses.

Stubble.

Mid-twenties.

Casually dressed.

No unusual stains.

Not carrying any fascist china.

He looked like a guy I'd probably meet for a drink, in a pub just like this.

Our eyes had met for just a fraction of a second too long when I'd recognized him, and, yes, I know that sounds romantic. But I could tell that he, too, had recognized me. The very fact that he was happy to send me a message like the one he'd sent, but still felt comfortable enough to stand next to me in a pub set something off in me.

So I quickly turned to him. I put my hand on his arm.

"Steve!" I said.

His eyes widened. He turned to look.

"Oh, hi . . . ," he said, confused.

"How *are* you?" I said.

He seemed shocked. Disconcerted. I moved my hand from his arm. He was starting to seem shorter. His eyes darted around for a second, before his brain found a viable explanation.

"Oh . . . you're a friend of Pete's, aren't you?" he said.

"I am," I said, nodding and smiling. "I *am* a friend of Pete's."

I did not know who Pete was. But Steve visibly relaxed. He'd found a connection. In that moment, he thought I didn't know.

But something didn't add up to him.

"But how did you know I was Steve?" he said.

And this is where I stepped forward.

Got closer to him.

Looked down at him.

"Because you said that you were going to punch my cunt face and that I deserve AIDS."

.   .   .

"Bullying" is an overused word these days. It's certainly not what Steve tried to do to me. But it's what the internet nevertheless allows us to have a fresh new-world attempt at. That's difficult to do to someone who can defend themselves, of course, but—not to get maudlin—we've all met kids who have been or were being bullied.

They look shattered by it. Fragile, like any beep of a mobile phone or ping of a tweet might bring fresh modern trauma. Imagine living your life that way. Constantly on edge, always waiting for the next unsolicited, faceless message, ready to tell you you're thick, or worthless, or friendless.

Those kids, not yet shored up by experience or confidence the way a canal bank can be shored up by interlocking sheet steel piles, aren't yet able to ignore it. They are surrounded by it, stuck in school-imposed social groups they can't get out of, enveloped by it, and the weirdest part is that it might well be at the hands of otherwise perfectly normal kids. Kids who now bully in a way that just couldn't have happened when I was at school. A modern, efficient, brutal brand of bullying that parents can empathize with, but never truly understand.

A quarter of all kids aged between 13 and 18 say they have been the victim of this kind of bullying.[3] That's one kid in four growing up with draining psychological pressure. Those most likely to be bullied? Kids with disabilities or from minority ethnic backgrounds.

It must be like having a dark ceiling constantly above you, which seems to get lower as you wake in the night, suffocating you with thoughts of the next morning at school. A few rude words, so casually dashed off, must make a kid feel the whole world is crashing in on them. A bully who can't see their victim dehumanizes them.

It's much harder to do that face-to-face with a grown man in a West End pub.

.   .   .

I watched as something exploded behind Steve's eyes.

It was pretty clear that he did not want to have this conversation. But I did.

And also, he'd ordered his pints. He was trapped. You cannot abandon unpaid-for drinks, in precisely the way you cannot abandon already-paid-for hotdogs. These are the values that make Britain great.

So I did two things as I stood inches from his face, making myself slightly bigger as I did so.

I kept using his *name*. And I kept using his *phrase*.

I wanted him to realize that right now he was a person, not a cocky profile picture. And I wanted him to know that these were the words *he* had brought into this world, not me. He couldn't fire off a tweet then run. He had to stand and wait for the reply.

"So when are you going to do it, Steve?" I said, keeping my voice steady, flat, unamused. "When are you going to punch my cunt face?"

Now, this is not like me. I hate that word. I'm not violent. I try to be nice to everyone I meet, and yet here I was, purposefully swearing in the face of a stranger.

This was changing me.

"Because you can punch my cunt face in here, or you can punch my cunt face outside."

A flash of mortification from Steve, and a moment of panic. But I wanted him to take responsibility for these words, to hear them. People will write anything on the internet and send it to a stranger. But ask them to read it out loud at a wedding . . .

"Who do you think *deserves* AIDS, Steve?" I asked, still jabbing his name at him, his actual name, not his username, and to his actual face, not his . . . user face. "Am I the only person who deserves AIDS or do you think other people deserve AIDS too? Does anyone actually *deserve* AIDS?"

"I was having a bad day," he said, looking small, awkward. "I'd been at an awards do and our magazine hadn't won . . ."

I'd been having a lovely day, I told him, until I got his tweet. I'd begun to feel adrenalized. Like I wanted to teach him a lesson.

"I gave you an out," I said. "You could have apologized."

He nodded, shrugged, glanced to see where his pints were, whether he could go yet.

"I'm really sorry," he said. "It's not like me."

His pints arrived. He put his hands around them, dragged them across the bar toward himself, then stopped.

"Look," he said, but I'd had enough.

"Take your pints, Steve," I said. "And fuck off."

.   .   .

My wife woke up at three in the morning shaking with laughter.

"It's just so unlike you," she said. "'Take your pints and fuck off!'"

She kept giggling then doing her new impression of me.

"Take your pints and fuck off!" she said, the bed now quaking.

Steve wrote an apology on his blog, but he never sent one to me. It turned out that once, a few years earlier, he'd written me a thank-you letter. He'd read one of my books while standing in a shop. (He didn't buy it, but I'm willing to let that go.)

I felt terrible about what I did to Steve maybe three microseconds after I'd done it. I suggested to the people I was with that we move pubs, and that's just what we did, squeezing past the actor outside still laughing with strangers.

But an hour later I felt great. I had exorcised something. I'd done the thing we all want to do when rudeness is left at our door like a dog turd in a brown paper bag. I had shoved it straight back through the owner's letter box.

But I also feel like what happened was important. I met one of those people who do those things you read about. He was an actual person. And by doing that, I sort of feel like I've met them all now. Not the ones who send awful messages to grieving parents, or the ones who tell soldiers to burn in hell, or the ones who threaten someone with rape because they have the ludicrous idea that one of the country's most celebrated literary icons might be a suitable candidate for inclusion on a banknote.

But the normal ones who make up the mass. The ones who find a voice online, but a voice that doesn't match the one they use in the pub. Those who have helped create a New Rudeness that no one would ever have chosen and people are still finding a way to stop.

There will be those among you who say, "Yes, but what about freedom of speech?," and that's a good point, but it's just one step away from thinking, "I'm only being honest" is a valid excuse for telling a kid at a bus stop she's fat.

We must praise the internet for giving us the right of reply. Steve thought I was a dick, so he got in touch to tell me. I thought Steve was a dick, so I told him face-to-face—though that was marginally less comfortable for him, and you might argue that it was me who became the bully.

I've been in email contact with Steve a few times since that day in the pub. He seems all right. Perhaps it's because we both now realize the other is an actual person. He told me he was genuinely horrified the day we met because he honestly didn't think he was that person. He's also read much of what you have just read. I told him I was writing it, and he said that was fine. I do have to say, he didn't seem to enjoy it very much, and I don't think there'll be another thank-you letter. He told me that the moment he realized he'd been uncovered, as I stood over him and made it explicitly clear I knew exactly who he was, "I was shitting myself . . . I was worried that exactly what went on to happen would happen."

Steve wasn't a troll in the traditional sense. He was being offensive, but he wasn't *trying to offend*, and I think there's a subtle but distinct difference. To try and shut down all people with opinions is ludicrous. The internet won't always be like this. It will get better as we work out a balance with our real-life interactions, and as we realize that even the faceless have a face.

According to the Wallace Report, 35 percent of people agree that the world is reaching a New Rudeness crisis point. And of those that feel the end is nigh, 65 percent place the blame squarely on social media.

We have to protect freedom of speech. But the best way to protect it is to use it wisely. For goodness' sake, don't run the batteries out.

We can be better, and we can do it every time we click "Send."

To those people who say about the internet, "It's like the Wild West. It'll never change," I say: why not test your theory by visiting the Wild West?

Which no longer exists.

Because it changed.

CASE STUDY: AGGRESSIVE POLITENESS

I am intent on buying a coffee and a sandwich from a well-known high-street bakers, but my hands are full, and although I've stopped listening to music I haven't taken my earphones out yet. There's no line and I get straight to the counter and the man behind it makes a real point of loudly saying, "Morning."

But it's not a "Morning!" with an exclamation mark. It doesn't represent or evoke joy. It is just the word "morning" said loudly.

"Morning," I reply, as a bus passes outside, and I put whatever I can into my pockets and look up to order my coffee.

It's then that I spot the man rolling his eyes. Why is he rolling his eyes?

He looks away, and I spy a slight shake of the head.

And then very quietly and hardly moving his lips he looks at the ground and says, "Oh, morning to you, too, how are you, I'm fine, thanks very much, nice to chat."

Then he plasters on a smile and looks back at me with dead eyes to await my order.

I realize exactly what has happened.

"I can hear you," I say.

"I'm sorry?" he says.

"I can hear you," I say, taking out an earphone. "There's no music. I've just got earphones in. I can hear you."

He thought I was a terrible man who would rather listen to music than engage on a human level with a member of the service industry! His paranoia was rampant!

"Well, it's just I said morning," he says, bristling, caught, but not backing down.

"I know you said morning and I heard you and I said morning back," I say.

He thinks I've been rude to him. He thinks I've walked in with my headphones on, stood there, and just ignored him.

"I didn't hear you say morning," he smiles, but still with those dead eyes, and I can't let it go. I must not allow him to think I was being rude. It was him who was the rude one, having a sarcastic conversation with himself. And then he adds: "I can *only* apologize."

Well, he doesn't *sound* like he is apologizing. He'd have just said sorry. Instead, he's all "I can only apologize," like he's a sarcastic butler, and we both know he thinks I'm lying and he'll bitch about me later. Also, all he's apologizing for is not hearing me say morning. What about his one-man play?

I seethe as I realize he thinks he's got one up on me.

"Well, I came in and you said, 'Morning,'" I say, not letting it go, "and then I said, 'Morning,' back, but I was putting things in my pocket and then I looked up and you were *impersonating* me."

Impersonating me! He was hardly impersonating me. But I was certainly supposed to be the other character in his amateur dramatics, and by pointing this out and feigning offense I've now got one up on him!

"I was not impersonating you," he says, and I make a face that says I think he was, even though I don't really.

A new customer walks in and starts looking at doughnuts.

"Well, it seemed like you were impersonating me," I say, quietly. "When you had that little chat with yourself."

The thing is, I get it. This poor guy must just get grunted at or ignored by a succession of early-morning men and women every day. But I wasn't being rude to him, and he didn't know he was being rude to me and yet we're both acting like we think the other is Pol Pot. We could have laughed it off. I could have said, "Oh, God, sorry, I did say 'Morning,'" and he could have said, "Oh, goodness, I'm so sorry, I didn't hear you and I thought your headphones were on," and I'd have laughed and said, "Yes, I should have taken them out!"

"*Morning*," he says, to the man looking at doughnuts, as if to make a point.

"Yeah," says the man looking at doughnuts, which isn't quite the response he was hoping for.

"A coffee, *please*," I say, and wow—my "please" is dripping with meaning. See? I'm saying please. I'm polite. But I'm not giving you the *polite* please, I'm giving you the pointed please.

"Any type in particular, sir?" he says, lightly, but look what he's doing. He's pointing out my muddle-mindedness *and* he's calling me "sir." He is distancing himself, showing how professional he is in the face of such callous arrogance, with his "Any type in particular, sir?"

"Yes," I spit, but I haven't decided yet and he's caught me on the back foot. "A flat white, if that's *okay*."

Oof. Take that. *If that's okay!* Politeness as a weapon.

The man at the doughnuts is just looking at us. He knows something's wrong but can't work out what. We're saying all the right things to each other, just not quite in the right way.

As he fusses over my coffee and taps the buttons extra hard to show how good he is at his job, I decide I'm not even going to buy a sandwich now. That is how I will punish him. I will not buy a sandwich he did not even know I was going to buy, and then I will not eat lunch because of it. That'll teach this rude idiot.

"£1.75, *please*," he says, and I will not dignify that with an answer. I just hand him the money and walk out of the shop.

"Good-bye!" he shouts after me, but he times it perfectly: I'm halfway out the door and striding. I look rude!

"GOOD-BYE!" I shout, madly, as I walk down the street. "GOOD-BYE!"

CHAPTER 11

Rude Rage

Didn't anyone tell you it's rude to cut people off?

When I was a kid, there was a woman who was not my auntie whom we nevertheless called Auntie Rosie.

We didn't really know many people in London, so if ever we went there we'd stop by and see her, and she'd make strong coffee and serve coconut macaroons.

She was lovely, and in my mind she drove a pale blue Citroën 2CV, though I've just checked with my parents and apparently it was a white Volkswagen Golf, which makes me question my other memories of her and worry perhaps she was not actually a diminutive Jewish retiree but a nine-foot black man called Bobby.

What I definitely remember is this: the way that woman drove.

We'd get in her car outside her Wembley terrace and drive to Brent Cross shopping center, and when we did, Auntie Rosie would change.

"LOOK AT THIS FACKING ARSEHOLE!" she would shout, banging her fists on her steering wheel. "YOU BLOODY BASTARD! YOU FACKING BASTARD!"

My dad would laugh awkwardly or make a "tsk" sound to show solidarity while my mum would glance fearfully at me.

"LOOK AT THIS ARSEHOLE! DRIVE, YOU BLOODY SIMPLE BASTARD!"

Then she would honk her horn. For ages.

"LOOK AT THIS PRICK!"

Auntie Rosie hated anybody who drove too slowly, too quickly, or in the same lane as her, even on a single-lane road. She hated male drivers, female drivers, young drivers, old drivers, and people who couldn't drive. She hated people who were parking, people who had parked, and especially people who couldn't park.

And the second we were in Brent Cross, she was lovely sweet old Auntie Rosie again.

What I can't remember, as I say, is precisely what the outside of her car looked like.

Turns out that if I could, this whole terrifying metamorphosis might be far easier to explain.

* * *

Since 2004, the number of deadly accidents a year involving furious drivers has increased nearly tenfold in the United States alone, from 26 to 247.[1] And those are just the fatal ones. That increase doesn't take into account the near-daily stories of road rage like the case of Tammy Meyers, who honked at a driver who had offended her by rudely speeding up behind her. She got out of her car, and the two drivers began shouting at each other. She drove off and picked up her son, who was armed. Then they went looking for the other driver. Meyers and her son couldn't find him, so they returned home. The other driver was waiting for her. He shot and killed her.

In Britain, more than 80 percent of drivers say they've been the victim of road rage at least once; 60 percent of people who have ad-mitted to committing it said their victims "deserved it."[2] It shows no signs of abating, either, if we look at the Wallace Report: nearly one in five people said that the last time someone was rude to them, it was while driving.

In London, a war between cyclists and drivers has gathered incredible pace in recent years. Both hate the other. Both see the other as a menace, as a danger, as "taking liberties." The rise in helmet cameras has led to a glut of YouTube videos of angry exchanges based on dangerous driving, thoughtless behavior and rude exchanges.

But my video favorite, if you can have one, is this.

Somewhere in London, a black BMW overtakes a cyclist but leaves him little space. The cyclist bangs his fist on the roof of the car as it gets nearer. The driver sounds his horn for 12 long seconds because he is absolutely furious and, in the confines of a car, this is the only way to let the world know.

He pulls up, cutting the cyclist off and forcing him from his bike.

What follows, which is verbatim apart from a boring bit I removed about traffic lights, is like a 1950s public information video on how people of different classes with different points of view should settle their differences.

The cyclist is posh. The driver is what a posh person would call "salt of the earth."

They come face-to-face and stand just inches from one another, each with a hand doubtless shaking from adrenaline and anger.

Separated by metal and glass, they *hated* one another.

Yet the first thing that is said humanizes a situation which moments before was simply man versus machine.

CYCLIST: I'm very sorry, my friend.

Look at that!
The driver is thrown.

He has come out with rage coursing through him, but now he doesn't quite know what to do with it. He's still angry, but it's crumbling, dissipating, evaporating.

DRIVER: If you hit my car again, yeah . . . ?

CYCLIST: Yes.

DRIVER: That's an offense!

CYCLIST: Yes.

DRIVER: You don't touch private property!

CYCLIST: I'm very sorry, my friend.

DRIVER: As you can tell, it's quite difficult driving in these roads. People do undertake and overtake, especially bicycles.

CYCLIST: Yes.

DRIVER: This lane goes to one lane from them traffic lights.

CYCLIST: Yes! That's quite correct.

DRIVER: I was just trying to move over; there was no need to bang on my car like that.

CYCLIST: My friend, I realized that you may not have observed me in your mirror . . .

DRIVER: Do you agree with banging on someone's car? I suppose if you're in a life-and-death situation . . .

CYCLIST: That is the only time.

DRIVER: Well, I didn't see any danger.

CYCLIST: That is the only time I will ever touch anyone's car. I don't have a horn. I can't alert you by any other means.

DRIVER: Okay . . . [pause] I understand.

CYCLIST: Okay?

DRIVER: Okay.

CYCLIST: All right. Thank you very much.

DRIVER: Thank you.

CYCLIST: Have a good day.

DRIVER: Yes, you too.

That could have ended very differently. Imagine what might have happened if the cyclist had opened with "Hey, dick-face!" instead of "my friend."[3]

Ordinarily, however, something very curious happens to us when we leave our homes and climb into a little metal box. We begin to take the most minor of rudenesses as the most startling of insults. We become furious when we feel disrespected, put down, moved in front of. Other drivers are idiots who aren't paying attention or "think they own the road." In fact, we're just as bad. How many times have we said, "Look at this jerk in my lane"? Well, it's not your lane, is it? Not unless you've been drunk-buying lanes on eBay again. This is *a* lane. Maybe *we're* the ones who think we own the road.

Scientists have already made the link between those who get angry in cars and parents who get angry at their children's sporting events.[4] They are the same sweaty, puce-faced breed, and strong research shows that, for many, our car becomes much more to us than a vehicle. It becomes, in fact, an extension of our home and our ego.

The problem is territory. We love it. Our ancestors fought for it, our contemporaries still do, and they'll still be at it next century. For a normal person, even tens of thousands of years ago, it was simply about survival, defense, control, and safety. The need for our own territory is in our biology.

But there are two types of space you and I both deal with every day: private and public. We would be furious if someone had a picnic on our front lawn, but we understand and accept that pedestrians might use the pavement beyond it.

Where the two spaces begin dangerously to cross over is when we start to think of our cars as private territory. Because we don't just drive our cars around our front lawns; we take them out into a shared world. Smart drivers know this.

But let me share a psychological secret with you: the drivers you have to watch out for are the ones with *bumper stickers*.

Putting a bumper sticker on your car is territorializing it. Same goes for window decals, fluffy steering-wheel covers, or stick-on insurance-company meerkats. And social psychologist William Szlemko and his colleagues at Colorado State University showed in a study that people who personalize their car with even just one bumper sticker are far more likely to engage in road rage than people who don't.[5]

You must avoid drivers of cars with bumper stickers.

> ## You must avoid drivers of cars with bumper stickers.

It doesn't matter what their bumper sticker says. If it's a political statement, it doesn't matter if you agree with it. It doesn't matter if it says they love cats and hey—you love cats too! Those people—the bumper stickered—not only become angrier when someone cuts in front of them or moves off too slowly, they are also far more likely to use their cars to express their rage.

Sounding their horn. Tailgating you. Screaming at you.

And depending where you are in the world, even loading their gun.

"The more markers a car has," Szlemko said, "the more aggressively the person tends to drive when provoked."

We share many of our instincts with animals. The need to protect our nest. If an outrage occurs while driving a car, we can respond as if that outrage had happened in our own home.

We are idiots who can't tell the difference between our bedrooms and a 2013 Volvo XC60.

.   .   .

Road rage was born in Los Angeles. Or at least the term was. A spate of shootings in the mid-1980s on freeways such as the 101 meant the locals had to find a term for it. "Road rage" was alliterative, and it was a lot better than "traffic tantrums," so road rage it was.

I decided to fly to LA to meet with Professor Jack Katz.

.   .   .

Now in his seventies, Katz has taught on and off at UCLA for nearly 40 years, and he's the guy who wrote the aforementioned "Pissed Off in L.A."—a chapter in his book *How Emotions Work*, which is a book title he now hates.

The chapter, on drivers and driving, gained enormous popularity because, for many, it sought to answer the question "Why do I become this way?"—a question I, too, would like answered.

One hundred and fifty drivers in LA were questioned about their driving experiences and found it only too easy to come up with examples of times they'd been pissed off. Times which Katz says, "the driver experiences a rude person as making a statement about his or her identity on the order of: You are a fool, a nobody, someone who deserves no respect, who need not even be treated as existing." Times in which people acted out of character. Flipped off a diner, say, or purposely made someone angry.

Like Catherine . . .

During stop-and-go freeway traffic, Catherine, a housing inspector, notices a car weaving around traffic behind her. "There was no way I was going to let him get in front of me," she recalled. "So I kept him boxed in by speeding up or slowing down when I had to. I felt an almost sick sense of pleasure in watching him get mad!"

Katz asked me to meet him at his favorite sushi restaurant in Oakland: a low and windowless brick building next to a Korean hairdresser's and opposite a garage that proudly advertises its excellent smog checks.

It's a breathtakingly hot day and I get there embarrassingly early, so decide to take a long drive around the city. I'm listening to National Public Radio when a fast-talking scientist called Sheyna Gifford is being interviewed. She has just spent 365 days confined in a small dome with just five other people as part of a NASA simulation. That's stress. I wonder to myself what must have happened if one of her colleagues had been rude.

On the roads, what I noticed immediately and jarringly, now that I was looking out for it, was how infrequently drivers in LA look at one another. On the freeway around Santa Monica it's a given, but as I drove up and down Laurel Canyon, or around the streets of Studio City, I was struck by how many times I actively helped another driver—and how nobody ever seemed to say thank you in return. Whether they had bumper stickers or not.

No nod of the head. No "Great Barrier Island" finger. No smile. No nothing.

As an outsider, you don't take offense, but at home in Britain this would drive me nuts. It is why I think something special has started to happen in the UK which is yet to happen in America. Something that as far as I can tell has evolved naturally between drivers over the years, and in my eyes has come to help temper road rage and aggression on our streets.

When I meet Jack, just a few feet from the well-armed sushi chefs in the chaos of a peak-hour restaurant stuffed with families, I ask him if he can guess what it is.

"No," he says.

So I tell him.

"We flash our hazard lights. Just for a couple of seconds. To say either 'thank you' or 'sorry.' And what's interesting is, now that we have this, we seem to give people a period of grace. After you've helped them or they've messed up, you wait four or five seconds to see if they acknowledge you."

This is something I don't remember anyone teaching me to do. I don't even think it's legal. It just began to happen, and there's a theory it began with truck drivers. They can't generally be seen by other drivers because their cabs are so high and their trucks so wide. So if they wanted to say "thank you" or "sorry," they couldn't just raise their hand and hope you were watching. They had to come up with another way.

"That's interesting," says Katz, nudging his squid, which is not a euphemism. "And most interestingly, it's a communally developed response without any leadership. But why should someone nodding at

you, or you catch their eye, and they let you in, why should that work
emotionally? What difference does it make?"

"I think because it's saying 'I see you.' It's saying 'you're someone.'
When they don't, it's like saying 'you don't matter.'"

And that does matter. How many times have you been in a car and
waited for the other person to say thank you? It's all you focus on. After
five seconds with no response, you immediately dismiss that person as
an absolute ninnyhammer. You hate them for their arrogance, for their
rudeness. And in that sixth second, when they *do* press their hazards
or raise their hand, literally everything is forgiven. You think they're
great again. You'd invite them around to your house, such is your relief.
You're just grateful they're grateful.

Katz loves this.

As he says in his book: "A driver who, in being cut off, had just
rushed to the brink of madness, often will be pulled back by nothing
more than a retrospective nod of acknowledgment."

That's us!

"This device of blinking," he says, leaning back in his chair as a
waitress brings him his third wrong order of the day. "It's like trying to
sustain a conversation with the world, that says 'you're okay.'"

Katz thinks we're constantly having a conversation with the world,
and that we need the world to reassure us. We get into our own flow—
and when that flow is interrupted, it's like realizing we don't have any
control. That jars us. Especially when we're in our own space.

"Somebody breaks that flow," says Katz, "then you have to make
sense of it."

So you're in control of your car. You're driving along, listening to
your music or thinking your thoughts, and someone jams on their
brakes in front of you or cuts you off. You're forced to respond, shaken
out of your comfort zone, and you take it personally.

"It's like you're in a computer-game mode," he says. "To get here today, I come through these really densely populated streets . . . and it's like a computer game. Kids running out into the street after balls. Someone's backing out of their driveway. There's somebody triple-parked waiting for somebody. A moving van over there, a garbage truck over here. And I'm scared to death, but I'm laughing at it. The way you avoid getting mad is you don't get into the environment. Stay out of that. Think of the passenger . . ."

One of the big revealing moments in Katz's work was realizing that the person sitting in the passenger seat doesn't get as offended or angered by "rudeness" as the driver.

"They look at you when you get mad, like 'Are you crazy?' But why shouldn't these things also be disrespecting the passenger? It affects their life and flow just as much. But it's the way the driver is embodying it."

Katz's idea of flow could apply to whomever your personal rudeness nemesis is. If you've ever been shocked at someone else's rude behavior, here's an explanation at least, which he offers me straight after I tell him about Madam Hotdog.

"Look, I'm a cook . . . ," he says. "I get really pissed off when people break my routine. I'm speculating, but I think she was trying to . . ."

He trails off, then points at the five Japanese men preparing sushi behind the bar, all concentration, white hats, and sharp knives.

"Look at these guys. They're under a lot of pressure. You have to get into a rhythm. You look at people working in the kitchen and it's athletic. To make things happen, you have to economize your emotions. Concentrate. Look at that short-order cook . . ."

I look at the short-order cook. He's fast and focused. Spinning a plate around, laying the food down, suddenly slowing to add some kind of garnish, then spinning it away again and straight on to the next one.

"These guys develop a way of working. They're all about not

touching something twice. You touch it once, you do it right. And you know you're doing a good job when you don't have to touch it again. So . . ."

He looks back at me.

". . . when that gets *interrupted*, even by someone who's not doing anything wrong—because I don't know that you were doing anything wrong just by showing up and ordering a hotdog—but it was interrupting her flow and you were there to get the focus of that kind of aggravation. [For the other person] it's a sort of fall from grace."

So maybe Madam Hotdog was just in her flow that day. She was thinking about the meals she had already had to cook, she was thinking about who needs cutlery or ketchup, she felt she had dealt with me already and my order was in hand . . . and then I turn up again unexpectedly.

Or maybe she was just grumpy, I suggest.

"Well, when children are misbehaving, parents often say, 'Oh, they're sleepy,' or 'Oh, they're hungry.' It's intuitive in a folk way that a child's body is no longer intertwined with the environment so they need to sleep or stop and eat. That makes emotional sense to people."

It's so rare that when a stranger behaves rudely toward us, we consider what was going on in their head or their body. It's much easier to reach for an instant response and place them in some easy category, like "rude." We react in the moment, I say—especially in cars.

Just then Jack Katz holds up his middle finger and flips me off.

"There's something called the Imitator Response. You throw the finger because that's what you imagine the person in the other car was doing to you. It is the most minimally creative response."

He's still flipping me off.

"You think, 'Oh, they're going to do that? Well, I'm going to do *this*!' And well . . . maybe they *didn't* do that."

"But we just take it that way?"

"And that explains why *you* flip them off," he says, and he stops flipping me off. "Again, it's sustaining the conversation. They threw me out of the conversation when they cut me off, I'm going to thrust myself back in. Like *this!*"

He flips me off again.

To anyone a few feet away from this table, it really does look like Jack Katz and I do not get on so well.

.   .   .

As I drive away from the restaurant, it's approaching mid-afternoon.

According to the Wallace Report, the "rudest" time of day is between 3 and 4 p.m. A time when traditionally we feel lower on energy in the workplace, we're at the school gates—or when traffic is beginning to increase on the roads.

As I head back to my hotel, I think about how a car is just a giant mute button.

We feel unseen and unheard in them, and when we feel disrespected by a thoughtless maneuver or a rude hand gesture, it's natural to want to feel heard. So we scream and shout at other drivers. We mouth obscenities at them. We make big crazy faces at them so they know we think they're mad. We shrug exaggeratedly and shake our heads to let them know they are terrible drivers and probably awful people. We flip them off.

But we don't talk to them. We don't call them "my friend." We project onto them the *idea* that they are rude, and we "even things out" by being rude back.

Like we've done since the dawn of time, we protect our territory.

Madam Hotdog had taken great care to personalize her diner. I think that for her, this diner wasn't just a business. It was an extension of her actual personality. A hobby and a job. It's like the restaurant was her car, and every little knickknack was a bumper sticker.

And here I was, striding into her territory, forcing her to defend it.

I was like a car, cutting her off, disturbing her flow. And she responded by verbally flipping me off. Because to her, I deserved it. I'm starting to understand her.

Turns out we can all be Auntie Rosie, whether in a 2CV, a Volkswagen Golf, or a small and drizzly diner far from home.

CASE STUDY:
GIVE ME SPACE

Sheyna Gifford, MD, MSc, MA, is a doctor, psychologist, journalist, and adviser to NASA. She's got degrees in neuroscience, journalism, biotechnology, and medicine. She's Scientist in Residence at St. Louis Science Center, she's a neonatal intensive care volunteer, and today she's in her bathrobe.

When I speak with her, she has only been home one day.

For an entire year before that, she was in a small dome, isolated 8,200 feet up a Hawaiian mountainside on a rocky lava plain.

She was there because she was chief medical officer on Project HI-SEAS, working with five other scientists from the U.S.A. and Europe to simulate what a NASA crew might go through on a mission to Mars.

They spent their days growing crops, designing space suits, repairing the hydrogen system, navigating their alien landscape, and having to get on in an unnatural, claustrophobic, diverse group dynamic.

Among the professionalism and the sense of duty, there must also have been bickering. Arguments. Rudeness. And cultural differences.

Today is Sheyna's birthday. She's just answered the door to a huge bunch of flowers wearing just that bathrobe, which, as far as she's concerned, is precisely how she wants to spend it.

DANNY: I'm interested in how we behave in confined spaces. There must be coping strategies for dealing with being with the same people in a small space for so long ...

SHEYNA: There are better and worse coping strategies. The worse coping strategy is just to say, "Whatever this person says or does, I don't care. I'm just gonna ignore it." Look at many marriages—they have that going on. They reach this point of emotional neutrality: "You know what, whatever this person says or does, I have decided I am not going to react." People employ this all the time. And if you look at people's faces, you wonder, "How have they gone behind that mask?" Bus drivers, cops, subway security guards, a lot of servers ...

DANNY: What's the better coping strategy?

SHEYNA: The more *functional* coping strategy is to say, "My goal is to make this work. So I'm going to listen to what you have to say, and if it's not working for me, I'm going to say something about it. I'm going to try to work with you to make it work." This is extraordinarily difficult and incredibly worthwhile.

DANNY: Was there rudeness on your mission?

SHEYNA: One of the things that the crew did not learn to agree upon was styles of leadership. What the Americans wanted was a leadership by permission; a very democratic style of leadership. The Europeans are more accustomed to a leader who actually makes decisions. He doesn't ask anybody else's permission. The leader makes decisions and then carries out the decision. So we were having a discussion [about this] and one person says to another, "Well, if you don't like it you can just leave. You can walk out of the dome. You're a volunteer and you can just go."

DANNY: Right.

SHEYNA: I think they were pointing out a fact. But it's *how* you point it out. This person is very cut-and-dry, and has a sense of humor but doesn't always exercise it.* The person who received that was like, "How *dare* you? That is a completely inappropriate thing to say!"

DANNY: And how did you deal with that?

SHEYNA: I said, "Hold the phone. Nobody is leaving. This person is correct. You could go, but you're not being asked to go. What we want is to try to come to an agreement." The rudeness was not intentionally perpetrated, but it was perceived as rudeness.

DANNY: So in confined high-pressure spaces—space missions, prisons, whatever—it's about defusing rudeness?

SHEYNA: What I did a lot of on the mission was beg for understanding and attempt to create context. Both someone's personality and someone's culture is context. Do you understand [the other person's] life story? Do you understand the day they're having? Do you understand the

---

* I refuse to speculate. I will simply say that the mission featured crew members from both France *and* Germany.

situation they're currently in? How deeply are you standing in that person's shoes? So now here's a great question: how often did I perceive straight-up rudeness? Very rarely.

DANNY: Really?

SHEYNA: I'm hard-pressed to say that I ever really perceived it once I understood what was going on. But I'm a deep believer in asking questions.

DANNY: I wonder if that's something I should have just said to the hotdog lady. Just said, "You're having a bad day. Why don't you tell me what's going on?"

SHEYNA: Yeah! Of course she could have turned to you and said, "Sir, fuck you. Leave."

DANNY: She pretty much did.

SHEYNA: Here's where rudeness came up most: when members of my crew were thinking the media were being rude. When somebody is sending you questions like "So sex in space, what's that like?" I only got this question once. From Irish radio. They were super nice to talk to, but they said, "What about sex?" And I said, "Well, what about it?" But my poor French crewmate got this question non-stop because the Continental Europeans talk about this stuff much more openly. He would say, "Well, as it is on Earth it is in space." But then sometimes they would press him for details and whatnot. Now, do you have to go around asking strangers about their sex lives?

DANNY: No.

SHEYNA: It's not polite [or professional]. Maybe if I'd only chosen to make one point talking to you, this would be it: no matter how much another crew person you're locked in the dome with, or on Earth with, or at the office with, or in the taxi with [is rude], I have yet to see a level of professionalism that couldn't overcome it.

DANNY: In what way?

SHEYNA: You seize upon your professionalism and you hold it like a beacon, like a torch in the darkness. And you follow it. "I am a consummate professional and really that means at the end of the day what you do doesn't matter. Only what I do matters because it's my professionalism on the line." So *be* a consummate professional. The most professional doctors I've ever seen, the firemen, police officers, teachers—you see them wielding that sword of professionalism. It's like watching a god. You understand that no matter what happens they are going to remain in a professional capacity. That used to be the way politicians worked. It used to be the way journalists were. It was the way a lot of people were. But like many arts, the art of being the consummate professional is not what it used to be.

DANNY: And professionalism has its own set of rules that cross boundaries, cultures . . .

SHEYNA: Maybe rudeness at its heart, if you're looking for the gestalt of rudeness, means you do have to look at culture. *Culture* is going to dictate what's rude and what's polite. [Sometimes] there's no rudeness. There's just the cultural gap, and I think you have a great story there to be told.

CHAPTER 12

Lost in Translation

Can we not help but clash?

In 2016, Queen Elizabeth II of the United Kingdom of Great Britain and Northern Ireland was standing on a wet patch of grass in a bright pink coat holding a giant umbrella.

At 90 years old, this woman remained the picture of protocol, of international grace and diplomacy—the very soul of decorum—with never a bad word to say about anybody, unless that word was extremely carefully chosen and not publicly spoken.

At a damp Royal Garden Party, she was introduced to Lucy D'Orsi, the police commander who had recently been in charge of a state visit from China's President Xi Jinping.

"Oh, bad luck," joked the Queen.

The cameras at these garden parties never normally capture much audio. The excuse this time was that the Queen's enormous umbrella was acting like a miniature amplifier. She was an oblivious one-woman royal broadcasting unit. But the Queen's joke laid the path for D'Orsi to take the conversation further. She told the Queen that the Chinese visit had been a very testing time for her. The Queen, in reply, said she thought the Chinese had been "very rude to the ambassador."

The police commander agreed. "It was very rude and undiplomatic, I thought."

A gentle garden party chitchat caught on tape.

The controversy was enormous.

Someone had called someone else . . . rude.

The power of the word and the weight it held was extraordinary. It was like international schoolyard gossip. The Queen thought the Chinese were *rude*! Spread it!

The reports went global. There was talk that the "golden era" of Anglo–Chinese relations was at an abrupt end. The Chinese state media panicked, censoring BBC reports in the country. Offended and hurt, the Chinese went on the attack, sarcastically saying there was *no way* the British could have leaked the video of the Queen on purpose, because that would be "truly boorish and rude."

Now *the British* were rude!

The Communist Party state media called the UK media "disrespectful gossipers," who "seemingly retain vestiges of the inelegance of barbarians."

The first bit is obviously startlingly accurate, but *barbarians*? Because they reported that the Queen said she thought someone was rude at a garden party?

Mind you, she did tell the police. Maybe Jinping thought she was an informer.

State visits like that are supposed to show us how alike we all are. How we have mutual interests, and respect each other's differences. Often, they show us how alike we aren't.

The Chinese were offended, doubtless because they saw nothing wrong or strange in the way they acted. It was the Queen who was rude for thinking it strange. It was the media's fault for telling the world. It's embarrassing to be treated rudely, but it's also embarrassing to be called rude in front of everybody else.

(It didn't help that the royals had history when it came to the Chinese. In 1997, when the UK handed back control of Hong Kong to the Chinese, Prince Charles was caught describing the Communist Party's lineup of very elderly leaders as "a group of appalling old wax-works." That's probably worse. And let's just skip over Prince Philip for now.)

· · ·

The scope for being misunderstood in a country not your own is obviously huge.

When my dad was teaching at an American university in the 1970s, there was a young student who was very worried about his upcoming exams. My dad took the man to one side, stared deep into his eyes, and gently said, "The most important thing is . . . you've got to keep your pecker up."

The young man nodded soulfully, then wondered why my dad was talking about his private parts in this way.

Language aside, the specificity of what is and is not deemed rude—considering we were once all just slathering apes, beating our chests and picking flies off one another—is bewildering.

In Brazil, never make the "okay" hand gesture, but feel free to tell people how you're feeling by giving them a lovely "thumbs-up."

Do not, however, *ever* give a lovely "thumbs-up" in the Middle East or Western Africa, because that's essentially flipping everybody off, and they'll break your nose.

In Britain, when someone's told you they're hoping for a promotion, or they've put an offer in on an apartment, you might be tempted to cross your fingers for them to show you're on their side. Do this in Vietnam, and they'll ask you why you've gone mad and made the gesture for a lady's private dealings.

Tip in America whether or not the person has actually done anything you consider of worth. Do not tip in South Korea, where they feel they're already paid and take pride in their work. Don't belch at your girlfriend's mum's house after you've polished off her lasagna. Belch like crazy if you've finished one in Taiwan.

Clear your plate if you're in France, because that means "I enjoyed that lots!" Don't do it in the Philippines, because what you are essentially saying is "I do not understand why you have failed to provide me with adequate sustenance and you are a terrible host."

It goes on and on.

Show up for a dinner party on time in North America, for example, but do not show up on time in South America. Be a few minutes late and bring some wine if you're in Britain. But if you're in Germany, be *absolutely punctual* but do not bring wine, otherwise they'll think you think your time is more important than theirs and you are saying: "I do not trust you to have bought wine of any particular quality for this evening's soirée."

Don't make too much eye contact in Mexico or they'll think you're belligerent. Don't eat a sandwich in Brazil unless you're holding it with a napkin. Don't wander about whistling in Haiti. Never turn down a vodka in Moscow. Put one hand in your pocket only if you want Turks to think you're arrogant. Use your left hand in India when greeting someone, eating, or giving a gift only if you definitely hate that person, because people tend to use that left hand for very unusual hygiene reasons.

Don't ask for ketchup in Spain. Don't sneeze in Saudi Arabia. Don't refuse food in Lebanon, but refuse all gifts in China a minimum of three times before relenting. Don't laugh with your mouth open in Japan. Or wear flipflops in public. Though that last one is one I think we can all get behind.

And sure, ask "What do *you* do?" at a party in Canada, but don't try that line in the Netherlands, where they may assume that because of their social-welfare systems you are attempting the classist move of arrogantly pigeonholing them to establish a party-based hierarchy.

Which you may well have been, knowing you.

But isn't it fun?

By which I mean—isn't it the opposite of fun?

And by the way, these and a million other things are all known by heart by the likes of the Queen. That there is a not an international diplomatic scandal every single week of the year—when the Queen takes someone else's beer at a barbecue in Norway, for example, or she eats an apple on a bus in Rwanda—is absolutely extraordinary.

Imagine if Britain had a Queen who did *not* respect diplomacy or the rules of not being rude. Imagine it had a Queen who said, "Your country's awful—I'm sorry, I'm *only being honest, #justsaying.*"

•   •   •

This was the moment that made me realize that it's not just what we think is rude that differentiates our cultures; it's also how we respond to rudeness.

Let's just say that in some cultures, people respond to rudeness better than in others.

> **Let's just say that in some cultures,
> people respond to rudeness better than in others.**

Stanford University's Robert M. Sapolsky is the author of *Why Zebras Don't Get Ulcers* among many more, and is a Californian academic who looks more like a Californian academic than any other

Californian academic in history. His next book, which he is in the throes of editing when I catch him, delves into cultures—and specifically cultures of honor.

"These are cultures with a huge emphasis on honorifics and hospitality, on one hand," he tells me, "and on the other, violent retribution . . ."

In other words, these are cultures to which you do not want to be rude.

This violent retribution tends to come about after an insult of some kind. An insult to you, to your sister, to the shoes you've decided to wear today, or more normally the honor of your family. Ordinarily, says Sapolsky, this kind of response is most common in "pastoralists living in tough environments"—sheep farmers, cattle wranglers, Saharan camel-herders.

But it is the American South that has arguably proved most intriguing.

In the original American colonies, Sapolsky tells me, the South was settled by herders from northern England and Scotland. Now, I'm saying nothing here, but a lot of my family live on the borders, and these are not people you want to get on the wrong side of.* And in the British borderlands of the early 1700s, life was violent. Blood feuds, revenge, retribution and finding and grabbing justice wherever you could were rife in the lives of those who fled one world for the uncertainty of another.

The northern colonies of the United States, on the other hand,

---

* Genuinely one of the most terrifying moments of my life was walking into the Crown & Mitre Hotel in Carlisle late on a Friday night and coming face-to-face with a group of angry, drunk men in fancy dress. Perhaps instinctively already aware of this culture of honor, I did not try and make light of the fact that they were all dressed as furious Smurfs.

found themselves peopled by the likes of literate Quakers, artisans, and puritans.

Even today, the South has much higher rates of violence than the rest of the United States. In 2016, Louisiana had the country's highest murder rate, of 11 people for every 100,000 (compared to 2.1 for *all* of Europe).[1] There were eight documented mass shootings that year, making them "relatively common," according to one news source.

But what stands out is that Southern violence tends to be of a different type than anywhere else in the country. Maybe it's the heat, maybe it's the economics, maybe it's the legacy of slavery and the Civil War. But in the rest of the States, a homicide is more likely to be undertaken by a stranger but begin with another crime—a burglary, a mugging, a carjacking, say. In the South, things get much more personal.

"The higher rate," says Sapolsky, "is entirely due to violence by white males in rural settings over issues of honor and insults— typically by people who know each other."

Insults.

"The whole thing is fascinating," he says. "I remember a lecture once by a scholar on the subject, who came from the South and described how bizarre it was for him to leave the South for the first time to go to grad school at Harvard . . . [He said:] 'It was so weird being in this alien culture. Extended families would get together for summer barbecues and, amazingly, *no one* would shoot someone else!'"

It sounds funny. Barroom brawls happening all over the country because someone called your mum a bit tubby. But rudeness strikes at the heart of those people brought up in a culture of honor in a

> **Rudeness strikes at the heart of those people brought up in a culture of honor.**

terrifying way. From street gangs all the way to the mafia, respect is currency, and the now clichéd mantra "Are you disrespecting me?" is too often quickly followed by the flick of a knife or the crack of a gun.

In 1996, a team of academics decided to investigate the differences between Americans from the north and south of the country properly.[2] This is where it gets really interesting.

A group of young men were gathered together in a now-famous experiment* by Richard Nisbett of the University of Michigan and Dov Cohen of the University of Illinois, Urbana-Champaign, and told they were to fill out a questionnaire and then drop it off in another room.

Ignore the questionnaire. The questionnaire was meaningless. It was what happened while they were dropping off that questionnaire that mattered.

As each man walked down a narrow hallway, papers in hand, one after the other, half the men simply dropped the questionnaire off and got on with their lives.

But the other half—the half Cohen, Nisbett, and their colleagues were really paying attention to—had their pathway blocked by a complete stranger. This stranger—quite a big man, and one you wouldn't want to mess with—was in on the experiment, and his job was momentarily to block their path. As each man struggled to get past him, the big guy would look and them and mutter . . .

"Asshole."

(I contacted Nisbett—still Professor of Psychology at the University of Michigan—to ask him why he'd chosen the word "asshole" specifically. Had there been a short list? What is it about the word "asshole" that cuts so deep? Is it the brevity, the simplicity, the dismissiveness? He replied and said "asshole" is simply "the canonical insult word in America." So now at least it's official.)

---

* Repopularized by the likes of Malcolm Gladwell in his excellent book *Outliers*.

According to their results, here's what happens when you call someone from Pennsylvania, Michigan, Maine ("2016's most peaceful state"), or anywhere in the north of America an "asshole."

Nothing much.

But if you call someone from Alabama, Louisiana, Georgia, or somewhere else in the honor-heavy South the same thing?

Stand back.

Not only were these men visibly angrier, but they were angry right down to the core of their neurochemistry.

Cohen and Nisbett tested each man's blood pressure, their testosterone levels, their cortisol, and even whether they were now more psychologically inclined toward aggression and violence after what was—in most people's eyes at least—a pretty mild provocation.

They were. Very much so.

For Nisbett, it was simple: "Males in a culture of honor feel obligated to respond physically to an insult from another male."

Obligated.

Now you can see why there is more violence in the Southern states. It is fortunate for those who act this way that it's been shown that "Southern juries are far more forgiving of such violence than elsewhere in the country," adds Sapolsky.

*   *   *

It is extraordinary that neighbors can be so similar and yet so different.

Take the French. Please.

Because what do you think of when you think of the French?

I'm not going to say it because I don't want to launch a full-scale international incident, but I'll say what you're thinking.

You're thinking they're rude. I can't believe you. You're so prejudiced.

But in many ways I see what you mean. Rudeness is something that for generations the French seemed almost to celebrate. Hundreds of years of finely-tuned incivility. Snootiness. Perceived arrogance. A weariness toward the neighbor Napoleon bitchily called "a nation of shopkeepers."

But being rude is exhausting and, just recently, it's gotten them down.

The French, like the Chinese, don't want the world to see them as rude. Deep down, they don't get it. It's like hearing someone's girlfriend has turned against you when you thought you got on fine when you met. You don't know that person very well, you feel they don't know you, and you're both offended and confused. You're not going to change just for them, yet you can't help but wonder if you should.

I remember once being driven in a fancy taxi from Disneyland Paris to the Gare du Nord with my then toddler son, who immediately became carsick. With seconds to go, I cupped my hands and allowed him to vomit into them. He did so with a force never before seen in Western society. Within microseconds my cup ranneth over. I simply poured what I was holding into my lap, glanced at the man now staring at me in his rearview mirror, then recupped for round two. There are those of you who may see this as a simple gesture of love from father to son. It was, in fact, what a British person does when they don't want to really piss off a Frenchman.

The French had to come to terms not with the way they felt they were, but with the way they were being seen. Because the reports were damning. One newspaper poll showed that Britons found the French the least welcoming nation of all. That's the same as saying most Britons find Basra more welcoming than Bordeaux. TripAdvisor users voted Paris the rudest city in Europe. More reports gleefully poured in: France had the least friendly locals, the most unpleasant waiters, the angriest taxi drivers.

There is even a recognized psychological condition called Paris Syndrome.

It was Professor Hiroaki Ota, a Japanese psychiatrist living in France, who first identified it, and since then it's found its place in science, officially documented by medical journals.

Affecting almost exclusively Japanese tourists, Paris Syndrome can cause an acute delusional state, anxiety, dizziness, hallucinations, and excessive sweating. Up to 12 Japanese tourists a year fall foul of "a transient psychological disorder exhibited by some individuals when visiting a place drastically foreign from their own."[3] They are generally women in their thirties on their first trip abroad—one which, crucially, does not match up to the magic promised in the guidebooks. They are put straight on planes and flown home accompanied by qualified nurses.

The Japanese love France. They send a million tourists a year. What they expect is a moonlit Seine, incredible food, cobbled streets populated by elegant women in Louboutin heels, artists sketching the Eiffel Tower under an ink-blue sky, and charming, attentive, model-quality waiters pouring fine champagnes and occasionally playing a romantic tune on a violin.

What a bunch of them get instead is some guy shrugging angrily and spitting in their laps when they ask for the bill for their overpriced ham and cheese toastie.

While a German or a Spaniard might laugh it off, the stress of someone shouting at you because you're still working out how the money works, or you don't speak fluent French, is too much for a nation of people generally famed for their politeness. The Japanese embassy has become used to this. They have a 24-hour hotline for those suffering from this precise kind of culture shock. And almost nothing shocks more than unexpected rudeness.

Now, if you've got a *whole syndrome* named after your nation's rudeness, chances are there's a problem.

Now, if you've got a *whole syndrome* named after your nation's rudeness, chances are there's a problem.

So much so that in 2015 the French government decided to make tackling rudeness a priority. The French foreign minister diplomatically suggested that the welcome tourists receive in France is "not always extraordinary," and urged his people to be nicer.[4]

The Parisian Chamber of Commerce developed a booklet aimed at helping French people cope with foreigners.

It told them that British people like to be called by their first names and eat dinner at an absurdly early time, but that this should not be mentioned.

Americans expect Wi-Fi in every nook and cranny of every nook and cranny and will immediately call you by *your* first name. Don't get angry with these clowns!

The Chinese are obsessed with shopping and will expect you to constantly smile at them.

The Germans like handshakes.

The Italians are impatient and move about in large groups.

It all sounds like a mildly racist nature documentary, but it was a genuine attempt to help build bridges. *Tell Chinese people where the shops are! Shake a German's hand!*

They went further.

Border control police were ordered to say both "hello" and "thank you" to people. That was an actual order. It's unclear what they were saying before.

Employees at four-star hotels were encouraged to know two languages. Employees at five-star hotels were encouraged to know three. Public transportation offices held "rudeness forums," where they discussed how they interact with passengers, but were probably just rude about them. Stickers were printed, saying "thank you, see you soon!" and put up at airports and train stations and other exit points. Floor-to-ceiling posters followed, saying things like "One *bonjour* doesn't cost a thing!"

A journalist from the New York *Daily News* was surprised to hear the following announcement on a train in the middle of it all: "Hello, welcome, greet your neighbor, and may you adopt a zen attitude!"

All this sparked a national conversation about rudeness. The French themselves opened up about how it made them feel: 60 percent of people asked in an Ipsos poll cited rudeness as the number one source of stress in their lives. That was higher than unemployment or debt.

France had had a rude awakening.

* * *

They don't always get it right, however.

The founder of one French fashion brand, announcing the opening of a new boutique hotel in Paris, made the mistake of going on record with: "We are going to select guests. It won't be open to Chinese tourists, for example."

Since then, he's clarified: he says he meant large groups of tourists in general. But it's fair to say the Chinese felt victimized once again, particularly when their tourists spent $105 billion in other countries in 2015 alone.

So imagine how they felt when a Swiss railway company proudly announced a brand-new service: carriages exclusively for Chinese people.

Mount Rigi in Switzerland is beautiful, and known as the Queen of the Mountains. A small cogwheel Rigi-Bahnen train pulls itself up to the summit for picture postcard views and sharp, clean air. You'd be forgiven for thinking that an Asian-only carriage had been put in place to reflect the growing presence of the Chinese tourist money, and that perhaps there would be announcements made in Chinese or signs written in Mandarin, and it was all an effort to make sure everybody was happy.

According to the newspaper *Blick*, it was actually because some Swiss people had accused the Chinese of being too rude.

They were crowding the corridors to snap photos, they said. Special signs had to be put up telling them not to squat on the toilets. And some were spitting on the carriage floors.

There was, quite justifiably, uproar. The company defended itself, insisting that complaints made about the tourists were in one isolated incident. But the damage had been done. Whether it was actually a problem or not, the Chinese had been tarred with the rude brush, in the way broad strokes are often used to make sense of a mass.

Mind you, I'm not saying the Chinese don't like to spit. I once recorded a radio documentary in Shanghai, and much of the work I did while editing it just involved taking out the sound of old men hocking up. It took ages. If I edited it all together and played it to you, you'd never talk to me again.

But before I go any further into this, it's important to say that culture clashes are a two-way street. What's essential, basic courtesy in one country is irrelevant in another.

When my Australian wife became a British citizen, we had to go to the local town hall to complete her citizenship ceremony. There was to be a speech telling the assembled former foreigners how to be British delivered by an elderly man dressed up like an army major. He

> What's essential, basic courtesy in one country is irrelevant in another.

stood up, looked everybody up and down, and began a ten-minute speech which can be boiled down to the following four words: "Look, just queue properly."

To the British, not to line up is appalling. It makes no sense. It is a proven, polite system that works. Just like saying "thank you, driver" when you get off a bus or using a tissue when you sneeze.

To many Chinese people of a certain generation, the fact that Westerners sneeze into that tissue, wipe their noses, crumple that tissue up in the palms of their hands, and then stuff it back into their pockets, next to their phones and wallets and keys, ready for a *second use* later on, is disgusting. Far better to spit. In a polluted city, spitting is seen as cleaning the body. It's *healthy*. Better out than in. Certainly better out than in your pocket.

In the West, to spit is to engage in a peculiar type of rudeness. It happens on every high street in Britain every day of the year and is largely seen as abhorrent, thanks to years of public health campaigns letting people know it's a wonderful way to spread disease. But it is also seen as simply disrespectful of public sensibilities and public spaces. We all have to use these pavements, these parks, these streets. Let's leave them saliva free.

Sun Yingchun, a professor at the Communication University of China writing in *Huanqiu* magazine, cited spitting, littering, and a disrespect of lining up as three of the major things Chinese people can do to earn them rude looks and make them feel unwelcome abroad.

. . .

The Chinese are by now acutely aware of this.

Before the Beijing Olympics in 2008, the government panicked about all the foreigners who would be pouring into China. The pressure to be their best was intense.

"Public awareness of manners needs to be improved!" said Wang

Tao, the man charged with the simple task of completely changing the way everybody had always done everything.

They announced "Queuing Day," in which people were encouraged to line up properly. It was to take place on the 11th day of every month, because an "11" looks a bit like two people in a line, even though now that I've added quotation marks it just looks like two people vibrating. Lining up was a major concern to the Chinese. Volunteers in special uniforms handed long-stemmed flowers to people they spotted lining up particularly well.

Foul language and littering were declared "stubborn diseases that stain the image of the capital city," and then Wang Tao had to tackle the spitting.

A hundred thousand paper bags were handed out to confused citizens for them to spit into.

"I spent six months trying to work out how to stop the spitting," Tao told journalists. "I first wanted to wipe their spit up myself, but just how much could I wipe? So I decided the best way was to ask the spitting person to stop."

In the end, Tao spent years doing this, setting up an anti-spitting club, gaining 4,000 members, and taking schoolchildren out onto the street to discourage grown-ups from their habit. But all this was hard work.

"Sometimes I feel lonely and upset when I get an unpleasant look as I persuade a person to wipe their phlegm off the street," he told *China Daily* at one point.

Incidentally, I convinced a Chinese journalist to give me Tao's phone number, and I gave him a ring. But Tao doesn't speak very good English, so if it was him, we just sort of made noises at each other for a few moments, and then I hung up.

He wasn't, though, the first to try to convince his countryfolk that there was another way. This goes back a century.

In 1924, in his final speech on nationalism, the first president of the Chinese Republic, Sun Yat-sen, made an impassioned plea for everyone to JUST BLOODY STOP IT.

He complained about long nails.

Belching in public.

Not brushing your teeth.

He talked about spitting and farting.

Things have to reach a certain point for world leaders to start making speeches about spitting and farting.*

Sun Yat-sen's aim was to re-energize the spirit of the nation. To explain why these things may seem completely normal in one place, but were still perceived as rude outside China.

In 1924, he talked about hotels just like the one in Paris nearly a hundred years later:

> Why did the foreign hotels not allow Chinese in? It is said that once there was a banquet in a very big hotel in a foreign country, where all people were quite elegant and enjoyed themselves, men and women alike. Suddenly a Chinese farted noisily, and all the foreigners fled and the owner drove out the Chinese. Ever since, the foreign hotel did not allow the Chinese to have meals at their establishment.[5]

Now, obviously, that's nonsense. No one has ever caused the decimation of an entire culture's right to decent hotel room service with a bottom burp, no matter the volume, even if it *was* in 1924 when it was probably deemed a scandal if you saw a goose not wearing a hat. But this was a problem from the top of society to the bottom, so to speak.

---

* By the way, I find it hard writing that F-word—I find it rude. I think you'll find it in only one other of my books, and that one's aimed at eight-year-olds.

"Even the Chinese scholars and literary men had such indiscreet behavior," he continued. "Some of them said that if they wanted to fart, they would fart. If they farted, they would fart noisily."

Sun Yat-sen said that they were wrong. That only by changing their behavior could they change Western perceptions of the Chinese. Only by winning respect, by not farting or spitting whenever they felt like it, would China avoid invasion. Changing behavior would, in the eyes of this revolutionary leader, help to rebuild a nation. Make it stronger.

The behavior as it stood, said Sun Yat-sen in words that would come to echo those later aimed at the press of Great Britain, was "barbarian."

I think his advice, from 1924 and meant only for the Chinese, applies to us all, and forever.

That, and line up properly.

CASE STUDY:
BEIJING'S SPITTING IMAGE

Wang Tao is the brave man who in early 2005 was charged with an intimidating and almost impossible mission: to stop all Chinese people spitting in time for the 2008 Olympics.

Today he's the head of the Green Woodpecker organization—a group of people dedicated to bettering people's manners, helping the environment, and not spitting.

After admiring his work but failing to talk to him once, I was thrilled when the Shanghai Daily *columnist and writer Ni Tao offered to step in as translator, meaning I could finally bond with another rudeness obsessive.*

DANNY: Now, you were charged with quite a task. How long did it take you to come up with your plans?

MR. TAO: Well, I did spend more than a year preparing for the campaign and making plans to be implemented. On the very day we embarked on this odyssey, May 4, 2006, I arrived at Tiananmen Square and tried to intervene when I saw people spitting. I put my plans to work, confronting the offenders and exhorting them to clear away gobs of spit they expectorated with the paper tissues I handed them. For those who refused to comply at first, I would squat down and remove the gobs myself. This worked, as many offenders voluntarily followed suit and did the same, out of a reawakened sense of dignity. Later on, I began to recruit volunteers and we worked as a group, which officially became the team of Green Woodpecker conservationists as we know it.

DANNY: Handing out spit bags was a good idea. Why do you feel they didn't catch on?

MR. TAO: Initially the spitting bag was thought to be an ingenious invention, but later we found that its upper part was too small, causing difficulty for people to spit into the bag. Then we tried distributing paper tissues, hoping that people would spit directly into paper tissues, wrap them up, and dump the waste where a garbage can can be found, or put it into their pockets or handbags where no garbage can is within sight.

DANNY: When you confronted people who were spitting, you must have had some bad reactions . . .

MR. TAO: Once when I confronted a man who spat, he was so angry he tried to hit me on the head with a water bottle in his hand. I narrowly escaped the attack. Another time, at a bus stop I saw a man spitting. He got on when the bus came. I followed him into the bus, whereupon I tried to talk sense into him, but the man grabbed me by the collar, ready to beat me. We were finally separated by other passengers.

DANNY: The rude behaviors you've tried to combat include spitting, of course, but also littering and not lining up properly. Which did you feel would be hardest to change?

MR. TAO: Of all the "rude behavior," spitting is the hardest to change, because some people are wired to think that they have the freedom to spit as they please, and seldom do they bother to find paper napkins to spit into. The social atmosphere is to blame. Since no one said "no" or challenged them when they saw others behaving rudely, a lot of the offenders felt no shame or guilt at all. This is why we at Green Woodpecker need to intervene, to help them shape up in terms of public manners. This is indeed quite challenging work, as it turned out, because it might offend some people and risk confrontation with them.

DANNY: People do spit more in China. What could others do to help you change this?

MR. TAO: Chinese people see their country as a civilized nation, and as such they should conduct themselves accordingly. Most people with cultivated public manners had better intervene at the first sight of rude behavior. Hopefully, more and more people will join our movement against public rudeness happening in our midst.

DANNY: Society just doesn't take rudeness seriously enough. Why don't we see it as dangerous?

MR. TAO: Ill-bred and uncouth people don't give much thought to their behavior; so long as it satisfies them, they hardly show any regard for other people. Sometimes the negative implication of their behavior is also lost on them when they go abroad, where some Chinese tourists tend to "be themselves" just like at home. At the very heart of this is selfish ego, a lack of overall environmental awareness, and a poor sense of public civility. Green Woodpecker and our government are sparing no efforts to promote environmental education, so as to help steadily raise citizens' awareness of correct manners. In Beijing we have a Public Civilization Guidance Office set up specifically for this purpose, namely: to encourage good behavior such as lining up for public transportation. All these years our campaign has received support from the government and society, and it has achieved fairly good results. Right now people properly waiting in lines have become a pleasant sight in Beijing, and spitting is considerably on the wane. Our society is becoming more civilized by the day.

CHAPTER 13

Juvenile Behaviors

Or: why I may have misjudged Madam Hotdog's sidekick

Once, my friend Marc was walking through a park and passed a group of teenage boys. Marc had just grown a beard, and was already a little self-conscious about it, which is fair enough, because it was a beard.

One of the lads nudged another and they pointed at Marc, who often wears a duffel coat and stares at the ground.

"All right, Granddad?" said the first boy, and the others all laughed.

Marc felt entirely disrespected.

We are raised on a maxim: *Respect thine elders!*

The social contract was broken, and Marc, in a flushed fit of rage fueled by the injustice of being called "granddad" while *still in his thirties*, was going to redress the balance.

"Shouldn't you be in bed by now?" is what he decided to say, at once establishing his superiority and also patronizing them. It would be a genius and withering move which would put the world back in order, and make him feel better about his new beard too.

Sadly, because of the unexpected rudeness, Marc got his words muddled up, stopped in his tracks, stared at the boys, and instead yelled, "It's *BEDTIIIIME!*"

They looked horrified and suddenly much younger than they had.

Marc was now just a bearded man on his own in a park in an oversized duffel coat staring at teenage boys and shouting, "It's BEDTIME!"

As they backed slowly away, Marc decided two things:

1: the youth of today need to respect their elders.

And 2: he should really try and find a pharmacy on the way home and stop for razors, because this beard was nothing but trouble.

• • •

Let's face facts: the sullen, moody, mouth-breathing youths of today *are* ruder than ever.

I'll prove it.

"When I was young," wrote a poet recently, "we were taught to be discreet and respectful of elders, but the present youth are exceedingly disrespectful and impatient of restraint."

Well, I say he wrote it recently. The poet was Hesiod and he's supposed to have written that in the 8th century B.C. I'm not sure if it was meant to be a poem or not, but it can't have been one of his most popular. I certainly wouldn't open a collected works with it.

Let's look a little more recently!

"What is happening to our young people? They disrespect their elders, they disobey their parents."

That was Plato. Who, by the way, had an enormous beard, so I think we can probably guess what happened there.

"We live in a decaying age. Young people no longer respect their parents."

That's on a 6,000-year-old Egyptian tomb.

Can you guess what I'm trying to say here?

. . .

If, as Wang Tao tried, we want to change behavior in society, it makes sense to try it when people are still young enough to change. A 90-year-old man who's been spitting all his life feels he has a right to coat the streets with spit. A five-year-old has a chance to learn not to.

As I thought more about behavior and rudeness, I remembered there was a bit-part player during the Incident. I'd also been reminded of her after talking with Jack Katz about the way we fear young drivers.

There was a teenage waitress that day, a little surly, not making eye contact with us, clattering plates down and wandering off again.

Perhaps she wasn't making eye contact because she found my exchanges with her boss awkward or perhaps this was always happening and she found it embarrassing.

What was interesting to me, looking back on it, is that I immediately tarred her with the same brush. I thought she was being rude too.

All she did was bring out my son's disappointing meal and walk off again, really. But because she wasn't a beacon of positivity, I made an unconscious decision: they're all like that here. And it's worse because she's a teenager.

Now I understand why I decided all that. It's what Darren Dahl, the man who smells of grapefruits, told me. I took against the "brand." I saw this girl as part of the team. My opinion of her was directly influenced by the place where she worked and the people with whom she worked.

This was unfair of me. She was just a teenager, probably earning minimum wage, forced to deal with customers already annoyed at a general lack of service. Perhaps she wasn't part of the problem. Perhaps we shared the same problem and were on the same side.

. . .

Historically, we do fear the young.

All of them. They're an irresponsible menace. Even the royals.

Prince William used to love an after-closing drink.

Prince Harry would get blind drink in Boujis and dress up as a Nazi.

Even the Queen, aged 19, is supposed to have knocked a police-man's helmet off on VE Day then run away, though I wouldn't ask her about it.

Sometimes they don't even grow out of it. Prince Jefri of Brunei is in his sixties and has a yacht called *Tits*.

Thing is, we think we know better than the youth of today, and that's because generally we do. Not because we're smarter, but just because it's an inevitable consequence of existing longer. It is conve-nient that we forget our own weaknesses, and we forget or ignore the fact that things move on. Just as teens are trying to make sense of the world, we're trying to keep it the same because we've only just made sense of it. Here we are, older, fatter, and pretending we're wiser, de-manding that the world stands still to the great frustration of the ones who want to know why.

Plato was annoyed that the young disrespected their elders. However bad it was for Plato, at least he didn't have to get on a bus and listen to someone else's confusing music blaring out of a phone, or meet a shop assistant who won't look up from Snapchat, or a blank-eyed kid who flat out refuses to eat dinner because he's planning his next Minecraft villa.

Every generation sees uncivil behavior in its youth, fueled by whatever they're just too old to be part of.

Punk. Rap. Teddy boys.

In 1926, the *Pentacostal Evangel* blamed "the Movies."

In 1859, *Scientific American* blew its top at a "pernicious" new game that stopped young people going outside and running around and having a clean mind. Chess.

In 1816, it was the waltz. "So fatal a contagion," said the *Times*, and so *"foreign."*

It goes on and on. In 1790, it was plays. In 1695, girls who swore.

So yes, we fear the young, and we fear their interests. And we hate it when they get together for chess or waltzing. So much so that we've developed subtle, hidden ways of moving them on. Antanas Mockus, a former mayor of Bogotá, would hate it.

Rude or "Hostile Architecture" is a style of city design that was aimed at our homeless first of all—councils claiming to be upgrading an area would by coincidence order new "types" of benches. These benches might be strangely shallow. Or have rigid metal armrests dividing them up. Or be unusually angled. But what linked each and every one of them was that they would be impossible to sleep on.[1]

Strange metal studs began appearing in alcoves outside banks. Immovable potted plants were placed on wide ledges, and we barely noticed. None of it was there for visual appeal—not unless you count removing the homeless.

We do the same to the young, and they hate it, but they take it.

In British towns like Mansfield and Scunthorpe, for example, strange pink lights began appearing in areas where young people might get together. The lights were supposed to be calming. They were supposed to lessen antisocial behavior and crime. What they also did, but which was not supposed to be the selling point, was highlight the blemishes on a teenager's skin.

One resident was quoted by the local newspaper as saying, "the lamps are the same ones that beauticians use to check for any abnormalities on the skin. So any teenager standing there trying to act big and tough will be seen as the spotty little herbert they really are."[2]

What this initiative did was say it's okay to embarrass kids. You can damage and shame them because it's better they feel bad about themselves than we have them hanging around.

> ## We don't know how to talk to the young; they don't know how to talk to us.

Granted, the residents in certain troubled areas might have been relieved, but the fact remains that we don't know how to talk to the young, they don't know how to talk to us, and, rather than try, we create new barriers.

.   .   .

I tried to talk to the teenage girl in the diner that day.

I hoped she might share something with me—a look of empathy, or maybe a roll of the eyes and a "Sorry, she's *always* like this!" about Madam Hotdog. I got nothing, and I took it almost as a slight. Couldn't she see? Why wouldn't she show me she knew this was crazy? I was no longer just a customer, but a customer who'd been treated rudely. I deserved recognition for that, I thought. But because I got nothing, I decided they must all be like that. *Rude.*

And that's what people think when they meet a surly teenage waitress, or a kid in a hoodie on his phone on the train.

The fact is, we're expecting too much of them. Because understanding the rules of society—and indeed feeling you are part of that society at all—is not instinctive. It's a behavior that takes a while to learn, and needs a brain that's ready for it.

That sounds patronizing. I cringed when I wrote it, but I had to, because there's truth in it.

Science shows us that when a teenager appears rude, it is often only because their brain is making it difficult for them to appear otherwise.

Sven Mørch is a lecturer in psychology at Copenhagen University and a man who's been investigating the teenage brain. When I get in touch with him, he immediately sends me a paper on youth life. It paints a stark picture.

We know that many young people are, in Mørch's words, "in difficulties"—feeling trapped in that troubling phase of being neither a kid nor a grown-up. Mørch says this can lead to "self-centeredness that does not promote the development of broader social responsibility." Like thinking about other people.

Shows like *The X Factor* at once say that anyone can be a star, but if you don't make it, it's your fault. You weren't popular enough, you weren't talented enough, you weren't special enough. Mørch suggests the fact that an ever-present media creates entertainment essentially out of inequality completely colors their worldview. It presses down hard on their shoulders.

And that's without adding in social media.

Remember: the Wallace Report states that if the world is indeed reaching a rudeness crisis point, 65 percent put it down to the rise of social media.

This was closely followed by celebrity behavior. Then reality TV stars. Then television in general.

The very things Mørch outlines.

Because just like *The X Factor*, social media trades on status, and what group of people is more worried about status, and their place in life, and where they fit in, than teens?

· · ·

But aren't they just rebelling? Finding their own feet? Aren't you *supposed* to be rude to your elders?

Often rudeness in teenagers is not about rebellion or disrespect. It's actually about not understanding, on some level, that there are even other people around. Bodies, yes—people, no. Often teens don't recognize authority, though not as a choice—they simply barely remember to care about it.

So when they play their music out of their phones on a bus, it's not because they're trying to be jerks, even though the immediate response from those around them is "they're trying to be jerks." It's not because they are bad people, or they wish you ill.

It's just because, from their perspective, there really *are* no other people on the bus. Just as there are no neighbors of any consequence who might object to an impromptu drum-and-bass party at twenty to three in the morning.

"Other people are irrelevant" to teenagers, Mørch has said. "They do not exist."

The young are drawn to friends like them, people of the same age who can reinforce their worldview and share their interests. The opinion of a peer is worth a thousand times that of the invisible old woman on the train. Obviously, that makes them sound as selfish as their reputation has long suggested.

But what this apparently rude behavior comes down to is empathy.

*   *   *

Frances Jensen is a pediatric neurologist at Boston Children's Hospital. She's also a Harvard specialist in epilepsy. But when her two sons became moody teenagers and almost immediately started putting red streaks in their hair and crashing cars left, right, and center, while expecting other people to pick up after them and tidy their rooms, she wondered what the hell was going on. We all ask questions, but Jensen is someone who then tries to answer them. She discovered that very little research had been done into the teenage brain, so she wrote a book, and called it *The Teenage Brain*.

Scientists used to think that by the age of ten or so, our brains had finished developing. They were fresh, yes, and they needed a little fine-tuning, but that was pretty much that. Done.

Jensen thinks not.

It's all to do with the frontal lobes. That's the part of the brain that asks some pretty big questions. "Should I do this? What will happen?"

Without fully functioning frontal lobes, you can be as smart as Einstein, but you won't be able to put that intelligence to proper use. You can get there—just more slowly. It's telling that a psychopath—who shows no empathy or compassion for others—has a brain that acts in the same way as that of a person with a frontal head injury.[3]

Teenagers don't yet have enough of the white matter that connects the frontal lobe with the rest of their brains. While they might seem self-centered and surly, it's because they are not yet able fully to appreciate the consequences of their actions or words on other people. It doesn't make sense yet. It doesn't *matter* yet.

Politeness is all about empathy. It's about understanding that there is another person, and that in their world they matter just as much as you do in yours. It comes with time. Teenagers can be rude because they've not had time to grow out of it.

For society not to immediately become Mad Maxian, we have to realize that there is an "other," and to care about what is happening to the "other."

American researchers studied 14,000 college students over a 30-year period. They were made to respond to questions like "I often have tender, concerned feelings for people less fortunate than me." Okay, it's strangely worded. It's like something you'd read on a dating website and then immediately burn your computer. But the results suggested that, since the year 2000, students have become 40 percent less empathetic than they were thirty years ago.[4]

The theories why are the usual: exposure to violent media helps numb people to the pain of others. It's been shown by the American Psychological Association, certainly, that violent video games boost aggressive behavior, and it's something I've felt myself after a long stint on *Call of Duty*. I have literally yelled at anonymous children in far-off lands through a headset when they've treated me with contempt or disrespect, and felt my blood still boil as I walked back downstairs to my normal grown-up life and kids and mortgage. But then, people got pretty het up about chess, and other multiplayer platformers like it.

Currently, with our love of labeling, we're looking at what we've reduced to "Generation Me." A self-obsessed, entitled, selfish bunch of boorish blank-eyes nitwits forever Instagramming knots they've tied in string, or petals. They stare at their screens, robbing us of the basic human comfort of eye contact. They're never "present"; always somewhere else, LOLing with avatars and little blue speech bubbles that matter more than the person standing in the same room as them.

Not like we did with video games or TVs.

That kind of reductionist nonsense is exactly why they shout "All right, Granddad" at us in parks, have done for generations, and will soon have it happen to them.

·   ·   ·

For some, though, those rude teenage years are not just a phase.

I mean, how can they be? Some people are just *rude*.

One recent ten-year-long study looked at the behaviors of 164 adolescents. What researchers found was that the teenagers who were particularly rude and argumentative often stayed that way into adulthood.

Researchers who spotted the early signs when someone was 14 or 15 would come back when that person was in their early twenties, and ask them to try and find a resolution to a subject on which they would often disagree with others.

What they found was that the people who were ruder as kids would very often find themselves unable to find a compromise or take other views on board. They'd instead try and ram their own opinions through with verbal force, calling the others names when they felt they were failing or becoming aggressive rather than playing as a team.

They had developed, the researchers concluded, a form of "relationship blindness." Their peers, families, and partners saw it clear as day—called them "impossible," for example. But the people themselves sensed nothing wrong at all. Them? Impossible? They thought everything was just dandy. The truly rude failed, then, to see their own behavior through the eyes of others.[5] And there it is again: empathy.

For years, we thought empathy was either something you had or you didn't. I suspect to a certain extent that is true. Anecdotal evidence will always show another side: the person who was a complete brat until a traumatic event made them reassess their lives; the former mugger who finds God; the anesthesiologist surrounded by demons, and so on.

But for those of us who lack empathy and see no way around it, can that be changed? Can we simply learn to be less rude? Deal with our own frontal lobes the way teens have to wait for theirs to catch up?

Psychological Science recently published a report that showed that after just seven hours of training, people could learn to be more compassionate toward others. For 30 a minutes a day for 2 weeks, participants were asked to do a variety of things: repeat phrases like "May you

Can we simply learn to be less rude?

be free from suffering" and "May you have joy and ease"; to think about rude colleagues or difficult "frenemies" and develop feelings of compassion toward them. FMRI scans of their brains at the end of their training showed that participants' brain activity had changed: those who were the "nicest" were the ones who had shown the most brain changes when viewing images of human suffering.[6]

Compassion, it seems, is a bit like a muscle. It's possible to build it up. It is a trait you can develop. And what this means for the future is that a form of kindness education might be possible in schools—a sort of empathy training.

It could help reduce bullying in the short term.

It could help reduce rudeness in the long.

It might even help the teens—so often belittled and blithely written off—get there a little quicker too.

. . .

The truth about that teenage girl in the diner is probably just this: as adults, most of us find it easy to talk with other adults about pretty much nothing. At the bus stop, in the break room at the school gates. We burble on about the weather. Teens need a *reason* for the conversation, otherwise what's the point of it? So when they fail to come up with an adequate response to our half-thought-out, just-being-sociable inanity about the weather, our conditioning means we are already expecting them to be rude and they "prove" it by not acting in the same dull, re-hearsed way we do. But these are scripts you learn with time. By the time you're 30 you've had the following conversation 8,000 times:

STRANGER: Gosh. This weather!

YOU: Oh, I know. But they say it's going to be a bit better at the weekend.

STRANGER: Let's hope so! Roll on, summer, I say!

YOU: Ha-ha, absolutely!

This is the same conversation we have over and over, at bus stops and in lines, whether it's about the weather, the town council or the unusual one-way system, because this is the basic script for social interaction with strangers we have developed and learned over the years. But a teenager hasn't seen that script yet; they haven't even entered drama school. All they hear is someone saying "weather" at them. Being a teenager is a bit like a nightmare you have where absolutely everyone else is in a Shakespeare play delivering complex lines they've all learned by heart, and occasionally one of them looks at you and nods expectantly because it's your turn. It feels like they want you to say "forsooth!" and start delivering a long soliloquy. They just want you to have a go. But the path of least embarrassment is just to nod and look away.

And that's why they think you're rude.

However, when it comes to the Wallace Report, things get surprising.

I asked 2,000 people what they thought the root cause of rudeness is.

Again and again, the word "parenting" came up. Dozens of times. Virtually never with further explanation. Almost like a knee-jerk reaction; an accepted truth. Blame the parents!

So if we think parenting is to blame for rudeness, it follows that it must be the kids who are being rude.

But when I asked those polled each to consider the age of the last person who stood out as rude to them, *only 3 percent of men and 4 percent of women said that the person who'd last been rude to them was aged 18 or under.*

It's not the young being rude.

A far greater 40 percent of men and 43 percent of women said the last person to have been rude to them was aged between 35 and 44.

I found that very strange. We instinctively think of the youth of today as being the problem. Yet the people being rude to us tend not to be the youth of today. Should we still blame the parents if a man in the parking lot at a KFC cuts you off? No. You flip him off and plan your revenge over a Zinger burger, because you're every bit as bad.

So in a battle between teenagers and office middle managers, the Wallace Report states that grown-ups are literally ten times ruder.

Maybe it's time we gave teens a break for their narcissism and took a long hard look in the mirror ourselves.

But let's not do it under that pink light, yeah? It's *so* unflattering.

CHAPTER 14

Policing Rudeness

Whose job is it to make sure we behave?

I was watching a grown man on the train the other day.

I realize this sounds like the beginning of a story that ends up with me in court, but I was watching him for good sociological reasons.

The man was in his thirties or perhaps early forties. Right in that Wallace Report rude age-bracket sweet spot. He was wearing a shiny gray suit, had a Bluetooth earpiece in, and was tutting at his phone. But the reason I was watching him was that he had two legs that apparently did not get on. So much so that they seemed actively to be trying to escape from one another.

One leg pointed east. One pointed west. And in the middle, something else was pointing out the south.

. . .

Recently, gentlemen travelers on trains, buses, and other forms of public transportation have come under fire for a grave crime indeed: manspreading.

Men sit with their legs far apart, taking up more space than is seen as necessary—sometimes most of two seats—and providing anyone sitting opposite with a view they'd rather not have.

It is invasive. It is rude. It is breaking a social contract.

No one is sure why men manspread. Some claim it to be of comfort to them. As a man myself, I'm not sure how my testes compare to the national average, but I'd say all three are perfectly normal.

But as this man sat on this train, and as this train filled up and space became scarcer, I wondered: is it my duty, as various experts suggest, to say something to him?

Or is it someone else's?

· · ·

Manspreading is not, as people tend to think, a particularly new thing.

As early as 1918, public transportation authorities have been trying to tackle it. One pamphlet in particular was handed out all across the Chicago subway system, with the following patriotic call to arms:

Men will give their sons to the service of their country [. . .] but will they disturb themselves and sit a little closer to give a seat to some poor tired girl? They sit there complacently, occupying twice the space they really require, while some other passenger is deprived of a seat through their selfishness.

The Japanese went further, in 1976, with huge red posters comparing men who spread their legs on trains to Hitler.

More recently, in 2014, it was New York that set the tone with the Metropolitan Transit Authority's "Dude . . . Stop the Spread, Please" campaign, which also condemned clipping your nails on the train, though of course that should also be eligible for the death penalty.

But in terms of literally policing rudeness, it was again New York that was about to take things further.

At 12:11 a.m. on an otherwise normal night, NYPD officers boarded a train on the New York subway and quickly arrested two men on the charge of "manspreading."

Now it was a crime.

Earlier, we saw how the Broken Windows theory led normal, everyday Dutch people to misbehave and steal from mailboxes—*if* those mailboxes seemed uncared for. Well, the idea behind Broken Windows policing is that by cracking down on petty offenses, you help reduce major ones. Treat a couple of guys spreading their legs with an iron rod, and you might stop something far worse from happening.

It's a simple idea, and so it's alluring. That allure made many want to believe its effects were huge. Particularly in New York, where in the 20 years since the petty-offenses scheme was introduced, the murder rate dropped from 26.5 per 100,000 people to 3.3 per 100,000 people.[1] That's lower than the national average.

In *New York*.

It's not so simple. The real reason is foggy, but critics have been quick to come up with other things that might have contributed to the dramatic downturn. There was less crack cocaine about. Legalized abortion led to fewer unwanted children and therefore fewer wayward young men. Longer prison sentences kept those committing the most crimes off the streets. Also, crime in most developed countries fell around the same time we started removing the lead from gasoline in cars. It's thought that lead is a neurotoxin that effectively changes who we are, what we react to, the decisions we make. With less lead in the air, there's less violence. With more, there's more. And if that works for serious crime, what impact might it have on low-level behaviors?

In the 1980s, New York was arguably the global benchmark for rude cities. It was the thing everyone said about New Yorkers. Nowadays, as we saw some pages back, inevitable cultural differences mean the West looks East to find rudeness. And you know what? I've just checked, and according to recent data from the World Health Organization, about 34 percent of children in China have blood-lead levels that exceed the WHO limit.[2] The effects of lead poisoning are permanent and irreversible.*

Broken Windows policing may not have had the huge and positive impact it was first believed, but it had a real and negative impact on some. The other side of the story everyone wanted to be true is that by cracking down on low-level "rude" behavior, authorities created huge friction between the police and the public. Particularly because a lot of the people seemingly targeted by them were in poorer areas populated largely by ethnic minorities.

Thanks to the Department of Criminal Justice Services, we know that of the 221,800 misdemeanor arrests in New York in 2015, 86 percent involved non-whites.[3]

Now, it's not like white people are wearing top hats and tails or ball gowns and sitting perfectly still on the subways of America, legs tightly clamped together, greeting each other with Victorian formalities and eating their Big Macs on little silver platters. Every race has rude people. But part of this was quotas. The police had targets to hit, and the best way to hit them was targeting minor rudenesses in poorer areas where the pickings were richer. Like the case of the young black college student with a part-time job and no criminal record who then spent 24 hours in jail because he'd been spotted on the subway with his foot on the seat opposite his.

Or the African American man riding his bike who was nearly hit by a car and swerved to avoid it, falling onto the pavement as he did so. Police arrested him for having a bike on the pavement.

---

* Oh, and I really can't imagine China's one-child policy helps. It's estimated that by 2020, there will be 55 million more men in China than women. And you think *you're* frustrated.

Now, we all hate cyclists who thoughtlessly bomb down the pavements. But I think we can forgive the ones who simply fall onto it while trying not to be killed.[4]

· · ·

I tell you this because in Britain, we had our own version.

The ASBO.

Antisocial Behavior Orders were introduced with a flurry of excitement in 1999. They would be brilliant. At last there was a way to punish people who spit in the street, or swear loudly in front of children, or refuse to turn down their thumping bass at night.

They were to cover things that were a nuisance. Things that weren't "criminal" but *were* criminally rude.

An ASBO could be given to anyone over the age of ten to tell them how not to behave.

And yes—ten years old. Children still at primary school, such as Alfie Hodgin, whom the *Liverpool Echo* saw fit to brand and dismiss as a "ten-year-old Wirral yob."[5]

An order could contain only negative prohibitions. You *can't* hang around the town center. You *can't* hang out with your best friend. You *can't* play your music after 9 p.m. It couldn't contain a positive obligation. And each one related to a very specific offense. So specific, in fact, that I can't help but think that's why they were doomed to failure. There was no such thing as a general rule or a general ASBO; the specificity of each was remarkable.

So you ended up with one teenage boy in Manchester who was banned from wearing only one glove, because not wearing two was seen as a sign of gang membership.

One woman was banned from making excessive noise during sex, but only in England. She could probably split the difference in the Borders.

Each ASBO lasted two years. But here's the thing: if in those two years you broke the conditions of the ASBO—you wore one glove when the government said you could only wear them in pairs, say— you now broke the law. Any adult who broke their ASBO could face up to five years in prison.

So you could get an ASBO for doing something everybody thought was rude. But break it and go to jail. This meant that for the first time, you could end up in prison for swearing at your neighbor, though not because you actually swore at them—but because you ignored the paperwork you were handed after you did.

Because they were so specific, the breadth of offenses ASBOs covered had to be breathtakingly wide: from fare evasion to spitting to "pedophilic activity." In some ways, an ASBO was a way of pursuing people for things for which they couldn't be charged, while pushing them in the direction of jail.

One of the mainstays was rudeness. As Henry Hitchings says in his 2013 book *Sorry!: The English and Their Manners,* "ASBOs criminalized what might previously have been classified as nuisance or rudeness."

Within six years, more than 4,100 people a year were getting ASBOs. But what little research was done on the behavior orders showed them to be next to useless in tackling the problems they were supposed to address. Simplistic instructions like telling alcoholics not to drink wouldn't actually stop them drinking, any more than they'd give bored kids something interesting to do in their own neighborhood other than just hang around. The Youth Justice Board, in 2006, found that nearly half of all ASBOs in England and Wales were broken—effectively creating brand-new criminals.[6]

Sometimes the ASBO'd couldn't help it. In 2004, an ASBO was given to a farmer because of the antisocial behavior of his pigs. In February 2005, a 23-year-old woman who repeatedly tried to take her own life was given as ASBO banning her from jumping into rivers and canals or onto railway lines. It's hard to imagine how a piece of paper, embarrassment, or threat of prosecution might seem more urgent to her. Nor keep a pig in line.

In 2010, a 47-year-old Loch Ness man named Stuart Hunt appeared in court in breach of an ASBO that banned him from laughing, staring, or slow-clapping at his neighbors. He was charged after chuckling in his car at a rude gesture his neighbors' young daughter made. He told papers at the time: "They charged me with laughing . . . I couldn't believe it."

One of the most celebrated and strange cases involved a man named Stephen Gough—the man who would become known as the Naked Rambler.

A former truck driver—and Royal Marine—in a country that traditionally has celebrated and adores the Great British Eccentric, Gough believed it was his human right to be naked.

But although the British love those who think differently or prick pomposity, we are an extremely strange country when it comes to nudity. Traditionally, we find it embarrassing. But we also find it silly. For years, no one seemed to mind a naked woman on page 3 of a newspaper. But at no point in history have we wanted to see a naked man on a bus.

> **At no point in history have we wanted to see a naked man on a bus.**

For other cultures, nudity is not a huge thing. When I was 12, my family moved to Germany for a year. As a treat, my mum and dad took me to the swimming baths one day. None of us realized that half the people in there would be completely naked. It was excruciatingly embarrassing. It wasn't just the pale naked bodies, although that was bad enough. It was also that if anything, with my Speedos *and* swim socks, I was entirely overdressed.

Gough couldn't see why people should be embarrassed. What's rude about the nude?

And it was that question that would see him spend around ten years in jail at a cost to the country of hundreds of thousands of pounds.

.   .   .

It's not like he didn't do things properly.

In 2003, a fully clothed Stephen Gough walked into his local police station in Eastleigh, Hampshire, and politely asked if it was illegal to walk around naked on the streets. The person on reception didn't seem sure. So Gough gave it a go. He went back to his mum's house and reemerged, all six-foot-four of him, completely naked except for boots, socks, and beard, to walk to Eastleigh town center.

Nothing much happened as he ambled about. One man shouted, "Disgusting!," but Gough claimed that's because the man was eating a sandwich he didn't like.

Then out of nowhere a bunch of policemen arrived.

That initial intervention might have stopped most people. But keen to explore his rights, Gough decided to go farther. Literally. He determined to walk from Land's End to John o'Groats—the length of Great Britain—and to do it as nature intended.

The world did not end. The sky did not fall in. Apparently, he was pretty much left alone in England. Every now and again the police might stop him, roll their eyes, and pretend this was just an everyday hassle, and then he'd put some clothes on and explain what he was doing. No one could really be bothered making much of a fuss about it.

But in Scotland, it was a very different story. He was picked up several times by police. Ordered to get dressed. And finally convicted of breach of the peace.

He served four months in Her Majesty's Prison Inverness.

When he got out, what did Gough do? He finished what he'd started. Gough made it, nude, to John o'Groats and a delighted media reception.

That should have been the end of it. He'd done what he'd set out to do, and struck a blow for nudity fans everywhere. Now, as we know from television editing, there is nothing ruder than a gentleman's penis. In fact, in 2015, the Federal Communications Commission in the U.S.A. doled out its highest-ever penalty—$325,000—for a three-second visual image of a penis run in a corner of a TV screen aired accidentally and just once during WDBJ TV's 6 p.m. newscast. Imagine what they'd make of Stephen Gough, wandering about, showing his to literally everyone around.

But Gough had the nagging feeling that he'd compromised himself. He wrestled with the question of why he'd felt the need to get dressed every time the police stopped him. That just wasn't who he was.

So he decided to do it all again—this time *his* way.

In 2005, he set off once more from Land's End. By now people knew who he was. He was a less startling, confrontational, and rude sight. In England, he would shop unclothed in supermarkets, and have pints bought for him while naked in pubs.

But in Scotland things went wrong again.

Arrested in Edinburgh, Gough decided that this time he would stay true to his brand and appear in court naked. He pleaded not guilty to breach of the peace. They weren't so sure. To make a long story a bit shorter, he found himself serving another five months at Her Majesty's pleasure.

He finally made it back to the windswept tip of Scotland in February 2006. Exposed to the elements, he'd walked through lashing rain, through the streets of towns and villages and over frosty moors and hills. And Stephen Gough had done it all with his gentleman's agreements bouncing happily along with him.

But just a few months later, on May 19, 2006, Gough boarded a 6:45 a.m. flight from Southampton to Edinburgh. Everything was pretty normal as they crossed the country in a fraction of the time it had taken him naked. Perhaps it was rebellion, perhaps it was nostalgia . . . but as soon as the pilot announced their descent, Gough stood up, walked into the bathroom, took off all his clothes, and returned to his seat *completely naked*.

The man next to him did the most British thing possible. Rather than react, or complain, or show acute embarrassment, or even just *admit* that the man next to him was now naked, he closed his eyes and just fell asleep.

In 2013, Gough was finally issued with an ASBO. It was tailor-made for him, and indeed is probably the only thing that ever was. It ordered him to cover his genitalia and buttocks whenever in public, unless in a changing room, at a nudist beach, *or* while having an intimate medical examination.

But moments after Stephen Gough received that ASBO, he walked out of court wearing just his socks and shoes. He was arrested on the steps outside—the ASBO still in his hands—and in June 2013 was sentenced to 11 months in prison.

But isn't this ridiculous? All in all, this prisoner of conscience has spent, by his lawyer's estimation, nearly nine years of his life in jail. I include his strange case not because I think he was "rude" for wandering around naked, but instead because it's an extreme example of the way the government effectively *criminalized* behavior the rest of us might see as, at worst, rude.

Former prime minister David Cameron is one of many statesmen to speak out on how people who didn't go to Eton should behave better.

"Swearing in public," he said while still in charge, "neglecting the elderly, being rude to shop workers or bus drivers—these should be as unacceptable as racism."

Mind you, he also once said "pissed off" and "twat" during the same early-morning radio interview broadcast to millions during the school run, and while at Oxford he was part of the Bullingdon Club: an organization that counted trashing the dining rooms of innocent restaurateurs among its high-class evening pursuits. And please don't tell me the landed gentry don't find public nudity hilarious. It's the best joke they've got.

Matthew Scott has fumed publicly about the strange case of Stephen Gough for a few years, and I meet the lawyer over a lemon tart in a patisserie in Bath, which by the way is the most middle-class sentence I've ever written.

Scott is a highly regarded and fully clothed lawyer with a nice line in self-deprecation. His Twitter bio lists some of the rude things people have said about him: "Contemptible vile views"; "morally dubious"; "no scruples, looks weird"; "greasy combover."

He is exceptionally polite and forthcoming about the strange case of Stephen Gough. As far as Scott can tell, Gough strikes him as a "perfectly sane, highly intelligent man." Just one who has absolutely no idea why people are forcing him to wear clothes.

"There is actually no crime of being naked," says Scott. "There's the crime of exposure. It used to be called 'indecent exposure.' But you've got to have some intent there, either sexual intent or some kind of hostile intent."

"So if you're hiding in a bush . . ."

"Exactly. If you're hiding in a bush and you leap out to frighten somebody, that's clearly an offense, under the Sexual Offenses Act. There's also outrage of public decency. And the reason [Gough] has never been prosecuted for that is that juries just say, well, that isn't an outrage. It's just someone being naked."

Juries, of course, often see far worse. But I ask Scott if he can understand the ASBO.

"Well, they say they've had complaints. I have to say I've never actually seen the evidence which gave rise to the ASBO, but apparently there were ten statements saying 'we find it deeply upsetting that this man walks around naked.' They always say 'close to where children might see him.' That's the clincher."

Yet almost literally everybody else didn't seem as if they could care less.

Scott calls the likes of ASBOs "very dangerous," "overused," and "like a sledgehammer to crack a nut."

"Quite often it's nothing 'rude' at all. It's just a little old lady who wants to feed the pigeons or something," he says. "Whatever you say to them, they're going to keep feeding the pigeons. And then they get locked up in prison."

"Has that kind of thing happened?" I ask, appalled.

"Yeah. Completely stupid."

It costs between £30,000 and £40,000 a year to keep a prisoner in jail in Britain. Stephen Gough has spent much of the last ten years locked up. This means we are effectively talking about the most expensive testicles Britain has ever seen.

And because of his ASBO, the only man in Britain who wants to walk around naked is now *the only man in Britain who would be breaking the law if he did.*

What I'm saying is that when it comes to antisocial or rude behavior, maybe we need to learn to self-police a little more.

The Wallace Report shows that only 18 percent of British people think that the government needs to take more responsibility for rude behavior. To me, that says one thing: we feel that there are rules, and that we should just get on and understand those rules. Most of us don't want punishments from on high. We want to take responsibility for our own behavior.

However, that doesn't always happen.

In the thick of the Hotdog Incident, I looked to my fellow customers for support, but what I got instead was grim joy. Their eyes were shining. They were watching a confrontation. Maybe they liked the fact that someone else was complaining. They were happy to be observers.

Darren Dahl, friend of the grapefruit, told me: "There are norms in society; rules we're supposed to live by. Don't cut in line. If you're in a shop and you mess up a display, fix it. There is an expectation that people will behave. And if they don't, often consumers will actually help discipline the situation."

But it's been shown that consumers feel a greater positivity toward a brand when they don't have to; when shop owners hold rude people to account themselves.

A shop owner is still "one of us." Like a hall monitor telling a kid not to run in the hallway because it's annoying everybody. It's like we're all still in the classroom. We are equal, but as soon as a social contract is broken, we feel the need for some kind of authority figure to step in before we do it ourselves.

If we don't, the lesson we teach each other is: what you're doing has no consequences.

"If you behave rudely and no one calls you on it," Amir Erez told me, "you simply continue to behave rudely. As soon as you are called on it, that behavior stops."

It sounds obvious. Simple. But just as Wang Tao believes, it needs saying: we must tell people off for their rudeness. Highlight it. Shine a spotlight on them. It's our duty.

. . .

In recent years, a group of young Russians took that sense of social responsibility to the extreme.

Moscow is notorious for its terrible, unthinking drivers. They block bus lanes, they drive through parks or on tramways, they park wherever they like, they bully and badger and belittle other people in cars.

A guy called Dmitry Chugunov had endured enough. He used to stand by the side of the road, watching cars thunder down the pavements, beeping their horns at elderly pedestrians or mothers with strollers and sending them running out of the way.

It was this sense of entitlement, this arrogant rudeness and complete disregard of both the law and basic common courtesy that led him to found the "Stop a Douchebag" movement: a vigilante movement dedicated to stopping "Хам" (literally "rude people" in Russian).

Chugunov's group set out to do exactly what I've just outlined: to expose rudeness, to humiliate the rude, stand up to them no matter how big or angry they seem, and to expose their unacceptable behavior. It caught on quickly, with satellite groups of volunteers popping up in more than 30 cities.

These people—furious at rudeness—approach cars and usually begin their exchange with a line like, "Hello, we're social movement Stop a Douchebag. Would you mind moving your car, please?"

Sometimes the person complies immediately.

Usually, there's a fight.

The rude, who are disrespecting everybody else, feel disrespected themselves.

"Who are you to tell me what I can do in my car?"

It's that ego again. It's that love of territory. It's that sense of entitlement.

Stop a Douchebag would take things further. They would stand in the way of speeding cars. They would clamber on top of their hoods when they tried to flee responsibility. And they almost always attached impossible-to-scrape-off stickers to the windshields, bearing legends like:

I spit on everyone! I drive where I want!

The rude, who have seen themselves as above everybody else in a traffic jam, now have to join the back of that very same line, rejoining a society that now mocks them, in a once-fancy car now ruined by a giant round sticker.

Stop a Douchebag activists catch bankers, thugs, hairdressers, cab-drivers, government officials—most of whom stand stubbornly behind their right to do whatever they want, no matter who it affects. Every confrontation is filmed, where together online they get hundreds of millions of views from others seeking the cathartic relief we all crave from seeing a genuinely rude person brought down a peg or 12.

It's dangerous work and visceral viewing. You could absolutely make the case that some members of Stop a Douchebag are just looking for trouble. But taken as a whole, the movement seems to capture the contained rage of the silent polite majority who've had enough. Who want to see someone stand up to the quick-to-fury aggression of those who think normal rules don't apply to them. Who fly off the handle the minute it's pointed out that they do. The rude react badly to humiliation—when they're caught, and by a bunch of nerds and sticklers they *know* are right.

It goes wrong all the time. Chugunov and his band of believers have been punched, beaten, had guns pulled on them by the side of the road, been dragged along by cars for hundreds of meters. They've been slapped, spat on, sworn at, threatened. But always—always—the rude lose, roaring off with a genuinely enormous sticker that marks them out as idiots to be mocked, or skulking off into the shadows like an impotent bully to lick their wounds.

Now, I'm not saying the whole world should adopt an aggressive approach to fighting rude behavior. But certainly this movement seems to suggest it has a right-thinking public on its side, and a public who crave that we challenge the rude on their behavior. It also has the tacit support of the Russian police, who have been known to follow up on their videos, or at least make some easy arrests along the way. Even the Kremlin itself, in 2015, gave Stop a Douchebag 8 million rubles (£85,000 at the time), which they mainly spent on stickers.

The world is coming to something when even Vladimir Putin is sick of rudeness.

But in 2016, it all stopped.

Feeling that the group had achieved its mission in its five years of harassing the harassers, the authorities finally shut it down. But Stop a Douchebag had made its point. They'd changed the way people think. Shown them that they could stand up to rudeness; that it wasn't okay. Councils reacted too, making parking bays much clearer and imposing greater fines. The police felt shamed into policing violations more effectively. Green tow trucks known as "vultures" began to parade around the cities, removing badly parked or abandoned cars. The public knew that others felt the way they did; that they had a right to speak up.

Self-policing rudeness *can* change attitudes.

.   .   .

But back to defense attorney Matthew Scott. I tell him about the Hotdog Incident to get the view of a noted legal mind.

I tell him that in films, a man making a stand against a petty tyrant would earn the standing ovation of every diner in the place. But

that my lot just stared. Even as I produced the evidence of my wait—
the receipt!—as if I was a clever young Southern lawyer who's just realized he's found the turning point of the whole case.

"I can't see how you could wait an hour for a hotdog," he says,
shaking his head.

"I know."

"Surely a hotdog . . . is it a boiled meat?"

"It was being grilled. She kept saying the same thing: 'You don't
understand how it works; we cook to order!'"

"Even so," says this highly respected lawyer. "I think that's too
long."

He leans forward and looks me in the eye. "A fundamental *breach
of contract*, I'd say."

"Really?" I say, excited, because now I'm starting to think this
might be something I could take to the European Court of Justice.

"My contract law is a little rusty, but I would've said there is an
implied term that you don't have to wait an hour for a hotdog. You are
entitled to a hotdog within a reasonable time."

And in his professional opinion? *Much less* than an hour.

I ask Matthew Scott whether he'd be interested in taking up the
case, but he just finishes his lemon tart and leaves.

CHAPTER 15

Rude by Nature

Could Madam Hotdog simply not help it?

In 2016, the mayor of Davao City, Rodrigo Duterte, was elected as the 16th president of the Philippines.

He understood that this office carried with it a special burden, and it was one he was prepared for.

"I am trying to enjoy the last days of my rudeness," he told a midnight press conference, who didn't look like they believed him.

This was the man who just a year before got so annoyed by a five-hour traffic jam caused by the pope's visit to Manila that he used an official campaign speech to call the infallible Holy Father a "son of a whore."

The pope was totally cool with it and sent him a note saying he'd pray for him.

But, Duterte insisted, calling the pope a son of a whore for unwittingly creating excess traffic was the old him. This mayor, sometimes pictured in newspapers showing the world his middle finger, and known for his rudeness, sarcastic jibes, and often foul mouth, assured the country he was ready to change.

Except even as he said it he seemed a little annoyed about it.

"Why would you criticize my cursing?" he complained to the journalists. "If I don't do that, I'm already dead. My language is like that because that is my universal identity given by God."

The pope probably had a few things to say about that.

But yes, okay, *fine*, Duterte would try. Things would be different.

"I can no longer be foolish when I'm president. I swear to God."

But like a lot of rude people, he saw abundant rudeness in others.

When a journalist innocently asked the next president about the state of his health, Duterte shot back: "Let's go to my house and I'll do the treadmill for one hour plus. I'll do the treadmill for one hour and thirty minutes. I will even do it longer than that. If I falter, I'll resign. If I do it for two hours, *you* resign. I challenge you. I am not the type of person who is almost *begging* for a position. *Bullshit.*"

.   .   .

The more research I did into rudeness—and the more people I spoke to—the more I realized there was one theory I hadn't explored yet.

I mean, the drivers in Moscow—where did that sense of self-entitlement come from? Did it develop, in the way a lack of rules in Bogotá helped the city descend into chaos? Had it evolved? Or was it somehow ingrained?

It was a theory so simple that I genuinely couldn't quite believe it hadn't occurred to me before.

It was this:

What if Madam Hotdog was just a jerk?

.   .   .

Looking back on that day, some part of me still blames myself for it. It escalated. I played my part in that. But I rigorously assert, also, that she started it.

Aaron James is a philosophy professor at the University of California, Irvine, with a PhD from Harvard under his belt.

I tell him all about my encounter with my hotdog nemesis and, based on the preliminary anecdotal evidence, he immediately feels confident enough to assert a theory: "It sounds like she was an asshole. It sounds like she definitely was."

James knows all about assholes. He is the author of *Assholes: A Theory*. He spots assholes everywhere he goes. He works out what makes them assholes. Consequently, he says "assholes" a lot.

"The basic definition of an asshole is someone who takes special advantages in cooperative life out of an entrenched sense of entitlement," he tells me when we speak. "That could be breaking rules of courtesy, maybe, or just being rude. But an asshole is immunized against the complaints of other people."

By cooperative life, James means normal, everyday events, in which we do all the little things that make it all a bit easier for one another. We ask permission. We say please, we say thank you. We hold a door open, we don't try and screw each other over.

The asshole has no time for that, and what's more, they absolutely don't care.

In the most basic form of capitalism, someone trades goods (hotdogs) and services (cooking those hotdogs) in a system of exchange and reward. If they do it fairly and well, they generate goodwill, and we pay them not just in money but in repeat trade and loyalty. But "assholery," says James, leads the person providing the hotdogs to act precisely as they feel like acting regardless of the actual value of their processed meat products and whether or not they were cooked to order. This behavior threatens the cooperative nature of capitalism which is so vital to its survival.

Yes. I am now saying that this woman was *acting in a way that could come to bring down the entire capitalist structure of life on Earth.*

He also seems very sure indeed that Madam Hotdog was an asshole, which I find a great relief and extraordinarily satisfying, although I must point out for legal reasons this is entirely his opinion and *absolutely* not mine.

"Buying a hotdog . . . that should have been a trivial occurrence that took just a few minutes of your day," he says. "But the display of disrespect . . . that was something you thought was worth fighting."

"It was!" I say, delighted to have found a kindred spirit.

"That's something we find really important: how we're seen in the eyes of others. Whether we're seen as an equal. Or whether we're seen as beneath the other person."

This was, once more, exactly why I fought to win her respect. Though James posits I wasn't trying to win her respect.

"You were trying to *exact* respect."

He has hit the nail on the head. I now realize I was trying to compel her to respect me. To force her to. When I stood up to her, just as we have all stood up to rudeness in the past, I was asserting my right to be respected and I knew it was something for which I would have to fight her. On some subconscious level, it was to be gladiatorial. There I was, standing on her territory, taking on the Queen of the diner, an outsider with no power other than a voice and a shaky grasp of consumer rights, observed by an audience of strangers baying for blood. She was in control. She was entitled to behave exactly as she pleased.

The sense of entitlement that rude people have often helps them get ahead, and, as we discovered earlier, it's a proven strategy for success in business. People act badly to assert themselves, though they also choose when to act in a nice or cooperative manner in a cynical attempt to further their own cause.

And sometimes the world needs an asshole. Sometimes, in fact, you need a *superasshole* to bring all the other assholes into line—for example, whoever runs Fox News. Without tyranny, the seventeenth-century philosopher Thomas Hobbes said, you get anarchy. And tyranny is better. Thomas Hobbes would absolutely have voted Trump.

And like Trump, often the "true asshole" will have one redeeming feature about themselves which helps balance things out. James tells me that to truly succeed as a genuinely rude person, they also need to have something . . . likable.

"Unusual intelligence," he suggests. "Money. Beauty. Or . . . hotdogs. I mean, they better be damn good hotdogs this woman was selling for her to act that way."

Maybe we'll never know.

Or maybe we will . . .

* * *

What James says about rude people being able to choose when to be rude and when to be cooperative jibes with the work of another American, this one a psychology student at Yale.

Adam Bear doesn't use the word "asshole" at all when we speak because he prefers "jerk." He attempted to develop a mathematical model to find out why some people are consistently jerks, while the rest of us are usually nice, even to people we don't know.

What he found was that people from a supportive background learn as they grow up to see the benefits in cooperation, politeness, and courtesy. They will instinctively act in a way that is good for the group.

However, if they take just a moment to think about things, they often realize that they *also* have the chance to act in a selfish manner. Guess what? Even for "nice" people, selfishness will therefore often overrule the "better" option if it turns out there's no real benefit to them.

Even nice people are jerks when no one's watching.

"If no one is watching," he tells me, "or if there are no long-term

> **Even nice people are jerks when
> no one's watching.**

repercussions for being a jerk, you'll be a jerk. If a homeless guy is asking you for money, and you're never going to see him again, and there's no one else around, you *know* that the selfish answer is you shouldn't give him any money."

So while your first instinct might be to open your wallet, just a moment's hesitation can reset the brain so that it refocuses on your own selfish wants and needs. And then it's a straight choice. Him or me. Most people will be ashamed to say they will cast their vote in their own favor.

I have seen this in my own life, I am ashamed to say. The other day I was waiting for an elevator in the lobby of a disappointing hotel. As I walked in, I noticed someone else approaching the elevator, suitcases behind them, from some way down the hall. We did not make eye contact. I could have waited—and had that guy seen me, I would of course have held the doors open. But he did *not* see me. In a microsecond, I realized this was something I could get away with. I pressed the button, the doors closed, I was off.

But I am not a true jerk. True jerks cut straight to the chase. They don't have that moment of thought. The wallet remains exactly where it was, opening it is never even considered—and even if they make eye contact with someone approaching "their" elevator, they'll press that button because only they matter.

That's pure, thoroughbred jerkery.

What Bear suggests is that people who grow up surrounded by boors learn intuitively the benefits of selfish behavior. Even when cooperating might pay off, they've already lost that chance because they've plowed straight on with the "rude" behaviour.

> **People who grow up surrounded by boors learn intuitively the benefits of selfish behavior.**

"The ones with an intuition to be nice sometimes end up selfish when they take a moment to stop and think," he says, to be clear. "But the jerks who are selfish never stop and think, so will always act selfishly."

But back to capitalism.

Had Madam Hotdog taken a second to think about our interaction, she might have realized that it wasn't wise to be rude to a customer and that she should take the edge off whatever her instincts were that day. She was being watched by other customers for a start, and as we've already established, customers who witness staff rudeness tend to leave with a much worse impression of the business and are much less likely to return. She was also risking the permanent loss of a brand-new customer, while also running the risk of having a whole bloody book written about her, but I think we can forgive her for not guessing that last one.

Perhaps it was because on some level, Bear and I decide, she instinctively felt that I didn't matter. She hadn't seen me before. I didn't seem local. I was an outsider of very little consequence, someone she could look down upon because I'm "probably the sort of people who queue up for *40 minutes* for FISH AND CHIPS."

By coincidence, Bear is working on a new model about just this thing.

"A person's intuition is sensitive to who's in their in-group, or who you've seen before. Sometimes only when you stop and think do you look at an outsider and realize that it is actually in your own self-interest to be nice to them . . ."

So if she had paused, she might not have been rude. But she saw me, sensed I was about to complain, decided I didn't matter, and instead went on pure instinct?

"Yes."

I don't know whether to be happy or sad about this.

I still can't help but feel that maybe I had done something to come across as rude myself. And yet I had done everything I could not to—a polite face, both hands up in the air, using noncombative, deflective words. Even mentioning a third party—my son—to distance the complaint from myself and make it less confrontational. So what goes through the head of an asshole when they behave like an asshole?

"For one kind of asshole," James says, "the way they rationalize things in their head is '*This person is mistreating me.*' There is a victim complex underlying it."

Aha!

"They see tiny slights everywhere. And so for them, their rudeness or brusqueness is justifiable. Their sense of entitlement can be a thin layer that spontaneously produces rationalizations."

"So she looked at me padding toward her, and immediately sprang to a conclusion?"

"And then they respond disproportionately, yes. It sounds like this hotdog woman was doing that. The bigger assholes act disproportionately."*

Why do these disproportionate reactions happen? We see it all the

---

* I should probably remind you, he hasn't actually met her.

time—road rage, fury erupting on the streets because someone's blocking the sidewalk, insane outbursts on public transportation.

James suggests something called victim-oriented narcissism. The sufferer becomes incredibly angry at the smallest perceived slight because in their heads it is far more: *it is an attack on them as a human being*. When I walked in and arrogantly asked how long my hotdog would be, I was not just asking how long my hotdog would be. I was launching an unwarranted and fundamentally abusive attack on her, her business, her choices, her personality. I was undermining everything she had done. I just did not appreciate it. I didn't *understand how it worked*.

"She thought, 'He thinks this late hotdog is my fault and he is getting at me,'" says James. "And then the real issue of where the hotdog is falls by the wayside. You have questioned her status. She can lash out."

"But she's retaliating at a shot that hasn't actually been fired," I say.

"But in her world, shots are always being fired. They're interpreted as threats to her worth. So even if you didn't say anything but you seemed slightly angry or perturbed, she would see that as an attack on her. It's not about the hotdog any more. It's about you and her."

Just look again at our favorite global rude man, Donald Trump, about whom much more in a moment. Consider the sheer amount of time he spent focusing not on the issues while campaigning, but on the attacks. How he constantly cried "unfair!" every time someone criticized him. Journalists were *unfair*. Celebrities were *unfair*. Judges and fellow candidates were *unfair*. Look at how he responded with wild sledgehammer blows when people suggested that maybe his fingers were slightly shorter than the national average. How he whined, yelled, whinnied, moaned, swore, and peacocked all the characteristics of low-self-esteem narcissistic rage.

A report in *Psychology Today* gives several indicators that someone might be suffering from narcissistic rage,* including:

An inability to apologize, or to do it sincerely.
Showing or feeling no remorse for their actions.
Quick to rage if you humiliate them.
Rarely saying "thank you."
Quick to becoming aggressively defensive if you call them on any deficiency, fault, or responsibility.[1]

The insecurity a narcissist feels means they have to show strength and power to make themselves feel stable. It's because often they're not just insecure, but brittle. The rage, the anger, the rudeness is all unleashed when—the way a wounded animal becomes more vicious as it realizes it needs to survive—the narcissist feels under attack and that the next insult may be the one to finish them off.

So they get in there first. They react in the moment. They attack.

Hey—Donald Trump is America's Madam Hotdog!

Jack Katz got the ball rolling, but I feel closer than ever to that woman while talking to Aaron James. In the course of one conversation, I tell him, we've gone from thinking she's an arsehole to realising that, actually, assholery might just be a behavioral side effect of something else entirely.

"Well," he says, smiling. "I think she's probably still an asshole. But she's not *just* an asshole."

There's a line for the headstone.

---

* Despite this, it should be noted that in February 2017, Allen Frances, the very man responsible for writing the criteria that define narcissistic personality disorder, wrote in a letter to the *New York Times* that while Trump is a "world-class narcissist," grandiose and lacking empathy, he is not actually mentally ill. Nor is it fair on the genuinely mentally ill to be lumped in with him. Instead, Frances later suggested in the *Los Angeles Times*, Trump is a "classic schmuck." *That's* a diagnosis.

· · ·

Both James and Bear think assholes and jerks, respectively, are not born, but made.

We learn how to be rude, how far we can push it, and what we can get away with. Some of us worry about it more than others, but for James, at least, it's getting worse.

> **We learn how to be rude, how far we can push it, and what we can get away with.**

"In politics, for sure. But also in the media."

"There are no assholes in the media," I reassure him.

"It's striking to watch," he says, a little lost in thought. "A lot of TV is about getting people to misbehave. We like people who lack inhibitions. It's attention-getting. That's what really sets the agenda these days. There is a lot of financial pressure in the world, which goes against cooperation. Certainly, in the U.S., there's more of an asshole culture that's taken hold. Success is about marketing, markets are about marketing, politics is about marketing."

And if you can still be elected president in a predominantly Catholic country like the Philippines after calling the pope a "son of a whore," then you've got to say it works.

But is it any way to behave?

And what might happen to the world if—God forbid—it went too far?

CHAPTER 16

Sense and Incivility

Or: the politics of rudeness

It was nearly 9 p.m. and I was in the Verizon Wireless Theater in Houston, Texas, waiting with thousands of others for his arrival: this enormously wealthy man who'd risen from American network television to full-blown international talking point in what seemed like the blink of an eye.

A star whose ranting and raving had blown up on Twitter. Who decried his enemies as "losers" or "clowns" or "turds." Who claimed to be winning whatever race he thought was running, even when logic dictated he simply couldn't be. Whose interview with the right-wing American conspiracy theorist and radio host Alex Jones had been played and replayed all over the globe.

"Look at what I'm dealing with," he'd tell anyone who'd listen, which was everyone. "I'm dealing with fools and trolls. I don't have time for their judgment and their stupidity, and you know they lay down with their ugly wives in front of their ugly children and look at their loser lives and then they look at me and they say, 'I can't process it.' Well no, you never will, stop trying, just sit back and enjoy the show."

I had found myself surrounded by his people, ready to enjoy his show. Men in cowboy hats. Frail old ladies in T-shirts bearing his name. A large black lady in her going-out top trailing an oxygen tank behind her like a little silver sausage dog. All looking to this strange man for . . . what? Hope? Leadership? A message?

In the foyer outside, I'd spoken with a few people. One Texan woman told me, "I love him because he tells the truth."

"How do you mean?" I'd asked, and I don't think she was ready to go into much more detail than that.

"Huh?"

"I mean, when you say he tells the truth. What truth is he telling?" She seemed confused.

"I don't understand," she said, then: "I just mean he tells it like it is."

It's true that here was a powerful man who had propelled himself forward on this wave of Telling It Like It Is, or Only Being Honest, or #justsaying; this furious railing against political correctness.

Another fan told me: "He's this big, rich guy but he still got screwed for it. So now he's giving the whole world the finger. He's still one of us."

This packed arena could not wait for its leader. I remember being stunned by the effect he had. How he had latched onto something and galvanized these people.

And, now, out he came, striding onto the stage to a deafening roar as people went nuts around me. I knew I was witnessing something unusual here. Something that shouldn't really be happening.

"HOUSTON!" he shouted into his microphone. "*We no longer have a problem!*"

And the crowd went wild as the show began. A show that would include endless, aimless, rambling rants. Sexism. Jingoism. A little bullying. At one point, he would tell a man in the crowd he should dump his wife because she doesn't earn the money and should be grateful, and this would be followed by stabs of non-ironic cries like "yeah, bitch!" from men (and women) somewhere behind me.

And just there, right there under a skin so thin it was translucent, I saw the paranoia, perhaps fueled by the fact that after 20 or so minutes of directionless fury, small pockets of people began to leave.

"The media reports on my show as though they were here!" he spat, shaking his head, pitying his enemy the media. "You will read things tomorrow about this show that did not happen. [. . .] They'll say half the fucking venue left early. [dramatic pause] Everyone still here as far as I can see . . ."

He said this as right before our eyes, people made their way through exits. But no one pointed this out. No one questioned him, for fear of angering their god.

And there was also the conspiracy.

"Run for president?" he said at one point, responding to a supporter in the crowd, willing the crowd to cheer. "At least I was *born* here . . ."

And cheer they did.

That night, I mingled outside, as midnight approached and his people waited patiently by an enormous black tour bus for a glimpse of him. An elderly woman clutched a handwritten letter she'd brought. A middle-aged man in the crowd passed the time watching porn on his iPhone as his wife rested her weary head on his shoulder.

The following evening, in Dallas, thousands more rallied to hear their leader's words, and as he stood before them he screamed, "We don't believe in emotion! We believe in *anger* and *resentment*!"

In front of a giant video screen bearing just his face, I watched as he stared soulfully out at his followers and then muttered, close to the microphone, "A movement can start with one man. Like it has with me. But unless anybody steps in behind me and follows, *regardless of the consequences*, unless people *come join*, then the movement is cut short.

Looks to me like the movement is in *full fucking force*, what do you think?"

It was April 2011, that man was Charlie Sheen, and what I saw was just a horrifying glimpse of what no one could guess lay ahead.

.   .   .

Charlie Sheen had been going through what we might politely call a rough patch.

As the star of the sitcom *Two and a Half Men*, he had been the highest-paid television actor in the world. But fired and unwanted, he had let rip like a jilted lover whose partner had been a little too quick to move on. I had been sent by GQ to cover his "Violent Torpedo of Truth" tour as it roared across America. I wanted to know who was going to see him—or paying $750 to meet him—and why. What I found was not arenas full of fans of gentle sitcom. What I found was a pocket of America brutally attracted to an unthinkably rich man taking on the "elites": his genteel, precious Hollywood bosses. A wounded, undeniably flawed, arguably unstable man theatrically lashing out, speaking his mind, taking no prisoners, he was also a man who'd go to great lengths to tell us he had all the answers without ever actually giving us one. Frighteningly, Sheen's fury was one somehow shared by those around me. I remember a tense, violent energy in the room. Sheen would talk endlessly about "truth" while insulting whomever he wanted. His unseen enemies, society, those who lived by liberal rules he no longer had any interest in.*

The crowds I saw at his shows—which were indeed more like political rallies—were vocal, angry, and blue collar, drawn to him because

---

* Just so you know, I paid my $750 and met him afterward, and he was lovely. He was warm and interested. But the stage Charlie, the Charlie of the people, the *rude* Charlie . . . not so much.

they felt they knew him and could trust him. Charlie Sheen, they had decided, was their America. A one-man movement. Relatable. Rich. Famous. Powerful. Angry.

And finally free to say whatever he wanted.

. . . .

Three weeks before the 2016 U.S. presidential election, I was at an upstairs table at Greenblatt's Deli on Sunset Boulevard in Los Angeles.

They do a brilliant pastrami on rye, and I was determined to have a pastrami on rye, because it would mean I would be able to say "I'll have a pastrami on rye" and not have anyone think I was just trying to be like someone out of a Billy Crystal film, which I was.

I was meeting the Republican political advisor Mike Murphy, a man I've known for a few years. He's a regular on NBC's *Meet the Press*, hosts the Radio Free GOP podcast, and among many others he's closely advised Mitt Romney, Jeb Bush, John McCain, and former governor of California Arnold Schwarzenegger.

As we order our sandwiches, I consider that, although Arnie made it through, a Trump presidency still feels like a bizarre, minor, outside chance.

"He doesn't know how anything works," says Murphy, as the potato salad arrives. "He thinks it's a movie. He thinks he'll show up and say, 'Bring me the aliens from Area 51. I want to see the spaceship.'"

I laugh, because that's probably true.

"He really thinks he can just call a number. He thinks he'll go to an underground tunnel at the White House and he'll get on a monorail to the CIA, and there he'll see the four most beautiful women he has ever seen in his life, and they're all deadly assassins. He doesn't know that if he's ever been to the CIA it's just a bunch of guys under bleary fluorescent lighting looking at Russian microwave-oven blueprints trying to figure out if they'll be able to make better radar next year."

It's funny because it'll never happen!

"But how can a man who says the things he says—who's so *rude*—have come so far?" I ask. "How does he get away with it?"

"Our trick with Arnold," says Murphy, "used to be, 'Well, he didn't *mean* to say that. If he had said it in German, it would have been crystal clear!' We said that like eight times."

"Really?"

"The press secretary would come out and say, 'Hey, Arnold got something a little bit off today,' and I'd say, 'Can we do ESL?'"

"What's ESL?"

"English as a Second Language. 'Oh, he got the *word* confused because English is his second language, and what this is when you really think about it is just a heart-warming immigrant story of success in America.' And they'd say, 'No, we can't use that for another six weeks.'"

We laugh.

"But in terms of a 'President Trump' . . . ," I say.

"Well, if you have a president of the United States sitting upon that throne we've created for the president, being rude every day . . . well, it would spread like a virus. It could be the first subversive plot to really bring America down from within. Forget Al-Qaeda; just rudeness. It's contagious. And he's the atomic plague of rudeness. That's his only way; he's made a profession out of it. And there you have another reason he shouldn't be president."

*   *   *

There are a thousand reasons why—even if it wasn't Donald Trump, a man whose own surname means "fart" in the playgrounds of Britain—the world simply cannot have a rude American President.

Let's say one day a rude president takes offense at, say, the President of Iran for calling him inept. A normal president taking on the most powerful job on the planet understands that democracy is, by its very nature, a sort of controlled rudeness. It affords us the ability to disagree with one another, in the strongest possible terms, and yet have a chance of departing as friends. And a normal American president also understands the value of freedom of speech, the benefits of diplomacy, and the knowledge that as you rise in power there will be more and more punches aimed at you. The smart person knows which to shrug off. You can't fight every battle, you can't acknowledge every swing someone takes, nor respond to every little criticism. You would have to be mad to do that.

A different type of president, however, would come out fighting before his brain's even had the chance to register the words properly. An unpredictable president might immediately and unthinkingly start threatening Iran.

"That's one thing serious people worry about," says Murphy. "Because America gets away with a lot. We're the big metronome beat. When the American president says something, people take it seriously."

"And if you make threats?"

"A little rule about Presidents 101. Never draw a red line. It's like with a toddler. 'If you throw that spoon again, you're not having dinner!' You now give the toddler the power to test you. So the kid throws the spoon. Now what? Now your wife is mad at you because the toddler is screaming, the spoon's on the floor, and the toddler isn't going to bed if you don't feed her . . ."

"And it's your fault because you drew that red line . . ."

"So don't make threats against Syria you're not willing to carry out. And because in the U.S. we get away with making threats, you always have to be ready to have your bluff called. And if you do nothing, it devalues our currency. If you get to the point where American presidents make threats and nobody believes them, what happens? We have to uncork the military and *do* something. The next thing you know, the skies are on fire."

. . .

Something to cling on to, however, is that the sheer scale of the United States government is awe-inspiring. While we might watch a rude president be sworn in, and hold our breath as he or she steps from Air Force One to meet with foreigners who also have a set of nuclear codes, we make a crucial mistake if we equate that display with absolute power. An insulted or angry president can't just do anything he or she feels like.

Congress can pass legislation to overturn a presidential order, for example, or the courts can declare a president's orders unconstitutional. Congress can impeach, taking you out of the game forever.

But what if a thin-skinned, impulsive president just decides unilaterally to invade Iran anyway?

Well, Congress has a trick. Like a dad with a credit card, it can pull funding.

Suddenly, you're a president sending 20,000 twenty-somethings to fight in a war only you believe in, but within days they're not being paid, there's no gasoline, no one can buy bullets, there's a power outage and they've run out of staples.

So just being president doesn't give you the power to do whatever you want.

But—and this is the part we should be worried about—being president does mean you can *say* whatever you want.

And if what you say is generally rude, that has consequences.

Just as a threat by an American president has consequences, and just as a promise by an American president has consequences, an *insult* by an American president has very real consequences.

When the president speaks, the world listens, because the words he chooses to use carry an enormous weight.

.   .   .

The effects, though, don't just travel overseas. Rudeness, base humor, disrespect, and incivility are likely to be just as devastating internally, because a president sets the very tone of a country.

Jack Marshall is an ethicist. He's also a former criminal lawyer and specialist in the ethics of leadership. He is passionate about rudeness and how to stop it, and is certain the world is getting ruder.

"I don't believe someone as intentionally and shamelessly boorish as Donald Trump would have been tolerated for a second even ten years ago," he tells me when we speak. "To me it's striking and shows just how quickly things have begun to deteriorate."

Marshall thinks that unless society fights to maintain standards, those standards slip.

"I think it's the nature of civilization—unless you really make an effort to fight it—to get ruder, to get cruder, to get more boorish."

Marshall's original area of expertise is American leadership, and how leaders set values and act as role models. In Britain, we seem mainly to think of soccer players as role models, which makes about as much sense as saying we look to our receptionists for quality meats. But for many Americans, the presidency is like a monarchy. The office of the president, the seal of the president, the concept of behaving "presidentially"—all of this is respected over and above whoever happens to be in charge.

But what if that person is as rude as Donald Trump?

"Disaster," says Marshall. "Policy mistakes we can fix. But if you corrupt the entire population, if you corrupt the *culture*, that is permanent and very hard to come back from."

We expect our leaders to be well behaved because our leaders have—at least in public—always been well behaved. If we have people in charge who behave rudely at will, then what we are allowing is the normalization of rudeness. We're saying it's fine. That you too can behave this way. That you can behave this way and still be president of the United States. And that therefore on some level, my child, maybe that is the way you *should* behave.

"And of course it means more vulgarians will get access to power," says Marshall. "The damage that someone like Trump can do is catastrophic. Having a president who does not embody the best of the country but actually celebrates the worst in the culture is a cataclysm, I think."

A rude president is like a rudeness bomb: one explosion and the fallout lasts for years.

> **A rude president is like a rudeness bomb:**
> **one explosion and the fallout lasts for years.**

Trump's casual misogyny and disrespect to his opponent meant that suddenly it was not at all exceptional to see a grown man at a political rally in Pennsylvania wearing a T-shirt bearing the words "She's a Cunt, Vote for Trump." While standing with his wife and *three kids*.

Probably just a normal guy, too. Someone who, on any other day, might help jump-start your car.

The rudeness of a leader leads directly to the rudeness of their followers.

The real problems occur not in those first flushes of liberating rudeness. The real problems occur when it becomes the norm.

. . .

People have issues with smooth politicians. They're too . . . professional. We don't like polish. It feels like a trick. Like they're up to something. And in 2016, a normally voiceless section of America yearned for change, and an abrasive politician felt like change. They could trust a man like that. It had to be genuine.

You didn't have to be a genius to see that no one could possibly be advising Trump to act in the ways he did. There was no spin doctor on the sidelines, saying, "Open on the rapist stuff, then close on the withered hand." There was no real PR department poring over every word, no meetings or scriptwriters or focus groups. Trump was no puppet, having his strings pulled by a hidden global elite. And that turned out to be his advantage. He was a streetwise scrapper, in charge of his own words, and the people read his rudeness as *honesty*. His brashness as *telling it like it is*. His misogyny as welcome relief from the stifling culture of political correctness gone mad. It wouldn't even matter if he said one thing then contradicted it just minutes later. People trusted Trump's honesty *in the moment* because even his lies were more honest than those pompous Washington elites with their long words and educated ways.

"Civility," says Marshall, "has managed to get itself associated with the so-called elites."

The elites are not to be trusted.

"Civility is for the *educated* people, the *rich* people, the *powerful* people, the people who don't have to *struggle* very much. The idea is that the people who speak well, who are so mannerly and so careful, are not liked. And all of a sudden those people who, with some justification, feel they've been looked down upon, are associating that very quality of incivility as something of a badge of defiance."

Screw your feelings. I'll wear whatever T-shirt I want.

. . . .

The terrifying truth is that however damaging we can say it is, however much we can warn people against it, however much it goes against basic decency and logic, the allure of rudeness can be almost uncontrollably powerful.

> **The allure of rudeness can be almost uncontrollably powerful.**

The "Civility in America" study is an ongoing poll by the PR firm Weber Shandwick which takes a look at American attitudes to rudeness year after year. Before the 2016 election, the poll showed that nearly all voters—93 percent—said that the civility of candidates *would* affect their vote.[1] And that seems about right, doesn't it?

"The American people are clearly watching not only what a candidate says, but how they say it," said the chairman of Weber Shandwick, Jack Leslie. "Our research shows that those perceived to behave uncivilly are less likely to be elected president in 2016."

Most of us didn't see it coming. We trusted our shared sensible instincts. We laughed about it while eating pastrami sandwiches in delis, even when it was just three weeks away.

And yet as much as people are likely to say the "right" thing when asked by a pollster, and as much as statistics on civility will tell you that ordinary, decent Americans do not want rude politicians, what we saw in November 2016 was that many of them *did*. They demanded it. They couldn't wait for it. Rudeness brings with it an entirely new set of advantages that smooth-talking politicians in shiny suits dripping with diplomacy, politeness, and pretty words just don't.

On some level, we suspect that to care, to be polite, is to be weak. True power means just not caring. Other people don't matter. Liberals. Immigrants. Asylum seekers. Do-gooders. Screw them, because *that's* how you get things done.

And screw the "experts," with their "facts." Go on gut instinct. Screw the media, too; those biased, overpaid, prissy liars. In fact, call them out on it. Call them *names*. Politicians have been scared of the media for too long, scared of saying just one wrong word and making endless headlines for it. Well, how about saying as many wrong words as you want and just not giving a damn? Being as rude as you like? Attacking without mercy? *This* is the new "presidential."

Trump's approach now seems genius in its simplicity. It's the bully in the bar. It's the guy we read about earlier, who by merely exuding a sense of power seems to deserve it. The guy who sets a whole new tone for the country: one in which civility, politeness, and respect are *disadvantages*. For losers and clowns.

And whenever Donald J. Trump was called out on his behavior by a dutiful media, his policy was simply to say "Yeah? So what?" as the cheers only grew louder.

The media loses its power over somebody when their attitude is "So what?" If anything, "So what?" makes for a better story. A better story gets more coverage; more coverage finds more supporters.

As frustrating as it is, as *wrong* as it is, what the U.S. presidential election showed us beyond doubt is that being rude is always much more exciting, fascinating, and attractive than being polite. Being rude is the brawn to diplomacy's brains.

And as that new tone starts to settle in, and all the data shows hate speech in schoolyards and streets beginning to rise, we either fight back or get used to it.

One week after Trump was elected the 45th president of the United States, the American Historical Association—the oldest and largest society of historians and professors of history in the States—put out a statement, the first paragraph of which ended: "Historians can say with confidence that this is not our nation's finest hour. Language previously relegated to the margins has moved out of the shadows, emboldening elements of American society less interested in a more perfect union than in division and derision."[2]

I began this book by saying that a New Rudeness was coming.

As I continued to write, it showed up at the door.

CHAPTER 17

The Honesty Clause

Should I just have told her to get lost?

In early 2015, a man named James Allen went for a job interview at a regional PVC windows installation company.

By all accounts, he thought it went quite well.

He emailed the company for feedback, and must not have done it quite right because he was surprised to receive the following reply.

> James,
>
> Sincere apologies for not replying to you today, as it happens I actually have a job, and other things to do with my day other than reply to you, when I already had the misfortune of wasting 30 very long minutes of my life speaking to you; not only the most inappropriate person for this job role, but probably for any job role you will spend the next few years applying for, only to get rejected as soon as they meet you.

As openers go, this one is confusing but strong.

It gets worse for James.

You are without a doubt one of the most irritating, rude, ob-
noxious, and arrogant people I have [had] the misfortune to
meet, and your email just solidifies this. Also, for an old, aes-
thetically challenged guy with no teeth you have an unbelievable amount of confidence!

I guess technically that's a compliment.

So you say, you didn't notice the word "professional" on our
website . . . believe me, if I had been anything other than "professional," I would have told [you] what I was actually thinking,
which was "this guy is an absolute cunt, get the fuck out." But
no, alas, I stayed "professional." I only wish I'd have seen your
CV beforehand, to save us both the time, as I would probably
have noticed your main job role was "professional prick."

And then she ends it, "good luck for the future, Sarah."

The woman who wrote that email was Sarah Haseler. She runs
the windows company and is a successful part-time weddings and corporate events singer too.

She had already taken against James Allen for the way he'd acted
in his interview. When she then received a terse and critical email
asking why she was yet to contact him—presumably to offer him the
job—she had just that day read an interesting article suggesting that
when you get angry, it is a good idea to write down all your feelings and
what you'd like to say. Better out than in. So she did.

She wrote her email and it felt good. Her fingers must have tapped
away at the keyboard in blind, glorious, cathartic fury. It was therapy.

And then she wrote a proper response, full of business-like phrases
along the lines of "Unfortunately, on this occasion," and so on.

And then she pressed "Send."

On the wrong one.

James Allen received the email reprinted here and probably had to read it a few times to make sure it was really happening. He started to show it around. The papers picked up on it. "Is this the rudest job response ever?" asked the *Mirror*, and just about everybody else.

People sided with Allen. But there are always two sides.

.   .   .

Although Sarah Haseler was wrong to send that email, she was right to write it.

At least if you go by the teachings of Dr. Brad Blanton, self-confessed "white trash with a PhD."

I first became aware of him in 2007 when I saw him interviewed by Nazanin Rafsanjani on Showtime TV's *This American Life*.

In Virginia, Blanton was running for Congress. He was a psychotherapist who practiced "radical honesty"—a form of only telling the truth, no matter how harsh, believing that to do anything else is to trap yourself in a web of self-deceit.

RAFSANJANI: Can I ask you any question, and you would tell me the truth?

BLANTON: Sure. Shoot.

RAFSANJANI: Have you ever had an affair?

BLANTON: Yes. I was also one time in a group marriage. I've had homosexual experiences, a number of homosexual experiences. I've actually literally slept with hundreds of women. I've had, like, gonorrhea, like, five or six times. I've had herpes for, like, 30 years.

RAFSANJANI: Have you ever tried drugs?

BLANTON: Yes I have. I've done heroin, I've done cocaine, I've done speed, I've taken peyote cactus, I've taken a lot of acid.

RAFSANJANI: Do you think America is the greatest country in the world?

BLANTON: No. I think America . . . I'm not proud to be an American. And I think anyone who says they're proud to be an American these days is an idiot.

It might surprise you to learn that Brad Blanton did not go on to become a member of Congress.

But what a startling and refreshingly direct route to take. In the end, Blanton's downfall seems to have been less about his insistence that anyone proud to be American is an idiot, but more the fact that in some of his workshops he'd been asking people to take their clothes off in order to discuss not just their bodies, but other people's too.

And not in a "nice" way, because being "nice" is a road to nowhere. Being truthful, open, and blunt is the only way truly to be free, says Blanton. Diplomacy is *lying*.

And he is right, to an extent. Diplomacy is the art of finding a smoother way. It is "the art of telling people to go to hell in such a way that they ask for directions," to quote Churchill, whom you could never really accuse of being Britain's most polite man himself.

· · ·

At first glance, the Radical Honesty website looks like it might be a cult of some sort. There are video testimonials, in which bright-eyed, perma-smiling converts talk in awe about how "being here and now with your own truth" is the only way to be.

Recently, Blanton also did what lots of great leaders do and decided to start his own country: the United States of Being. He asked people to forever pledge their "lives," "sacred honor," and "fortunes" to his cause, and so far 52 have thought that was absolutely fair enough.

Though it's 51 if you don't count Brad.

But there's demand for radical honesty. There are people who feel they need it in their lives. A nine-day workshop costs $3,000 per person. Each participant gives a detailed account of their sexual history, then "stands naked in front of the entire group, who are also naked, recounting these details while being recorded on video."[1]

Then the next day, they all sit around and watch the videos together, looking at their bodies and pointing out the flaws.

That seems like something I could do myself for free.

· · ·

I admit I have mixed feelings toward Blanton's work, because I feel it gives genuinely rude people an immediate exit clause. A way of distancing themselves from their behavior. That exit clause is admittedly genius: whether famous or at school, rude people have found a way to say whatever they like, so long as they then claim it as honesty.

You can't argue with "honesty."

But it's not honest. Sandra is not a bitch. You're *saying* Sandra is a bitch.

With the "honesty" clause, we have tricked ourselves into thinking that we somehow have to take other people's opinions as fact. But it gets worse. Because we then have to *applaud* that person for having the guts to call it like it is.

You and I both know that's not calling it like it is.

You're not *Only Being Honest*—you're stating an opinion and shutting down the conversation. It shows a lack of confidence in your own argument. You don't want to talk about it any further; you just want that cathartic release and to reach for the high ground. You have nothing more to say. You're not *Just Telling It Like It Is*—you're being an idiot and asking people to praise you for it.

(I'm sorry. I'm only being honest.)

And more often than not, these "honest" statements aren't challenged, and that is something that can only come from fear. Fear of being the next person to receive an "honest" assessment. Fear in our own, less strongly held opinions in a world where suddenly everyone's got to have one about everything and they *must be heard*. Fear in putting our head above the parapet to offer an opposing view from a far weaker standpoint.

We admire those with confidence—we invite them to be our bosses, to lead our countries—but a whole lexicon of stock phrases has developed from this unpleasant conceit.

If you're *Only Saying What Everyone Else Is Thinking*—then consider the reasons why they're only thinking it.

If you're someone who says *I'm Sorry, Don't Suffer Fools*—then you must have a very hard time when you're on your own.

If you're *Not Being Funny* . . . you're right.

And if you end by waving your hand around and saying *That's Just Me, It's Who I Am, I Won't Change for Anybody*, then well done, Kanye, but please know that everyone would like you more if you did.

One day, when I am in charge, anybody who has ever written or tweeted #justsaying will be gathered together, quickly executed, and forgotten—and yes, I fully realize I sound like your mad grandpa on Facebook after six Jagerbombs.

·   ·   ·   ·

For each and every statement I have just made, Brad Blanton would give me a small sticker to wear, on which he'd written "I am a repressed moron."

I freely admit I don't want to be videoed naked talking about my body with strangers or having to comment on theirs. I think I would struggle, focusing on whatever positives I could: "you have terrific nipples, sir!"; "what wonderfully smooth shins!"

Fact is, I probably do worry too much about other people's feelings. But Blanton thinks I *should* hurt them. Because by hurting their feelings, I will be able to help them get past that hurt. He is on record on the Radical Honesty website as saying we should *actively* offend one another because "on the other side of that reaction is a conversation in which your mutual honesty creates an intimacy not possible if you are hiding something for the sake of someone's feelings."

So in my world, you're a friend if you look after your pal's feelings. But in Blanton's, you're a far better friend if you call it as you see it and trust you'll be able to take the friendship further and deeper.

It is such an intriguing idea with a real logic behind it that I find myself wondering if I've been doing it wrong all these years.

It isn't just toward friends and family either. Blanton says that if he sees someone—a stranger, say—whom he finds tremendously ugly, he will stride up to that person and say, "I find you tremendously ugly." Not just that, but he will then go on to give his detailed account of precisely why he finds that person so hideous.

Not because he's a sociopath, but because he truly believes that while everyone else dances around the topic, the person he's telling needs to hear the "truth" and that their life will be better for it.

If you're rude but you don't worry about it, you're free.

Free to say what you want, and free not to care when someone else is rude to you.

I get it. And yet it goes against everything that is ingrained in me.

But what if I could immunize myself against rudeness? Or understand that I shouldn't worry too much about it? What if I *am* a repressed moron?

So I decide to attend a meeting.

. . .

Seminars espousing Blanton's teaching have sprung up all over the world in recent years, taking their inspiration from his book, also called *Radical Honesty*.

They take place in Prague. Copenhagen. Munich. Nottingham. Everywhere.

I find one happening soon in Dortmund, Germany, and then I realize that if I'm going to end up naked and videoed, I think that is an experience I should like to share with a friend. So I book two places on a three-day intensive Radical Honesty workshop taking place in a small room above a shop and then face the unusual task of convincing my friend Marc to accompany me.

The first night is what I imagine will be a cheese and wine and chitchat evening in which the participants—about ten of us, it seems—will get to know one another.

The following two days will be made up of eight or nine hours of solo exercises, one-on-one sessions, and intensive group confessions.

. . .

A week or so later we arrive in Dortmund, and it's only now that I'm in the taxi on the way to the seminar that I begin to feel nervous.

I want to talk to Marc—who still doesn't know he might end up naked this evening, talking eloquently about his genitals to strangers—but our driver is extremely chatty and angry about the amount of genetically modified food he predicts will soon be pouring into Germany.

As we speed through the streets, he tells us many intricate details surrounding international meat-based trade deals. Over and over. And every time he repeats a fact or finds some new meat-based trade deal fact to get all worked up about, I keep wanting to shout SHUT UP, YOU BORING MAN.

But instead I say, "Oh, really?"

"Yeah, man!" he says, shaking his head in fury. "To get a 'made in Germany' stamp on your food it must have 80 percent domestically produced content!"

OKAY! I want to shout.

"But soon it will be 60 percent!"

DON'T CARE!

"So we could have burgers which are 30 percent Venezuelan beef!"

THAT'S AN ODDLY SPECIFIC EXAMPLE! I want to shout, but again, I say, "God! How terrible," and hope he won't start again, but of course he does, almost every time saying one of the same three things in a slightly different way.

The problem is, Marc and I still haven't sorted out our story yet. What's our excuse for turning up to a Radical Honesty workshop in Dortmund? In reality, I want to see Radical Honesty in its purest form. By admitting I'm investigating rudeness I worry I might dilute that. I am beginning my radical honesty lessons, ironically, on a lie.

On that note, I will tell you what happened in this workshop, but out of complete respect I will change the names and identities of the people involved and anything at all that might identify them to others. What I will remain absolutely true to is what happened, what I learned, and how it made me feel.

The first thing it made me feel was entirely awkward.

As we walked into a narrow beige hallway in what appeared at first to be an apartment, we were welcomed in by our course leader, whom I shall call Horst.

Horst was wearing a joyless fisherman sweater, and he talked very quietly. He did not seem particularly pleased nor displeased to see us. He was entirely nonplussed by our presence. In that moment, I realized the radical honesty had already begun.

Horst led us into a small tiled kitchenette and pointed at a small plate of sliced apples.

"You can have some," he said, with all the enthusiasm of someone pointing at a turd. Then he waved a bored hand over a jar of instant coffee, to which he said we were free to add thick, beige, vegan milk.

I began to realize this wouldn't be a cheese and wine night. It'd be a coffee and sliced apple and beige vegan milk evening. And it was then that I noticed how silent the place was, which was all the more un-nerving, as through a door in the hallway I now saw six or seven men and two or three women sitting in complete silence on small plastic chairs. One guy wore slippers, but apart from him, no one wore any shoes.

Sitting in silence wearing no shoes, apparently, allows you to feel the floor, and if you can feel the floor, says Horst, you are more aware of your feet. Being more aware of your feet is really important, they say, though at no point does anyone explain why.

As we take our chairs in a room that looks a lot like the TV room from *One Flew Over the Cuckoo's Nest* had it been furnished by IKEA, it quickly becomes apparent that this evening will not be a casual meet and greet.

This evening will be starting at 70 miles per hour.

"So, ladies and gentlemen, we will begin by going around the room, and you will tell us your name, what you are scared of, how much per year you earn, and how many sexual partners you have had," says Horst, and his deputy—Anders—gets his notepad out.

The room bristles. I bristle. I can feel Marc bristling next to me. I don't think he realized I was taking him to Dortmund so he could tell people how many sexual partners he's had.

But this is good. This is getting stuck straight in. I have never really known precisely where my comfort zone ends. Now I know for sure it ends somewhere just before Dortmund.

A young man decides to go first. He's traveled a hundred miles to be here, and he says he can't understand why people have a problem with him. He is very direct all the time, and tells them *exactly* how he feels. This, I suspect, is why people have a problem with him. Anders does not write down any of this, which I find odd. But as soon as the guy talks about how much he earns and how many people he's slept with, Anders writes it down so quickly I worry he'll break his wrist.

The next guy is in his fifties. He's nervous. Finds it difficult to speak at first. But when he begins to talk of his colleagues, something crackles and slowly opens up inside him.

"I can't talk to them," he seethes. "I can't tell them how I feel. I just remain silent."

The room nods its understanding.

"What do you *want* to say to them?" asks Horst.

"I want to be honest," he says.

"*Be* honest," replies Horst.

"I want to say . . . ," begins the man, and then he grimaces and starts to wildly mime violently slapping his colleagues from left to right. "You are STUPID! You are BENEATH ME! I don't talk to you BECAUSE YOU ARE NOTHING."

We sit in tense silence for a moment.

"Very good," says Horst.

The man goes on to say how many people he's slept with and Anders nods a thank-you, before—out of nowhere—the man goes one step further and tells us a very clearly defined thing he likes to do in private involving bottoms, and it is so shocking that even Anders forgets to write it down.

"*There it is*," I think. "*Radical honesty.*"

But the man is scared. He has been truly open with a roomful of strangers. And it is oddly inspiring because we tell him how well he did and how difficult we knew that was.

The room, like a bottom, begins to open up.

People take their turns, talking of prostitutes, sexual encounters, loneliness, and lost love. Of losing jobs because they didn't speak up when it mattered. Of relationships with parents based on lies and despair. Of what they wished they'd said when they'd had the chance and what they'd like to say now.

One man pipes up to say he was doing a crossword puzzle recently and around 14 minutes in became sexually aroused, "which, I must be honest, I'm still working through."

He finished on that, but Anders still wanted more.

"And how many partners have you had?" he said, pen ready.

At this point I became a little suspicious of Anders and his motives. Why wasn't he writing down people's feelings, or why they'd joined the course? Why was he only writing down things that people might naturally feel could be weighted toward blackmail? Was he going to get his video camera out in a minute?

But perhaps it was a trust issue. By being honest about these very confronting, personal things, why not be honest about everything else, to anyone else? Why not tell the world exactly how you feel?

"Hey!" says the younger guy suddenly, pointing at the man on my left with an accusing face. "Why are you wearing *shoes?*"

Everyone looks at the man's feet. It's the slippers guy. He is immediately caught off guard. He looks at everyone else's feet and realizes with absolute horror that he's the only one wearing shoes.

"These are *haus-schus!*" he says, desperately, guilt flushing his face.

"Those are *haus-schus?*" says the young man.

"The email said we could wear *haus-schus!*" he replies, panicking, looking around the room for support, hoping he hasn't ruined everything by wearing *haus-schus.*

"It did," I say, supporting him. "The email said you could wear slippers."

"No, I'm just saying, is there a *reason* why you are wearing them?" says the young man. "I am just interested in why you are wearing shoes specifically."

"These are *haus-schus*," replies the other guy again, and you get the sense that he is almost welling up, that he is always under attack. "I went to the store and they were in the *haus-schus* section!"

The young man sits back, confused that he's offended someone yet again. He wasn't trying to be rude, he thinks; he was just being direct. Why is everyone so touchy?

The offended man scowls and stares at his *haus-schus*, thinking, "Why me? Why are people always rude to *me*?"

They are on opposite ends of society, and each brings brittleness.

I'm starting to wonder whether honesty is really what these people need.

And then it is my turn.

"I'm Danny," I say. "And I am not an honest man."

Strong start, right?

I tell them why.

"On the way here there was a taxi driver, and he was so boring, he just kept going on about genetically modified food. And I wanted to say, 'SHUT UP! I did not ASK you about genetically modified food. I am NOT INTERESTED in your talk of trade deals. I want you to BE QUIET and LEAVE ME ALONE.'"

A lady opposite nods.

"But I didn't. I just kept saying, 'Oh, that's interesting.' And so did my friend Marc here. And both of us let the man dominate our journey, instead of just being honest and a bit rude and letting him know he had to stop."

And as I speak, I begin to realize that I'm not actually making up an excuse for being here. This is genuinely how I feel. I'm talking about one journey but, really, I'm talking about all of them. I'm talking about my whole life. I was more concerned with being polite to that man than I was with creating a situation that would more deeply benefit me and my friend. I should have told him to shut up, or come up with a way of letting him know on an honest level that I was not interested in engaging with him right then.

Okay, I'm not revealing that I'm investigating rudeness, but it was rudeness that brought me there, and maybe it's rudeness that will help me when this is done.

Because how many days of my life have been wasted with interactions like the one in the cab? Listening to opinions someone's copied off the radio? Enduring tedious tales from a guy I've only just met and will never see again? Going out of my way not to appear rude?

"I think I need to learn how to be more honest for my own sake," I say, and this is where it gets a bit weird for me, because I do start to feel a bit emotional. All these stories I've listened to—yeah, they were a bit weird, like the crossword one, but they were from the heart and they've opened up something in me.

So I talk about that. Then I realize I've finished.

"And in the spirit of honesty and openness," I say as I end, holding up my coffee cup. "I have to say that vegan milk is fucking disgusting."

It gets a laugh. Horst nods at me with a dead smile, acknowledging the stab at "humor," then quickly looks away.

"Well, you *could* have asked for other milk," he says.

He's offended. He's the leader of a radical honesty workshop. He's supposed to be unoffendable. He's supposed to be encouraging my honesty.

"We do have other, *normal* milk," he spits.

Horst is acting like this milk was *his* milk. Like someone milks him before every session.

"But thank you for sharing how you feel about it," he adds, which is definitely something he's read off a radical honesty techniques pamphlet.

We move on. Throughout the milk exchange, one man has been looking my way the whole time.

He has an open, honest face. He looks like a really nice guy. Someone with whom I'd like to be friends.

He takes a moment, then says, "I am going to be very honest now."

"Good," says Horst, though part of me thinks he's probably had enough of the group's honesty by now. Anders gets his pen ready.

The man takes a breath.

"I have been with very many women," he begins, leaning forward and for some reason now ignoring everyone else but looking straight at me. "I have been with *many* hundreds."

I nod at him, as if to say "okay," though I'm confused by why he's aiming this at me.

"And of these women," he says, before going on to spell out exactly what happens when he is with them, for a very long time, in great detail, while *never once taking his eyes off me.*

I do not quite know how to act anymore.

All I can do is keep nodding like I completely get it.

It's like I've been mistaken for the course leader or some kind of "woman" expert, and now I just have to pretend I am. And because of this, because of these very intimate details being directed solely toward me, I can feel Marc next to me beginning to shake with silent laughter. But no one is looking at Marc. Everyone's looking at the guy. And the guy is looking straight at me.

"Sometimes they want me to do these strange things with them and I'm not into that," he says, and then he tells us what these things are, and I can sense Marc gripping his mug tighter.

I glance to my left, and Anders is writing everything down as fast as he can.

And when the guy finishes, he looks straight at me and, welling up, says the thing he's most scared of.

"I worry that you and other people think that I'm a slut."

And I gently and truthfully say, "Honestly: I don't."

And he thanks me and has to catch his breath so that he doesn't cry.

·   ·   ·

"Okay!" I say, at about ten o'clock that night, in the hallway, to the small group of radical honesty candidates with whom I'm standing. "See you guys tomorrow!"

I skip down the steps with Marc.

"And that," he says, putting his hand on my shoulder, "is the only lie you told this evening."

And he's right.

I couldn't discuss it with Marc in the room for obvious reasons, but there was no way we could return for a further 16 hours of intensive radical honesty.

The selling point for the idea is being open with others and getting all your feelings off your chest.

"We all lie like hell," Blanton has said. "It wears us out. It is the major source of all human stress. It kills us."

I see the value in that now, far more than I did when I first started looking at rudeness. I was dismissive of what I saw as pointless honesty in its entirety. How could you live that way? You would have to be sociopathic, unfeeling, uncaring.

But none of the people I met in the workshop were truly there for that. It wasn't about dealing with other people. It was about dealing with themselves. I ended up genuinely liking every single one of them, and going back would have compounded my own dishonest reasons for being there and stood in their way.

I don't believe in radical honesty, though; I don't believe that your life will be better if you disregard the feelings of others. I don't believe slapping your colleagues from left to right and telling them they're beneath you will really help you. I don't think we should think it's fine to be as direct as we want the whole time with never a thought to the other person's feelings, even if they are wearing *haus-schus*. I don't believe we should encourage a scheme that propels a new rudeness to dominance.

What I think I found was that many of the people there that night were looking for "how to be." They're trying radical honesty because thus far they've lacked the tools that we've evolved over time to smooth out our relationships.

Diplomacy is lying, Blanton asserts. But diplomacy works. A world without diplomacy is a world at war. A society without diplomacy is just a load of rude people walking around insulting each other in the hope of being "free."

The problem is, I think they just end up in a different type of prison.

Had I been radically honest with Madam Hotdog, what might have happened?

I think it would have ended far worse. She might have stuck a fork in my hand.

Perhaps, though, I could take just an element of what I'd discovered and apply it.

Maybe it was time to be not radically honest, but just a little more forthright.

I email the godfather of Radical Honesty, Brad Blanton.

Maybe it was finally time to act.

CHAPTER 18

Rude to the End

The choice we have to make

B rad Blanton's pleasant, friendly face fills my screen, and his Texan drawl—the only word society has yet come up with to describe that accent—booms through my office.

He looks like a man who should constantly be holding a whisky tumbler.

We like each other immediately, but he still thinks I've been "a goddamn idiot."

This whole thing could have been avoided, he tells me, if I hadn't.

Me? I want to say. Has he taken nothing in?

I've told him all about Madam Hotdog. I've explained precisely what happened. I've painted the picture as accurately and honestly as I could. And yet still he thinks all this is somehow my fault.

"What you did is, you lied," he says, accusingly. "You lied from the beginning!"

"I lied?"

"You lied! You should've said, 'GET ME MY GODDAMN HOTDOG, BITCH!'"

Has he gone mad?

"You should have said, 'This is a PROBLEM. I'M a problem. I'm going to BE a problem. And you're going to HAVE a fucking PROBLEM. We have a PROBLEM. Fuck you, bitch!'"

That seems a little strong, I tell him. I'd only just met her.

"But that would be the first honest response," he says, suddenly calm again. "So she took your typical British politeness as what it is—which is a goddamn lie."

"But politeness is a virtue," I say, pathetically, and he waves this away like a king waving away an unpleasant potato.

"Most politeness is just lying. Often, the truth *is* rude. And what's important is that you stick with people beyond the initial rudeness and don't just do a drive-by. Don't just be rude and run off. You say, 'LISTEN, BITCH: I don't know what your goddamn problem is, but you better GET MY HOTDOG for my son or I'm gonna go in the goddamn kitchen and get it myself!'"

I'm slightly startled by this. I remind Blanton that all this took place in a very middle-class town in Britain.

"EXACTLY. Everyone in Britain is pissed off about the politeness. Everyone is pissed off in Britain and they're pissed off from overly polite people. Politeness is a goddamn cover story for goddamn lying."

There is something incredibly liberating about speaking with Brad.

It's cathartic, listening to him rail against the hotdog-based injustices I have faced and my subsequent attempts to make sense of them. But I tell him that despite attending a radical honesty workshop in Germany, this level of "honesty" is not in me.

"You probably haven't done it before, but it would be good for you. Actually, you know what?"

"What?"

"I recommend you go back and tell her you resent not getting your goddamn hotdog for 60 fucking minutes and to *kiss your goddamn ass!*"

I want to! I want to do just that!

"And tell her, what she said about you being the kind of people who'd wait 40 minutes for fish and chips? Tell her 'Stick 'em up your goddamn ass!'"

I'm starting to laugh hard, and so is Blanton, because maybe he's right. I didn't see it during the workshop, but maybe sometimes the truth can set you free. Maybe I am all those things I thought I wasn't. Maybe I thought my standards were just high, but what if in fact I *am* repressed? What if I worry too much? What is the worst thing that could have happened if I'd done exactly what Blanton is suggesting and then got on with my day?

I mean, this would have been a pretty short book, but we all make sacrifices.

Wait, though—my *son*.

What would I be teaching that little guy—all big brown eyes, sponge-soaking this in—if that's what I'd done? Isn't being a grown-up about suppressing those urges? Not calling people bad words? Isn't it about teaching others the right way to act, not selfishly doing whatever you want? Every young parent instinctively tries to make kids understand the correct way to behave by wheeling out "How would you like it if someone behaved that way to you?"—the parental equivalent of "Treat others as you would wish to be treated." It is *in* us.

Unexpectedly, this throws Blanton.

"Uh, well, don't do any of that in front of him," he says, his "flow" broken. "I mean, if you go in and he's still outside, *then* give her all kinds of shit."

"That's interesting," I say. "So I can be honest . . . but not in the company of children?"

Does he believe in radical honesty or not?

"Well, I mean, you don't wanna scare your son . . . basically . . . you have to do *something* . . ."

He resets.

"I think being a good role model of impoliteness would be a good virtue to have, for your son. I think it would be of benefit to him. Don't be such a lying, polite person."

Thing is, I don't want my son to be the type of man who walks into diners and immediately blows up at people and calls them "bitch" and threatens to stick French fries in their bottom.

"I don't think many kids *need* lessons in rudeness," I say.

"That's what I love about them!" booms Blanton. "We should be modeling ourselves after them. Not the other way around. Kids tell the truth."

I tell Blanton that my son did, in fact, call the woman rude, though not to her face. But he did go further and told strangers he didn't even like his hotdog. A sense of injustice at inexplicable rudeness begins at a very young age, and when he hears this, Blanton nearly implodes with joy.

"Good for him!" he says, laughing and applauding. "Do what your son does! *He* was the role model that day!"

Again, he urges me to go back to the diner one last time and make my feelings known.

"It's been about six months," I tell him, hoping I can get out of it.

"Well, that hotdog is cold now," he says. "But it would be good practice for you. You really want to become knowledgeable about rudeness? The reason that you've done all this work is that there is something about rudeness which *attracts* you. It's not just repulsion. It's also attraction."

He leans forward, now much more serious.

"If I can connect with someone, and say, 'I resent you for making me wait while you had your thumb in your ass while I stand there waiting for a goddamn hotdog' . . . if I can say that and just stay there . . . and she yells at you, and you yell back, and then you just stare at each other . . . you can get beyond rudeness. One of you smiles, and you say, 'Okay, where's my hotdog?,' and she says, 'Okay, I got it.' You can get beyond rudeness, but you can't get beyond goddamn lying phony politeness."

I think about how to do it and pitch it to Blanton.

"So I return to the diner, I order a hotdog, and I say, 'I think you were a terrible woman that day, and I would like your response to that'?"

His face falls.

"Yeah, that's . . . okay. But it's still a little . . . look, just walk in and say this: 'I resent you for the goddamn hour I wasted in your shitty little restaurant.'"

.   .   .

Deep down, I knew Blanton was right. I had to confront this head on.

I tell my son we're going for a hotdog, and he looks delighted.

He runs through a few of his favorite places. Ed's Diner? Dog Eat Dog on Essex Road? Herman ze German?

"No," I tell him. "Do you remember that place last year when we tried to buy a hotdog?"

He scrunches up his nose. *Vaguely.* It's almost as if he has not been thinking of nearly nothing else since it happened.

As I fire up the GPS and we start the drive—and my son points out we seem to be going a very long way for a hotdog—I go over the lines Blanton gave me.

"*Tell her you resent not getting your goddamn hotdog for 60 fucking minutes and to kiss your goddamn ass!*"; "*I resent you for the goddamn hour I wasted in your shitty little restaurant.*"

I think about how they would go down with some of the people I've met recently.

A thought comes into sharp focus; something that had occurred to me around the time of my trip to Germany. I'd struggled to articulate it properly to anyone before now but, after speaking with Blanton, I worked it out.

What if, actually, we *need* rudeness because rudeness keeps us in check? Only if we have something to rebel against can we rebel against something.

When I talked with the ethicist Jack Marshall about the crazy world of Donald Trump, he told me about the day, decades ago, he met a man named Herman Kahn.

Kahn was widely regarded at the time as the smartest man alive. He was a futurist who helped develop America's nuclear strategy, and was the inspiration for the title character of the 1964 film *Dr. Strangelove*.

"By dumb luck," Marshall told me, "the U.S. Chamber of Commerce had this mini-conference of about 20 people, and I was supposed to be at it. By a complete mess-up, the only two people who showed up in this big room were Herman and me. So I got to spend two hours with him waiting for everybody else to show. Herman used to charge $25,000 an hour for people to come and talk with him. So he and I just sat there chatting, and he was just sending ideas out into the air."

One of these ideas really resonated with me.

The two had begun talking about a time of huge cultural change—the 1960s.

Marshall said it struck him that the 1960s were a time in which people took established behaviors and just threw them out the window. Did things differently. What you wanted to do took precedence over what you were "supposed" to do.

"And Herman said, 'Yes—the sixties was a period of mass stupidity where everyone suddenly forgot everything they learned and *why* they had learned it.'"

The idea was: only once you've thrown all the rules out of the window—when you're running around in the street screaming obscenities while drunk in your underpants—do you realize why those rules were there in the first place.

"They learned very quickly why it's a bad idea for people to take drugs. They discovered that, actually, dress codes were a good idea to demonstrate mutual respect. And also why it's not a good idea to run out into the street yelling 'fuck' all of the time."

Herman laughed and said, "The problem with cultural tradition and civilization is that after a while they just become tradition and no one actually understands *why* they have become tradition."

It is natural for us to want to do things differently and to see rebellion as attractive and refreshing. It's what appeals to Brad Blanton. It's certainly also what led to a glut of by-the-number bad guy TV judges; what appealed to those who ticked "Trump." They rail against do-gooders. New men. Caring and sharing. Pompous left-wing sensibilities, all. They find considering the feelings of others annoying, restrictive, weak. It stops them enjoying themselves.

In each generation is a movement of people who want to change the status quo.

But I have come to conclude, and I put it to you, that some ideas are so good—and so useful—that they *have* to stay in place. They are tradition because they have earned it; they work.

"People say, 'Why do we have to be civil?'" Marshall said. "'What difference does it make?' Well, there's a good reason why all these various traditions of respect for each other—holding doors open for each other—come about. And reasons for the many things that built a culture of kindness and mutual respect. But people take it for granted, and say, 'This is what *old* people do. *We* don't have to do it anymore.'"

*   *   *

As we left the city and found the highway, I thought about how, whether we realize it or not, we're all suffering.

The week before, I met a London cabbie who told me that that very day a man in a braying, drunken mob outside a pub had shouted, "Fuck you!" at him as he drove past and it was so confusing that five minutes later he had absolutely no idea where he was or where he was going. Instinctively, I explained to him why this had happened: his frontal lobes had been fiddled with. He looked at me oddly.

In Los Angeles, I'd spoken with a hotel concierge who told me, very specifically, that in his experience Brazilian women are the rudest. His friend agreed. "Brazilian women, yeah."

But let us not forget that cultures differ; in Brazil the "okay" sign is considered the very height of rudeness. Maybe those guys were over-using it.

The day I'd left Germany, I spoke to a team of Spanish air steward-esses waiting for their airport shuttle bus. "Parents" can be the rudest passengers, apparently. It's the lack of space, the lack of air, the sheer *stress* of not being able to shut off in an environment in which shutting off is what everybody else does to survive it.

One day I'd talked with a team of similarly stressed, baggy-eyed moving men. They told me that moving house is commonly thought to be the most stressful time in a person's life, and they see that every day. Mind you, they told me, it was the wealthier people you had to watch out for. Their version of rudeness is that they simply won't ad-dress you—they'll just complain about you to your boss behind your back, and that's worse. (And as we've discovered, they're also far more likely to steal sweets from children.)

And outside a shop near New York's Columbus Circle, I'd spoken with a homeless guy who told me it's the "people in suits" who are rudest. They look down at you, pretend you're not there: "You don't matter."

Again and again, it seems rudeness is often about not seeing others, not feeling you've been seen, and our fundamental human need for respect—something the city often allows us to step around.

Blanton didn't want me to step around anything. He wanted me to stride back into this diner and offload more rudeness in the most forthright way possible. I realized this was just a way of making sure I was seen. Making sure I was listened to, that I had my say, that I fought for my honor. It's all I'd wanted that first day, after all.

But I was concerned that just offloading more rudeness was the wrong thing to do. I wondered whether there was a higher ground to be taken.

I remembered the limo driver called José I'd met outside my hotel in LA, who told me he encounters rude people almost every few hours. How wearing it gets. How bruising. How disappointing. And how he gets back at them with the only power he has. "You just ignore them, give them the silent treatment."

As you know, the Wallace Report backs this up as one of the world's number one ways of dealing with the rude.

But I knew absolutely that the silent treatment would not satisfy me *one bit* when it came to Madam Hotdog. Walking back in there and saying nothing would not make my point at all. And this entire endeavor has been about making a point that I want heard.

Because, why give the silent treatment—when you have a voice?

* * *

This book, I have to admit, began for a silly reason. It could have been a silly book. But more than ever I've come to see that civility is not just important, it's not just the right thing to do. I've come to see that it is *vital*.

Rudeness is a form of rebellion that we must rebel against. Not because it weakens us, but because politeness makes us stronger. It gels us.

And this means that all of us—you, me, your uncle's great-aunt—have a moral obligation to Say Something. To not just say we hate rudeness, but to call people out on their terrible behavior wherever

> ## Rudeness is a form of rebellion that
> ## we must rebel against.

we see it happen: the line for coffee, the passive aggression in the office, the muttered insult to a retiree.

Civility is at the foundations of our society. Remove those foundations and let's watch it all come tumbling down.

And yet those who understand this are seen by others as weak, or too precious, or old-fashioned, or "politically correct."

What I see in those very same people is not weakness, but an underlying fury. A desperation from my fellow rudeness nerds, who talk softly and politely but with quick and sharp exasperation about the people who just don't get the *obvious*: that life would be better if *we* were better.

And yet still we don't take rudeness seriously.

Remember what Amir Erez said when I asked him why?

"They find it amusing," he said, "until they're on the operating table."

If we allow the New Rudeness to overwhelm us, to choke us, the whole world will soon find itself on a metaphorical operating table. And as I let my obsession take hold, and traveled around or hammered the phones, I raised the same point with expert after expert. Why not act when the impact is obviously so great?

Health. Wealth. Self-worth. Friendship. Family. The state of the world in general.

All of it chipped away at and damaged by the draining, wearing, corrosive effects of pointless incivility.

I've learned that we can be bad by accident or design. But I've also learned that we can be better. We can be more patient, more understanding, less knee-jerk. We can train ourselves to be more compassionate. We can *just be polite*.

Rudeness, it seems to me, happens in the gaps between people. That microdistance, that little misalignment of thought or direction. The gap that makes someone a stranger. Within that gap is a very thin layer of civility. Just enough to get by. Like cartilage cushioning the bones. We are each of us isolated, but we don't have to be. We can choose to be part of civilization. We can *choose* to be *civil*.

. . .

As I parked up near the diner, I felt nervous. But more than ever I felt I had right on my side. My head had cleared. I was armed with knowledge. I was even armed with my own national survey, which, I have to tell you, I don't think anybody in there would have seen coming.

And let me share something else with you: the Wallace Report goes far deeper than I've let on. Because right at the end of that national survey of 2,000 UK adults, I asked several more questions.

Each and every one of them concerning *current and prevailing public attitudes toward the acceptable time limits we place on the order and provision of cooked meats.*

Here is what is now *official data.*

The longest an average Briton is willing to wait for a hotdog—*even if it is "cooked to order"*—is 11 minutes.

Eleven.

Not well over an *hour*—which *I can prove* because I have the receipt because she made me pay UP FRONT.

Eleven minutes is the *maximum.*

Again—*even if that hotdog is COOKED TO ORDER.*

Even then, that's from a European perspective. I didn't tell you this before, but while I was in Los Angeles I hopped on a five-hour flight to New York. In Times Square, I saw a hotdog vendor standing under a sign that read WORLD'S BEST HOTDOGS. I ordered one and timed precisely how long it took to reach me. It took 32.57 seconds from start to finish. I asked the vendor how long it would have taken had it been "cooked to order." He said I could "add five minutes." So that's the *world's best hotdog* in just five minutes thirty-two-and-a-half seconds.

Can you imagine what New Yorkers would say to this man if he took over an hour?

And look at this.

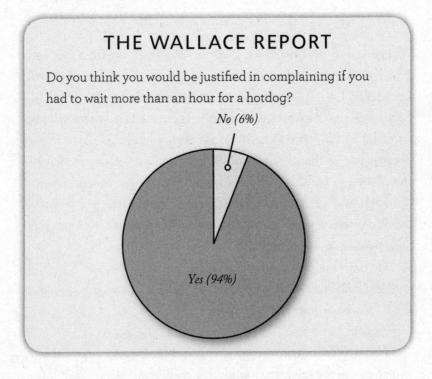

THE WALLACE REPORT

Do you think you would be justified in complaining if you had to wait more than an hour for a hotdog?

No (6%)

Yes (94%)

Ninety-four percent of those surveyed are with me!

Now I was walking down a quiet street and into that diner accompanied not just by a six-year-old boy—but by 61.1 million other people who've had enough.* Ninety-four percent of my countryfolk.

---

* If the same statistic works globally, I was also walking back into that small diner with 6,956,000,000 people right behind me. We'd definitely need to bring our own chairs.

And as I pushed open the door, and I thought of Antanas Mockus and his mimes, and Jack Katz and his sushi flow, and grapefruit cologne and unfair umpires and 101 creative uses for a brick, I braced myself.

This was the moment I would be putting into practice what I'd learned.

This was the moment I would do something.

Because there she was.

My old enemy.

The reason for all of this.

Madam Hotdog.

Just a fleeting glance of her, admittedly, before a gentleman stood in my way, blocking my view.

"Take a seat," he said, and while to some ears he may have said it perfectly pleasantly, for a man we have learned was now inevitably subconsciously primed for rudeness I could not help but detect some weary passive aggression.

So "Get out of my way!" I yelled, pushing him hard in the chest and vaulting over the counter in one heroic move. He grabbed a French fry pan and swung it at me wildly, but I was ready and countered it brilliantly, before grabbing a knife block and throwing each individual knife—small, medium, large, and extra-large—with such speed and accuracy that he immediately found himself pinned hard against the wall.

"YOU!" he said, realizing.

Actually, I'm a bit fuzzy on that, I think I may just have taken a seat.

"What would you like to order?" said the man.

Well, there was only one option, really, wasn't there?

"A hotdog, please," I said. "And one for my son."

I kept glancing over his shoulder in case I should see her again. This specter that had haunted my life all these months.

"Any drinks?" he said, and we ordered a Diet Coke and a lemonade, and he nodded and left.

"This is the place that takes ages," said my son, physically deflating.

"We'll see," I said in a mysterious voice, but I was beginning to feel nervous.

I wanted to have it out with this place. With Madam Hotdog. To say, "It's me, I'm back, and here's what I've learned."

I had stats.

I had anecdotes.

I had world-renowned evolutionary psychologists, psychiatrists, and lawyers on my side.

I thought again about how Brad Blanton had told me to be confrontationally honest. How it complemented the view of Aaron James, author of *Assholes: A Theory*, when he'd said I'd felt this need to *exact* respect. I remembered Paul Ford telling me we all feel the injustice of random rudeness, and how natural it is to want to fight for balance.

After 5 minutes and 34 seconds, our drinks arrived.

I tapped my chin with my pen. *Five minutes and 34 seconds.* As a new expert in both rudeness and hotdogs cooked to order, I considered this acceptable. Although of course in New York, you'd already be one bite into the world's best.

I kept one eye on the timer on my phone as the wait for my great British hotdogs continued.

Eleven minutes came and went: the time limit most Britons would be happy to wait, even if the hotdogs were cooked to order.

Part of me was thrilled about this.

Fifteen minutes passed.

Wales would have been incandescent.

Twenty.

And then, after 25 minutes and 44 seconds . . .

"Here you are!"

I looked down. It was a bloody miracle.

Two hotdogs. *Cooked to order.* By a man with manners. In less than half an hour!

My son's—plain.

Mine—with cheese and jalapeño peppers.

There were even fries.

"Thank you," I mumbled, not quite willing to give credit, which was very ungenerous of me.

And still Madam Hotdog remained nowhere to be seen, perhaps plotting in the shadows, sharpening her knives.

My son and I ate our hotdogs in silence. Hotdogs that tasted all the sweeter because they were hotdogs it had taken so long to get.

And they were pretty good. A strong 3 out of 5.

But as we ate them, the weight of responsibility grew heavier on my shoulders. The time was upon us. It was my duty to Say Something.

For me, for Britain, and for the world. To make Wang Tao proud. To make Jack Marshall proud. For every person who's ever encountered rude service that seemed to come from nowhere and been hamstrung by slow-moving frontal lobes. For every Japanese tourist sent home from Paris confused and sedated and accompanied by nurses, carrying a rudeness contagion they then spread to a whole new set of strangers. To make my case.

But make it politely; nonconfrontationally; *better* than she had.

And, I had decided, to make it in a way that would kill the virus dead: no witnesses, no rudeness hangover, no neurotoxic butterfly effect to make the world microscopically worse. Only I, Danny Wallace, could end the strain.

But how?

I caught sight of the "TIPS" jar on the counter—the one that had made me laugh that first day because of its apparent arrogance and pointlessness.

It gave me an idea. I *would* give them a tip.

I got out a fiver.

And I began to write on it.

25 minutes and 44 seconds is a perfectly reasonable time to wait for a hotdog.

But 94% of 2000 UK adults asked said that one hour and one minute is <u>NOT.</u>

Even if it is cooked to order.

You're headed in the right direction.

I paused. And I realized what I had to say next. A sentence that was mine alone to write; a sentence I had *earned*.

I smiled, and wrote . . .

I now consider the matter closed.

I initialed and dated it.

I placed my knife and fork back on my plate, stood up, pushed my chair back in, and walked over to the "TIPS" jar.

I neatly folded the five-pound note, and quickly dropped it in.

"Oh, that's very kind of you," said the man, with a warmth I hadn't been expecting.

"Not at all," I replied, bowing my head very slightly.

"Thank you," he said, and somewhere in the back I heard the sound of heavy approaching footsteps.

"That was very nice," said my son to the man, and as those footsteps got louder, I patted him on the back with pride.

Acknowledgments

It's impossible to write about rudeness without also talking about it. I'm indebted to my friend, the writer Marc Haynes, for being a sounding board and discussions partner, and for his help with extra research on some of the topics in this book. Also, as always, to my brilliant editor Jake Lingwood and agent Robert Kirby. Greta, Elliot, Clover, and the Bump—thank you so much for listening to me talk so much about hotdogs. Thanks to Howard Watson and Laura Horsley. Wag and Sara Marshall-Page—who would have thought it?! Thank you, Phil Hilton.

And thank you in particular to Amir Erez, Christine Porath, Robert M. Sapolsky, Nate Fast, Jack Katz, Aaron James, Sheyna Gifford, Mike Murphy, Adam Bear, Robin Dunbar, Antanas Mockus, Rodrigo Sandoval, Ni Tao, Wang Tao, Paul Ford, Trevor Foulk, Jack Marshall, Sven Mørch, Darren Dahl, Matthew Scott, Richard Nisbett, Kieran Snyder, Paul Piff, Lauren Emberson, and Brad Blanton—all of whom were happy to talk with me about their fascinating work, and only one of whom was rude about it.

THE WALLACE REPORT

Are you rude?

In order to find out where we should be, I decided I might need to find out where we already were. And so the Wallace Report was commissioned—a survey of 2,000 adults on the subject of rudeness:

 1 in 5 (21%) Brits consider themselves a rude person.

 38% of Brits said that they had been rude to someone in the past seven days, even if only slightly.

 54% of Brits said that someone had been rude to them in the past seven days, even if only slightly.

Those polled who said someone had been rude to them in the past seven days were most likely to have been rude to while at work (27%). This was closely followed by:

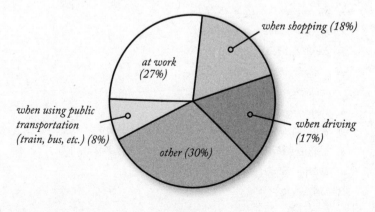

How are people rude?

Those polled who said someone had been rude to them in the past seven days were most likely to have the person be rude to them by having an "attitude" (47%). Here are the figures in full:

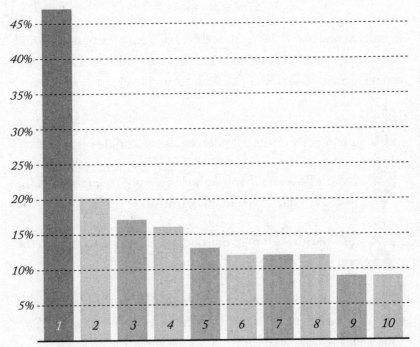

Respondents could give more than one answer.

1. *having an "attitude" (47%)*
2. *talking down to them (20%)*
3. *being passive aggressive (17%)*
4. *ignoring them (16%)*
5. *shouting at them (13%)*
6. *swearing at them (12%)*
7. *mumbling something under their breath (12%)*
8. *blaming them for something they didn't do (12%)*
9. *calling them something rude (9%)*
10. *other (9%)*

How do you react?

Those polled who said someone had been rude to them in the past seven days were most likely to react to the person who was rude to them by ignoring them (45%). Here are the figures in full:

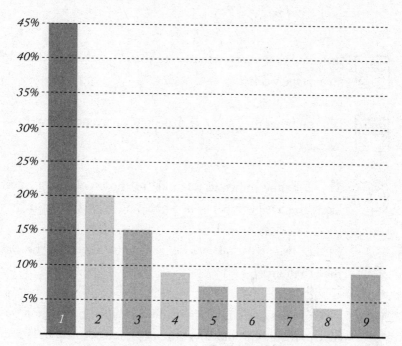

Respondents could give more than one answer.

1. *ignoring them (45%)*
2. *giving them a "look" (20%)*
3. *being rude back (15%)*
4. *being passive aggressive (9%)*
5. *shouting back at them (7%)*
6. *trying to respond with a "clever" comeback (7%)*
7. *trying to make them feel guilty (7%)*
8. *mumbling something under their breath (4%)*
9. *other (9%)*

Other results

Those polled who said someone had been rude to them in the past seven days were most likely to say that the person who was rude to them was between the ages of 35 and 44 years old (25%).

Brits said that people are rude to them, on average, twice in an average week.

Brits said that they are rude to people, on average, once in an average week.

The last time someone was rude to those polled was most likely to have been between 3 p.m. and 3:59 p.m. (6%).

14% of Brits have taken revenge against someone who was rude to them.

70% of Brits said that if someone in a brand-name shop was rude to them, it would affect their opinion of the brand itself.

18% of Brits agree that the government should do more to punish rudeness.

More than a third (35%) of Brits agree that the world is reaching a rudeness crisis point.

More than half (56%) of Brits have felt that the rudeness of others has affected their mental well-being, no matter how briefly.

Of those polled who agree the world is reaching a rudeness crisis point, 65% think social media (Twitter, Facebook, etc.) is to blame. Here are the figures in full:

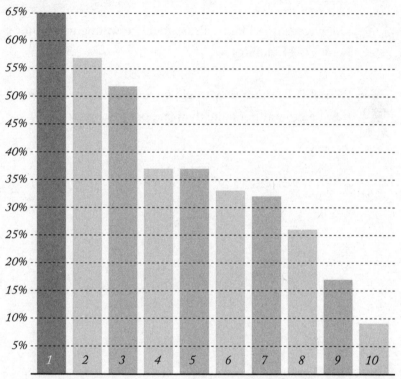

Respondents could give more than one answer.

1. *social media—Twitter, Facebook, etc. (65%)*
2. *celebrity behavior as seen in gossip columns, etc. (57%)*
3. *reality TV stars (52%)*
4. *TV in general (37%)*
5. *schooling/education (37%)*
6. *soccer players (33%)*
7. *stressful jobs (32%)*
8. *politicians—government cuts, how they come across on TV/radio (26%)*
9. *not having to do national service (17%)*
10. *other (9%)*

Only 8% of Brits believe that it is acceptable to wait in excess of one hour for a hotdog, even if that hotdog has been cooked to order.

 On average, the longest Brits would be willing to wait for a hotdog is 11 minutes.

 94% of Brits think they would be justified in complaining if they had to wait for more than an hour for a hotdog.

Notes

CHAPTER 2

1.   T. Foulk, A. Woolum, and A. Erez, "Catching Rudeness is Like Catching a Cold: The Contagion Effects of Low-Intensity Behaviors," *Journal of Applied Psychology* 101, no. 1 (June 2015): 50–67.

2.   R. McDermott, J. H. Fowler, and N. A. Christakis, "Breaking Up Is Hard to Do, Unless Everyone Else Is Doing It Too: Social Effects on Divorce in a Longitudinal Sample" (18 October 2009), available at https://ssrn.com/abstract=1490708.

3.   C. L. Porath and A. Erez, "Overlooked but Not Untouched: How Rudeness Reduces Onlookers' Performance on Routine and Creative Tasks," *Organizational Behavior and Human Decision Processes* 109, no. 1 (May 2009): 29–44.

4.   M. L. Ambrose, M. Schminke, and D. M. Mayer, "Trickle-Down Effects of Supervisor Perceptions of Interactional Justice: A Moderated Medium Approach," *Journal of Applied Psychology* 98, no. 4 (July 2013): 678–89. Ambrose, Schminke, and Mayer are a team of academics whose names sound like they should be creating quality gourmet sausages.

5.   M. Ferguson, "You Cannot Leave It at the Office: Spillover and Crossover of Coworker Incivility," *Journal of Organizational Behavior* 33, no. 4 (May 2011): 571–88.

6.   T. Nicholson and B. Griffin, "Thank Goodness It's Friday: Weekly Pattern of workplace incivility," *Anxiety, Stress, & Coping* 30, no. 1 (June 2016): 1–14.

CHAPTER 3

1. As well as watching footage from a Danish documentary by Andreas Dalsgaard called *Bogotá Change*, you can read all about what else Mockus did in *Taking Power Back: Putting People in Charge of Politics* by Simon Parker, *Happy City: Transforming Our Lives through Urban Design* by Charles Montgomery, and *Incivility: The Rude Stranger in Everyday Life* by Philip Smith, Timothy L. Phillips, and Ryan D. King.

2. From the brilliantly named academic paper by I. E. Hyman et al, "Did You See the Unicycling Clown?: Inattentional Blindness While Walking and Talking on a Cell Phone," *Applied Cognitive Psychology* 24, no. 5 (July 2010): 597–607.

3. L. L. Emberson et al, "Overheard Cell-Phone Conversations: When Less Speech Is More Distracting," *Psychological Science* 21, no. 10 (October 2010): 1383–8.

4. A. Monk, E. Fellas, and E. Ley, "Hearing Only One Side of Normal and Mobile Phone Conversations," *Behaviour & Information Technology* 23, no. 5 (September 2004): 301–5.

5. K. E. Mathews and L. K. Canon, "Environmental Noise Level as a Determinant of Helping Behavior," *Journal of Personality and Social Psychology* 32, no. 4 (October 1975): 571–7.

6. Kikumoto has written a whole book about this, *Date Mask Izonsho*.

7. S. Milgram, "The Experience of Living in Cities," *Science* 167, no. 3924 (March 1970): 1461–8.

8. Malcom Gladwell discusses the Broken Windows theory in chapter 4 of *The Tipping Point: How Little Things Can Make a Big Difference* (London: Abacus, 2002).

9. K. Keizer, S. Lindenberg, and L. Steg, "The Spreading of Disorder," *Science* 322, no. 5908 (December 2008): 1681–5.

CHAPTER 4

1. P. Gallagher and A. Delmar-Morgan, "Rudeness is Off the Menu: The Notorious Wong Kei Restaurant Is under New Management—and Pledging to Improve the Quality of Its Service," *Independent*, February 23, 2014.

2. M. K. Ward and D. Dahl, "Should the Devil Sell Prada?: Retail Rejection Increases Aspiring Consumers' Desire for the Brand," *Journal of Consumer Research* 41, no. 3 (October 2014): 590–609.

3. J. Katz, "Pissed Off in L. A.," *How Emotions Work* (Chicago: University of Chicago Press, 2001), ch. 1.

4. N. Brookes, "The multibillion Dollar Cost of Poor Customer Service," *NewVoiceMedia* (January 8, 2014), available at: http://www.newvoicemedia .com/blog/the-multibillion-dollar-cost-of-poor-customer-service-infographic.

5. S. Barbera, "Customer Experience Guide: What Millennials Expect in 2016," *CGS* (October 19, 2015), available at: https://www.cgsinc.com/en /customer-experience-guide-millennials.

6. C. L. Porath, D. MacInnis, and V. S. Folkes, "Witnessing Incivility among Employees: Effects on Consumer Anger and Negative Inferences about Companies," *Journal of Consumer Research* 37, no. 2 (August 2010): 292–303.

CHAPTER 5

1. Just in case you don't know, though I'm sure you do: the Stanford Prison Experiment took place in a university basement in 1971. A professor named Philip Zimbardo assigned two different roles to two sets of college students—prisoner and guard—to test the effects of power, roles, and social expectations on the human psyche. Each student was paid $15 a day. It was supposed to last two weeks but was abruptly stopped after six days. The simulation had become too real; the pretend guards too realistically abusive.

2. N. J. Fast, N. Halevy, and A. D. Galinsky, "The Destructive Nature of Power without Status," *Journal of Experimental Social Psychology* 48, no. 1 (January 2012): 391–4.

3. "Census of Fatal Occupational Injuries," *Bureau of Labor Statistics* (2015), available at: http://www.bls.gov/iif/oshcfoi1.htm.

4. "How to curb job violence? Watch for stressed workers," *USA Today* (April 16, 2016).

5. G. A. van Kleef et al, "Breaking the Rules to Rise to Power: How Norm Violators Gain Power in the Eyes of Others," *Social Psychological and Personality Science* 2, no. 5 (2011): 500–7.

6.   P. K. Piff et al, "Higher Social Class Predicts Increased Unethical Behavior," *Proceedings of the National Academy of Sciences of the United States of America* 109, no. 11 (January 2012): 4086–91.

7.   G. A. van Kleef et al, "Power Gets You High: The Powerful Are More Inspired by Themselves than by Others," *Social Psychological and Personality Science* 6, no. 4 (May 2015): 472–80.

8.   B. J. Tepper et al, "On the Exchange of Hostility with Supervisors: An Examination of Self-Enhancing and Self-Defeating Perspectives," *Personnel Psychology* 68, no. 4 (Winter 2015): 723–58.

CHAPTER 6

1.   A. Frankenberry, "Do More, Apologize Less—How Bitches Get Ahead in Business," *The Content Factory* (2012), available at: http://www.content fac.com/boss-bitch-manifesto-why-nice-girls-finish-last-in-life-and-in -business.

2.   T. A. Judge, B. A. Livingston, and C. Hurst, "Do Nice Guys—and Gals—Really Finish Last?: The Joint Effects of Sex and Agreeableness on Income," *Journal of Personality and Social Psychology* 102, no. 2 (February 2012): 390–407.

3.   R. Lakoff, "Language and Woman's Place," *Language in Society* 2, no. 1 (April 1975): 45–80.

4.   J. M. Salerno and L. C. Peter-Hagene, "One Angry Woman: Anger Expression Increases Influence for Men but Decreases Influence for Women, during Group Deliberation," *Law and Human Behavior* 39, no. 6 (December 2015): 581–92.

5.   Survey administered by the Economic and Social Research Council, in conjunction with Lancaster University and Cambridge University Press. The full results will be published in 2018.

6.   S. Sandberg and A. Grant, "Speaking While Female," *New York Times* (January 12, 2015).

CHAPTER 7

1.   The best book on Whitehouse and her campaign is her own: M. Whitehouse, *Cleaning Up TV: From Protest to Participation* (Blandford, 1967).

2.   Quoted by G. Levy, "Who's Mocking Mary Whitehouse Now?," *Daily Mail* (November 10, 2012).

CHAPTER 8

1.   Y. Chida and A. Steptoe, "The Association of Anger and Hostility with Future Coronary Heart Disease," *Journal of the American College of Cardiology* 53, no. 11 (March 2009): 936–46.

2.   M. H. Teicher et al, "Sticks, Stones, and Hurtful Words: Relative Effects of Various Forms of Childhood Maltreatment," *Journal of American Psychiatry* 163, no. 6 (June 2006): 993–1000.

3.   J. T. James, "A New, Evidence-Based Estimate of Patient Harms Associated with Hospital Care," *Journal of Patient Safety* 9, no. 3 (September 2013): 122–8.

4.   C. Andel et al, "The Economics of Health Care Quality and Medical Errors," *Journal of Health Care Finance* 39, no. 1 (Fall 2012): 39–50.

5.   "Data and Statistics," World Health Organization, available at: http://www .euro.who.int/en/health-topics/Health-systems/patient-safety/data-and-statistics.

6.   A. H. Rosenstein and M. O'Daniel, "A Survey of the Impact of Disruptive Behaviors and Communication Defects on Patient Safety," *Joint Commission Journal Quality on Patient Safety* 34, no. 8 (August 2008): 464–71.

CHAPTER 9

1.   You can read Paul Ford's "Why Wasn't I Consulted?" (2007) here: http:// www.ftrain.com/wwic.html.

2.   B. Gardiner et al, "The Dark Side of *Guardian* Comments," *Guardian* (April 12, 2016).

3.   M. Wang et al, "Daily Customer Mistreatment and Employee Sabotage against Customers: Examining Emotion and Resource Perspectives," *Academy of Management Journal* 54, no. 2 (April 2011): 312–34.

CHAPTER 10

1.   Kick It Out statistics reported in D. Conn, "Kick It Out Calls for Collective Action on Social Media Abuse Towards Players," *Guardian* (April 16, 2015).

2. N. Lapidot-Lefler and A. Barak, "Effects of Anonymity, Invisibility, and Lack of Eye-Contact on Toxic Online Disinhibition," *Computers in Human Behavior* 28, no. 2 (March 2012): 434–43.

3. UK Safer Internet Centre Survey (2016), information available at: http://www.saferinternet.org.uk/safer-internet-day/sid-2016/safer-internet-day -2016-press-release. See also: "One in Four Teenagers Suffer Trolling Online," *Telegraph* (February 9, 2016).

CHAPTER 11

1. National Highway Traffic Safety Administration statistics. See: C. Ingraham, "Road Rage Is Getting Uglier, Angrier and a Lot More Deadly," *Washington Post* (February 18, 2015).

2. *Max Power* survey of 1,035 drivers, in association with the RAC. See M. Oliver, "Poll Reveals Prevalence of Road Rage," *Guardian* (August 13, 2003).

3. You can watch the entire exchange by typing "Road Rage British Edition" into YouTube, or a longer version on the channel of the cyclist—"kmcyc"— available at: https://www.youtube.com/user/kmcyc.

4. J. D. Goldstein and S. E. Iso-Ahola, "Determinants of Parents' Sideline-Rage Emotions and Behaviors at Youth Soccer Games," *Journal of Applied Social Psychology* 38, no. 6 (June 2008): 1442–62.

5. W. J. Szlemko et al, "Territorial Markings as a Predictor of Driver Aggression and Road Rage," *Journal of Applied Psychology* 38, no. 6 (June 2008): 1664–88.

CHAPTER 12

1. 24/7 Wall Street's index statistics, see: T. C. Frohlich, S. Stebbins, and M. B. Sauter, "America's Most Violent (and Peaceful) States," *Evansville Courier & Press* (July 29, 2016); United Nations Office on Drugs and Crime statistics, see: A. Kirk, "Which Countries Have the Highest Murder Rates?," *Telegraph* (December 11, 2015).

2. D. Cohen et al, "Insult, Aggression and the Southern Culture of Honor: An Experimental Ethnography,'" *Journal of Personality and Social Psychology* 70, no. 5 (May 1996): 945–60.

3. There's more about Paris Syndrome in M. Robinson and D. Picard, eds., *Emotion in Motion: Tourism, Affect and Transformation* (Ashgate, 2012).

4. D. Bolton, "French Foreign Minister Encourages Countrymen to Be More Polite to Foreigners, as France Tries to Boost Tourism," *Independent* (June 14, 2015).

5. Sun Yat-sen, 1924, "Speech on Nationalism" in Y. Hu, *Rural Health Care Delivery: Modern China from the Perspective of Disease Politics* (Springer, 2013).

CHAPTER 13

1. A book on this entire subject is G. Savičić and S. Savić, *Unpleasant Design* (GLORIA, 2013).

2. "Spotty Teens Deterred from Underpasses by Acne Light," *Daily Telegraph* (March 26, 2009).

3. S. G. Shamay-Tsoory et al, "The Role of the Orbitofrontal Cortex in Affective Theory of Mind Deficits in Criminal Offenders with Psychopathic Tendencies," *Cortex* 46, no. 5 (May 2010): 668–77.

4. S. H. Konrath, E. H. O'Brien, and C. Hsing, "Changes in Dispositional Empathy in American College Students over Time: A Meta-Analysis," *Personality and Social Psychology Review* 15, no. 2 (May 2011): 180–98.

5. C. A. Hafen et al, "Conflict with Friends, Relationship Blindness, and the Pathway to Adult Disagreeableness," *Personality and Individual Differences* 1, no. 87 (July 2015), 7–12.

6. H. Y. Weng et al, "Compassion Training Alters Altruism and Neural Responses to Suffering," *Psychological Science* 24, no. 7 (July 2013): 1171–80.

CHAPTER 14

1. Division of Criminal Justice Services, "New York State Crime Report" (September 2015), available at: http://www.criminaljustice.ny.gov/crimnet /ojsa/indexcrimes/nys-crime-report-2014.pdf.

2. S. Wang and J. Zhang, "Blood Levels in Children, China," *Environmental Research* 101, no. 3 (January 2006): 412–18.

3. V. Bekiempis, "Why Do NYC's Minorities Still Face So Many Misdemeanor Arrests?," *Newsweek* (February 28, 2015).

4. Examples from the Police Reform Organizing Project, who regularly attend court hearings to see the mountains being made out of molehills. See: http://www.policereformorganizingproject.org.

5. Rob Pattinson, "Wirral Yob, 10, Slapped with ASBO Weeks after His Brother Received Similar Order," *Liverpool Echo* (December 11, 2014).

6. S. Macdonald and M. Telford, "The Use of ASBOs against Young People in England and Wales: Lessons from Scotland," *Legal Studies* 27, no. 4 (December 2007): 604–29.

CHAPTER 15
1. M. Goulston, "Rage—Coming Soon from a Narcissist Near You," *Psychology Today* (February 9, 2012), available at: https://www.psychologytoday.com/blog/just-listen/201202/rage-coming-soon-narcissist-near-you.

CHAPTER 16
1. "Nearly All Likely Voters Say Candidates' Civility Will Affect Their Vote," Weber Shandwick press release (January 28, 2016), available at: http://www.webershandwick.com/news/article/nearly-all-likely-voters-say-candidates-civility-will-affect-their-vote.

2. "AHA Statement in Aftermath of 2016 Election," American Historical Association statement (November 18, 2016), available at: http://blog.historians.org/2016/11/aha-statement-aftermath-2016-election.

CHAPTER 17
1. "9-Day Course in Honesty Workshop," Radical Honesty (2016), available at: http://radicalhonesty.com/9-day-course-in-honesty-workshop-deposit.

About the Author

Danny Wallace is a *Sunday Times*–bestselling author who lives in Los Angeles and Suffolk. His award-winning column in *ShortList* magazine reaches more than 1.3 million readers weekly. He has made comedies and documentaries for television and radio, and won the Arqiva Award for Presenter of the Year as host of the *Xfm Breakfast Show with Danny Wallace*. GQ magazine has called him: "One of Britain's great writing talents."

www.dannywallace.com